# Modern Perl
## 2014 edition

chromatic

# Modern Perl
2014 edition

Copyright © 2010-2014 chromatic

**Editor:** Shane Warden
**Logo design:** Devin Muldoon
**Cover design:** Allison Randal, chromatic, and Jeffrey Martin

**ISBN-10:** 0-9779201-7-8
**ISBN-13:** 978-0-9779201-7-4

Published by Onyx Neon Press, http://www.onyxneon.com/. The Onyx Neon logo is a trademark of Onyx Neon, Inc.

Onyx Neon typesets books with free software, especially Ubuntu GNU/Linux, Perl, PseudoPod, and LaTeX. Many thanks to the contributors who make these and other projects possible.

2010 - 2011 Edition October 2010
2011 - 2012 Edition January 2012
2014 - 2015 Edition January 2014

Electronic versions of this book are available from http://onyxneon.com/books/modern_perl/, and the companion website is http://modernperlbooks.com/. Please share with your friends and colleagues.

Thanks for reading!

# Contents

# Preface

*Modern Perl* is one way to describe the way the world's most effective Perl programmers work. They use language idioms. They take advantage of the CPAN. They show good taste and craft to write powerful, maintainable, scalable, concise, and effective code. You can learn these skills too!

Perl first appeared in 1987 as a simple tool for system administration. Though it began by declaring and occupying a comfortable niche between shell scripting and C programming, it has become a powerful, general-purpose language family. Perl has a solid history of pragmatism and a bright future of polish and enhancement.

Over Perl's long history–especially the 19 years of Perl 5–our understanding of what makes great Perl programs has changed. While you can write productive programs which never take advantage of all the language has to offer, the global Perl community has invented, borrowed, enhanced, and polished ideas and made them available to anyone willing to learn them.

## Running Modern Perl

The `Modern::Perl` module from the CPAN (The CPAN, pp. 15) asks Perl to warn of dubious constructs and typos and will enable new features introduced in modern Perl releases. Unless otherwise mentioned, code snippets always assume the basic skeleton of a program:

```
#!/usr/bin/env perl

use Modern::Perl '2013';
use autodie;
```

... which is equivalent to:

```
#!/usr/bin/env perl
```

```
use 5.016;      # implies "use strict;"
use warnings;
use autodie;
```

Some examples use testing functions such as ok(), like(), and is() (Testing, pp. 203). These programs follow the pattern:

```
#!/usr/bin/env perl

use Modern::Perl;
use Test::More;

# example code here

done_testing();
```

At the time of writing, the current stable Perl release family is Perl 5.18. If you're using an older version of Perl, you may not be able to run all of the examples in this book unmodified. The examples in this book work best with Perl 5.14.0 or newer, though we recommend at least Perl 5.16. While the term "Modern Perl" can refer to any version of Perl from 5.10.1, several features added in newer versions are essential to modern development.

If you have no Perl installed (or if you have an old version installed), you can install a newer release yourself. Windows users, download Strawberry Perl from http://www.strawberryperl.com/ or ActivePerl from http://www.activestate.com/ activeperl. Users of other operating systems with Perl already installed (and a C compiler and the other development tools), start by installing the CPAN module App::perlbrew[1].

perlbrew allows you to install and manage multiple versions of Perl. This allows you to switch between versions as well as to install Perl and CPAN modules in your home directory without affecting the system's version. If you've ever had to beg your system administrator for permission to install software, you know how much easier your life can be now.

## Credits

This book would not have been possible without questions, comments, suggestions, advice, wisdom, and encouragement from many, many people. In particular,

---

[1] See http://search.cpan.org/perldoc?App::perlbrew for installation instructions.

Preface

the author and editor thank:

John SJ Anderson, Peter Aronoff, Lee Aylward, Alex Balhatchet, Nitesh Bezzala, Ævar Arnfjörð Bjarmason, Matthias Bloch, John Bokma, Vasily Chekalkin, Dmitry Chestnykh, E. Choroba, Tom Christiansen, Anneli Cuss, Paulo Custodio, Steve Dickinson, Kurt Edmiston, Felipe, Shlomi Fish, Jeremiah Foster, Mark Fowler, John Gabriele, Nathan Glenn, Kevin Granade, Andrew Grangaard, Bruce Gray, Ask Bjørn Hansen, Tim Heaney, Graeme Hewson, Robert Hicks, Michael Hicks, Michael Hind, Mark Hindess, Yary Hluchan, Daniel Holz, Mike Huffman, Gary H. Jones II, Curtis Jewell, Mohammed Arafat Kamaal, James E Keenan, Kirk Kimmel, Graham Knop, Yuval Kogman, Jan Krynicky, Michael Lang, Jeff Lavallee, Moritz Lenz, Andy Lester, Jean-Baptiste Mazon, Josh McAdams, Gareth McCaughan, John McNamara, Shawn M Moore, Alex Muntada, Carl Mäsak, Chris Niswander, Nelo Onyiah, Chas. Owens, ww from PerlMonks, Jess Robinson, Dave Rolsky, Gabrielle Roth, Grzegorz Rożniecki, Jean-Pierre Rupp, Eduardo Santiago, Andrew Savige, Lorne Schachter, Steve Schulze, Dan Scott, Alexander Scott-Johns, Phillip Smith, Christopher E. Stith, Mark A. Stratman, Bryan Summersett, Audrey Tang, Scott Thomson, Ben Tilly, Ruud H. G. van Tol, Sam Vilain, Larry Wall, Lewis Wall, Paul Waring, Colin Wetherbee, Frank Wiegand, Doug Wilson, Sawyer X, David Yingling, Marko Zagozen, Ahmad M. Zawawi, harleypig, hbm, and sunnavy.

Any remaining errors are the fault of the stubborn author.

# CHAPTER 1

# The Perl Philosophy

Perl gets things done–it's flexible, forgiving, and malleable. Capable programmers use it every day for everything from one-liners and one-off automations to multi-year, multi-programmer projects.

Perl is pragmatic. You're in charge. You decide how to solve your problems and Perl will mold itself to do what you mean, with little frustration and no ceremony.

Perl will grow with you. In the next hour, you'll learn enough to write real, useful programs–and you'll understand *how* the language works and *why* it works as it does. Modern Perl takes advantage of this knowledge and the combined experience of the global Perl community to help you write working, maintainable code.

First, you need to know how to learn more.

## Perldoc

Perl has a culture of useful documentation. The `perldoc` utility is part of every complete Perl installation[1]. The `perldoc` command-line utility displays the documentation of every Perl module installed on the system–whether a core module or one installed from the Comprehensive Perl Archive Network (CPAN)–as well as thousands of pages of Perl's copious core documentation.

> http://perldoc.perl.org/ hosts recent versions of the Perl documentation. CPAN indexes at http://search.cpan.org/ and http://metacpan.org/ provide documentation for all CPAN modules. Other distributions such as ActivePerl and Strawberry Perl provide local documentation in HTML formats.

---

[1]However your Unix-like system may require you to install an additional package such as `perl-doc` on Debian or Ubuntu GNU/Linux.

Use `perldoc` to read the documentation for a module or part of the core documentation:

```
$ perldoc List::Util
$ perldoc perltoc
$ perldoc Moose::Manual
```

The first example displays the documentation embedded within the `List::Util` module. The second example displays a pure documentation file, in this case the table of contents of the core documentation. The third example displays a pure documentation file included as part of a CPAN distribution (Moose, pp. 165). `perldoc` hides these details; there's no distinction between reading the documentation for a core library such as `Data::Dumper` or one installed from the CPAN. This consistency is a benefit to you–Perl culture values documentation so much that even external libraries tend to follow the good example of the core language documentation.

The standard documentation template includes a description of the module, demonstrates sample uses, and then contains a detailed explanation of the module and its interface. While the amount of documentation varies by author, the form of the documentation is remarkably consistent.

---

**How to Read the Documentation**

Perl has lots of documentation. Where do you start?
`perldoc perltoc` displays the table of contents of the core documentation, and `perldoc perlfaq` displays the table of contents for Frequently Asked Questions about Perl. `perldoc perlop` and `perldoc perlsyn` document Perl's symbolic operators and syntactic constructs. `perldoc perldiag` explains the meanings of Perl's warning messages. `perldoc perlvar` lists all of Perl's symbolic variables. Skimming these files will give you a great overview of the language.

---

The `perldoc` utility has many more abilities (see `perldoc perldoc`). To search the Perl FAQ, use the `-q` option with a keyword. For example, `perldoc -q sort` returns three questions: *How do I sort an array by (anything)?*, *How do I sort a hash (optionally by value instead of key)?*, and *How can I always keep my hash sorted?*.

The -f option displays the documentation for a builtin Perl function. perldoc -f sort explains the behavior of the sort operator. If you don't know the name of the function you want, browse the list of available builtins in perldoc perlfunc.

The -v option looks up a builtin variable. For example, perldoc -v $PID displays the documentation for the variable which contains the current program's process id. Depending on your shell, you may have to quote the variable appropriately.

The -l option causes perldoc to display the *path* to the documentation file rather than the contents of the documentation[2].

The -m option displays the entire *contents* of the module, code and all, without performing any special formatting.

Perl uses a documentation format called *POD*, which is short for *Plain Old Documentation*, or *POD*. perldoc perlpod describes how POD works. Other POD tools include podchecker, which validates the structure of POD documents, and the Pod::Webserver CPAN module, which displays local POD as HTML through a minimal web server.

# Expressivity

Larry Wall studied linguistics and human languages. Then he designed Perl. Unlike other languages designed around a mathematical notion, Perl takes into account how people communicate. In return, you get the freedom to decide how to arrange your programs to meet your needs. You may write simple, straightforward code or combine many small pieces into larger programs. You may select from multiple design paradigms, and you may eschew or embrace advanced features.

Where other languages claim that there should be only one best way to solve any problem, Perl allows *you* to decide what's most readable, most useful, most appealing, or most fun.

Perl hackers have a slogan for this: *TIMTOWTDI*, pronounced "Tim Toady", or "There's more than one way to do it!"

Though this expressivity allows master craftworkers to create amazing programs, it also allows the unwary to make messes. Experience and good taste will guide you as you design your code, but the choice is always yours. Express yourself, but be mindful of readability and maintainability, especially for those who come after you.

---

[2]Be aware that a module may have a separate *.pod* file in addition to its *.pm* file.

Learning Perl is like learning any spoken language. You'll learn a few words, then string together sentences, and then enjoy simple conversations. Mastery comes from practice of both reading and writing code. You don't have to understand every detail of Perl to be productive, but the principles in this chapter are vital to your growth as a programmer.

Perl novices often find certain syntactic constructs opaque. These idioms (Idioms, pp. 247) offer great (if subtle) power in the hands of experienced programmers, but it's okay to avoid them until you're comfortable with them.

As another design goal, Perl tries to avoid surprising experienced (Perl) programmers. For example, adding two variables ($first_num + $second_num) is obviously a numeric operation (Numeric Operators, pp. 101); the addition operator must treat both as numeric values to produce a numeric result. No matter the contents of $first_num and $second_num, Perl will coerce them to numeric values (Numeric Coercion, pp. 79). You've expressed your intent to treat them as numbers by using a numeric operator. Perl happily does so.

Perl adepts often call this principle *DWIM*, or *do what I mean*. You could just as well say that Perl follows the *principle of least astonishment*. Given a cursory understanding of Perl (especially context; Context, pp. 5), it should be possible to understand the intent of an unfamiliar Perl expression. You will develop this skill as you learn Perl.

Perl's expressivity allows novices to write useful programs without having to understand the entire language. This is by design! Experienced developers often call the results *baby Perl*. This is a term of endearment, because everyone begins as a novice. Through practice and learning from more experienced programmers, you will understand and adopt more powerful idioms and techniques. It's okay for you to write simple code that you understand. Keep practicing and you'll become a native speaker.

An experienced Perl hacker might triple a list of numbers with:

```
my @tripled = map { $_ * 3 } @numbers;
```

...and a Perl adept might write:

```
my @tripled;

for my $num (@numbers)
{
    push @tripled, $num * 3;
}
```

4

... while a novice might try:

```
my @tripled;

for (my $i = 0; $i < scalar @numbers; $i++)
{
    $tripled[$i] = $numbers[$i] * 3;
}
```

Every program does the same thing, but each uses Perl in a different way.

As you get more comfortable with Perl, you can let the language do more for you. With experience, you can focus on *what* you want to do rather than *how* to do it. Even so, Perl will happily run baby Perl just as well as expert Perl. You can design and refine your programs for clarity, expressivity, reuse, and maintainability, in part or in whole. Take advantage of this flexibility and pragmatism: it's far better to accomplish your task effectively now than to write a conceptually pure and beautiful program next year.

# Context

In spoken languages, the meaning of a word or phrase may depend on how you use it; the local *context* helps clarify the intent. For example, the inappropriate pluralization of "Please give me one hamburgers!"[3] sounds wrong, just as the incorrect gender of "la gato"[4] makes native speakers chuckle. Other words do double duty; one sheep is a sheep just as two sheep are also sheep.

Context in Perl is similar. It describes the *amount* as well as the *kind* of data to use. Perl will do what you mean to do to data if you choose the appropriate context for that data.

For example, several Perl operations produce different behaviors when you expect zero, one, or many results. A specific construct in Perl may do something different if you write "Do this, but I don't care about any results" compared to "Do this and give me multiple results." Other operations allow you to specify whether you expect to work with numeric data, textual data, or true or false data.

Context can be tricky if you try to write or read Perl code as a series of single steps in isolation. That's not how Perl works! Every expression is part of a larger context. You may find yourself slapping your forehead after a long debugging

---

[3] The pluralization of the noun differs from the amount.

[4] The article is feminine, but the noun is masculine.

5

session when you discover that your assumptions about context were incorrect. If instead you're aware of context, your code will be more correct–and cleaner, flexible, and more concise.

## Void, Scalar, and List Context

*Amount context* governs *how many* items you expect from an operation. The English language's subject-verb number agreement is a close parallel. Even without knowing the formal description of this linguistic principle, you probably understand the error in the sentence "Perl are a fun language"[5]. In Perl, the number of items you request determines how many you get.

Suppose the function (Declaring Functions, pp. 105) called `find_chores()` sorts your household todo list in order of task priority. The number of chores you expect to read from your list determines what exactly the function will do. If you expect nothing, you're just pretending to be busy. If you expect one task, you have something to do for the next fifteen minutes. If you have a burst of energy on a free weekend, you could get all of the chores.

When you call a function on its own and never use its return value, you've used *void context*:

```
find_chores();
```

Assigning the function's return value to a single item (Scalars, pp. 59) enforces *scalar context*:

```
my $single_result = find_chores();
```

Assigning the results of calling the function to an array (Arrays, pp. 61) or a list, or using it in a list, evaluates the function in *list context*:

```
my @all_results           = find_chores();
my ($single_element, @rest) = find_chores();

# list of results passed to a function
process_list_of_results( find_chores() );
```

The parentheses in the second line of the previous example group the two variable declarations (Lexical Scope, pp. 119) into a single unit so that assignment assigns

---

[5]In terms of amount context, you could say that the verb "are" expects multiple nouns.

to both of the variables. Note that a single-item list is still a list, however. You could also correctly write:

```
my ($single_element)    = find_chores();
```

.... in which case the parentheses give a hint to the Perl parser that you intend list context for the assignment even though you assign only one element of a list. This is subtle, but now that you know about it, the difference of amount context between these two statements should be obvious:

```
my $scalar_context = find_chores();
my ($list_context) = find_chores();
```

Evaluating a function or expression–except for assignment–in list context can produce confusion. Lists propagate list context to the expressions they contain. Both of these calls to find_chores() occur in list context:

```
process_list_of_results( find_chores() );

my %results =
(
    cheap_operation     => $cheap_results,
    expensive_operation => find_chores(), # OOPS!
);
```

The latter example often surprises novice programmers, as initializing a hash (Hashes, pp. 68) with a list of values imposes list context on find_chores. Use the scalar operator to impose scalar context:

```
my %results =
(
    cheap_operation     => $cheap_results,
    expensive_operation => scalar find_chores(),
);
```

Why does context matter? A context-aware function can examine its calling context and decide how much work it must do. In void context, find_chores() may legitimately do nothing. In scalar context, it can find only the most important task. In list context, it must sort and return the entire list.

## Numeric, String, and Boolean Context

Perl's other context–*value context*–governs how Perl interprets a piece of data. You've probably already noticed that Perl can figure out if you have a number or a string and convert data between the two forms. In exchange for not having to declare (or at least track) explicitly what *type* of data a variable contains or a function produces, Perl's value contexts provide hints about how to treat that data.

Perl will coerce values to specific proper types (Coercion, pp. 78), depending on the operators you use. For example, the eq operator tests that strings contain the same information *as strings*:

```
say "Catastrophic crypto fail!" if $alice eq $bob;
```

You may have had a baffling experience where you *know* that the strings are different, but they still compare the same:

```
my $alice = 'alice';
say "Catastrophic crypto fail!" if $alice == 'Bob';
```

Where the eq operator treats its operands as strings by enforcing *string context* on them, the == operator imposes *numeric context*. In numeric context, both strings evaluate to 0 (Numeric Coercion, pp. 79). Be sure to use the proper operator for the type of context you want.

*Boolean context* occurs when you use a value in a conditional statement. In the previous examples, if evaluated the results of the eq and == operators in boolean context.

In rare circumstances, you may need to force an explicit context where no appropriately typed operator exists. To force a numeric context, add zero to a variable. To force a string context, concatenate a variable with the empty string. To force a boolean context, double up the negation operator:

```
my $numeric_x =  0 + $x;  # forces numeric context
my $stringy_x = '' . $x;  # forces string  context
my $boolean_x =    !!$x;  # forces boolean context
```

Value contexts are easier to identify than amount contexts. Once you know which operators provide which contexts (Operator Types, pp. 101), you'll rarely make mistakes.

# Implicit Ideas

Programmers who understand Perl's linguistic shortcuts can glance at code and instantly understand its most important characteristics. Besides context, Perl has default variables–the programming equivalent of pronouns.

## The Default Scalar Variable

The *default scalar variable* (also called the *topic variable*), $_, is most notable in its *absence*: many of Perl's builtin operations work on the contents of $_ in the absence of an explicit variable. You can still use $_ as the variable, but it's often unnecessary.

Many of Perl's scalar operators (including chr, ord, lc, length, reverse, and uc) work on the default scalar variable if you do not provide an alternative. For example, the chomp builtin removes any trailing newline sequence from its operand[6]:

```
my $uncle = "Bob\n";
chomp $uncle;
say "'$uncle'";
```

$_ has the same function in Perl as the pronoun *it* in English. Without an explicit variable, chomp removes the trailing newline sequence from $_. Perl understands what you mean when you say "chomp"; Perl will always chomp *it*. These two lines of code are equivalent:

```
chomp $_;
chomp;
```

Similarly, say and print operate on $_ in the absence of other arguments:

```
print;   # prints $_ to the current filehandle
say;     # prints "$_\n" to the current filehandle
```

Perl's regular expression facilities (Regular Expressions and Matching, pp. 145) default to $_ to match, substitute, and transliterate:

```
$_ = 'My name is Paquito';
say if /My name is/;
```

---

[6]See perldoc -f chomp and $/ for more precise details of its behavior.

9

```
s/Paquito/Paquita/;

tr/A-Z/a-z/;
say;
```

Perl's looping directives (Looping Directives, pp. 45) default to using `$_` as the iteration variable. Consider `for` iterating over a list:

```
say "#$_" for 1 .. 10;

for (1 .. 10)
{
    say "#$_";
}
```

. . . or `while`:

```
while (<STDIN>)
{
    chomp;
    say scalar reverse;
}
```

. . . or `map` transforming a list:

```
my @squares = map { $_ * $_ } 1 .. 10;
say for @squares;
```

. . . or `grep` filtering a list:

```
say 'Brunch time!'
    if grep { /pancake mix/ } @pantry;
```

As English gets confusing when you have too many pronouns and antecedents, so does Perl when you mix explicit and implicit uses of `$_`. If you use it in multiple places, one piece of code may silently override the value expected by another piece of code. For example, if one function uses `$_` and you call it from another function which uses `$_`, the callee may clobber the caller's value:

```
while (<STDIN>)
{
    chomp;

    # BAD EXAMPLE
    my $munged = calculate_value( $_ );
    say "Original: $_";
    say "Munged   : $munged";
}
```

If `calculate_value()` or any other function changed $\_$, that change would persist through that iteration of the loop. As of Perl 5.10, you can declare $\_$ as a lexical variable (Lexical Scope, pp. 119) with my to prevent clobbering an existing instance of $\_$:

```
while (my $_ = <STDIN>)
{
    . . .
}
```

Unfortunately, this construct has a few edge cases related to how existing functions behave when they expect $\_$ to be a global variable. As of Perl 5.18, the Perl 5 Porters consider this feature experimental. Use it with caution. Besides, using a named lexical may be even clearer:

```
while (my $line = <STDIN>)
{
    . . .
}
```

Use $\_$ as you would the word "it" in formal writing: sparingly, in small and well-defined scopes.

---

**The . . . Operator**

Perl 5.12 introduced the triple-dot ( . . . ) operator as a placeholder for code you intend to fill in later. Perl will parse it as a complete statement, but will throw an exception that you're trying to run unimplemented code if you try to run it. See `perldoc perlop` for more details.

---

## The Default Array Variables

Perl also provides two implicit array variables. Perl passes arguments to functions (Declaring Functions, pp. 105) in an array named @_. Array manipulation operations (Arrays, pp. 61) inside functions operate on this array by default. These two snippets of code are equivalent:

```
sub foo
{
    my $arg = shift;
    ...
}

sub foo_explicit_args
{
    my $arg = shift @_;
    ...
}
```

Just as $_ corresponds to the pronoun *it*, @_ corresponds to the pronouns *they* and *them*. *Unlike* $_, Perl automatically localizes @_ for you when you call other functions. The builtins shift and pop operate on @_, if provided no explicit operands.

Outside of all functions, the default array variable @ARGV contains the command-line arguments to the program. Perl's array operations (including shift and pop) operate on @ARGV implicitly outside of functions. You cannot use @_ when you mean @ARGV.

> **readline**
>
> Perl's <$fh> operator is the same as the readline builtin. readline $fh does the same thing as <$fh>. As of Perl 5.10, a bare readline behaves just like <>, so you can now use readline everywhere. For historic reasons, <> is still more common, but consider using readline as a more readable alternative. (What's more readable, glob '*.html' to <*.html>? The same idea applies.)

ARGV has one special case. If you read from the null filehandle <>, Perl will treat every element in @ARGV as the *name* of a file to open for reading. (If @ARGV is empty, Perl will read from standard input.) This implicit @ARGV behavior is useful for writing short programs, such as a command-line filter which reverses its input:

```
while (<>)
{
    chomp;
    say scalar reverse;
}
```

Why `scalar`? `say` imposes list context on its operands. `reverse` passes its context on to its operands, treating them as a list in list context and a concatenated string in scalar context. If the behavior of `reverse` sounds confusing, your instincts are correct. Perl arguably should have separated "reverse a string" from "reverse a list".

If you run it with a list of files:

$ **perl reverse_lines.pl encrypted/*.txt**

...the result will be one long stream of output. Without any arguments, you can provide your own standard input by piping in from another program or typing directly. That's a lot of flexibility in a small program, but Perl's only getting started.

# CHAPTER 2

# Perl and Its Community

Perl's greatest accomplishment is the huge amount of reusable libraries developed for it. Where Perl 4 had forks to connect to databases such as Oracle and Sybase, for example, Perl now has a real extension mechanism. Larry wanted people to create and maintain their own extensions without fragmenting Perl into thousands of incompatible pidgins–and it worked.

That technical accomplishment was almost as important as the growth of a community around Perl. *People* write libraries. *People* build on the work of other people. *People* make a community worth joining and preserving and expanding.

The Perl community is strong and healthy. It welcomes willing participants at all levels, from novices to core developers. Take advantage of the knowledge and experience of countless other Perl programmers, and you'll become a better programmer.

## The CPAN

Perl is a pragmatic language, and the availability of tens of thousands of freely reusable Perl libraries demonstrates that pragmatism. If you have a problem to solve, chances are the global Perl community has already written–and shared–code to solve it.

Modern Perl programming makes heavy use of the CPAN (http://www.cpan.org/). The Comprehensive Perl Archive Network is an uploading and mirroring system for redistributable, reusable Perl code. It's one of–if not *the*–largest archives of libraries of code in the world. The CPAN offers libraries for everything from database access to profiling tools to protocols for almost every network device ever created to sound and graphics libraries and wrappers for shared libraries on your system.

Modern Perl without the CPAN is just another language. Modern Perl with the CPAN is a powerful toolkit for solving problems.

CPAN mirrors *distributions*, or collections of reusable Perl code. A single distribution can contain one or more *modules*, or self-contained libraries of Perl code. Each distribution occupies its own CPAN namespace and provides unique metadata.

> ### The CPAN is Big, Really Big
>
> The CPAN *adds* hundreds of registered contributors and thousands of indexed modules in hundreds of distributions every month. Those numbers do not take into account updates. In January 2014, search.cpan.org reported 11021 uploaders, 129039 modules, and 29068 distributions (representing growth rates of 15.1%, 21.2%, and 18.1% since the previous edition of this book, respectively).

The CPAN itself is merely a mirroring service. Authors upload distributions which get sent to various mirror sites from which CPAN clients download, configure, build, test, and install them. This simplicity has served Perl well, by enabling the contributions of thousands of volunteers. In particular, community standards have evolved to identify the attributes and characteristics of well-formed CPAN distributions. These include:

- the behavior of automated CPAN installers
- metadata to describe what each distribution provides and expects
- machine-readable documentation and licensing

Additional CPAN services provide comprehensive automated testing and reporting to improve the quality of packaging and correctness across platforms and Perl versions. Every CPAN distribution has its own ticket queue on http://rt.cpan.org/ for reporting bugs and working with authors. CPAN sites also link to previous distribution versions, module ratings, documentation annotations, and more. All of this is available from both http://search.cpan.org/ and http://metacpan.org/.

Modern Perl installations include a client to connect to, search, download, build, test, and install CPAN distributions; this is *CPAN.pm*. With a recent version (as of this writing, 2.0 is the latest stable release), module installation is reasonably easy. Start the client with:

```
$ cpan
```

To install a distribution within the client:

```
$ cpan
cpan[1]> install Modern::Perl
```

... or to install directly from the command line:

```
$ cpan Modern::Perl
```

Eric Wilhelm's tutorial on configuring CPAN.pm[1] includes a great troubleshooting section.

> Even though the CPAN client is a core module for the Perl distribution, you will likely need to install standard development tools such as a `make` utility and possibly a C compiler. Windows users, see Strawberry Perl (http://strawberryperl.com/) and Strawberry Perl Professional. Mac OS X users must install XCode. Unix and Unix-like users often have these tools available (though Debian and Ubuntu users should install `build-essential`).

## CPAN Management Tools

If your operating system provides its own Perl installation, that version may be out of date or it may have its own dependencies on specific versions of CPAN distributions. Serious Perl developers often construct virtual walls between the system Perl and their development Perl installations. Several projects help to make this possible.

App::cpanminus is a newer CPAN client with goals of speed, simplicity, and zero configuration. Install it with cpan App::cpanminus, or:

```
$ curl -LO http://xrl.us/cpanm
$ less cpanm # review the code before running
$ chmod +x cpanm
$ ./cpanm
```

App::perlbrew is a system to manage and to switch between your own installations of multiple versions and configurations of Perl. Installation is as easy as:

---

[1] http://learnperl.scratchcomputing.com/tutorials/configuration/

```
$ curl -LO http://xrl.us/perlbrew
$ less perlbrew # review the code before running
$ chmod +x perlbrew
$ ./perlbrew install
$ perldoc App::perlbrew
```

The `local::lib` CPAN distribution allows you to install and to manage distributions in your own user directory, rather than for the system as a whole. This is an effective way to maintain CPAN distributions for individual users without affecting the system as a whole. Installation is somewhat more involved than the previous two distributions, though `App::local::lib::helper` can simplify the process. See https://metacpan.org/pod/local::lib and https://metcapan.org/pod/App::local::lib::helper for more details.

All three projects tend to assume a Unix-like environment (such as a GNU/Linux distribution or even Mac OS X). Windows users, see the Padre all-in-one download (http://padre.perlide.org/download.html).

# Community Sites

Perl's homepage at http://www.perl.org/ links to Perl documentation, source code, tutorials, mailing lists, and several important community projects. If you're new to Perl, the Perl beginners mailing list is a friendly place to ask novice questions and get accurate and helpful answers. See http://learn.perl.org/faq/beginners.html.

The home of Perl development is http://dev.perl.org/, which links to relevant resources for Perl's core development.

Perl.com publishes articles and tutorials about Perl and its culture. Its archives reach back into the 20th century. See http://www.perl.com/.

The CPAN's (The CPAN, pp. 15) central location is http://www.cpan.org/, though experienced users spend more time on http://search.cpan.org/. This central software distribution hub of reusable, free Perl code is an essential part of the Perl community. MetaCPAN (https://metacpan.org/) is a recent alternative front end to the CPAN.

PerlMonks, at http://perlmonks.org/, is a community site devoted to discussions about Perl programming. Its decade-plus history makes it one of the most venerable question and answer sites for any programming language.

Several community sites offer news and commentary. http://blogs.perl.org/ is a free blog platform open to any Perl community member.

Other sites aggregate the musings of Perl hackers, including http://perlsphere.net/, http://planet.perl.org/, and http://ironman.enlightenedperl.org/. The latter is part of an initiative from the Enlightened Perl Organization (http://enlightenedperl.org/) to increase the amount and improve the quality of Perl publishing on the web.

Perl Buzz (http://perlbuzz.com/) collects and republishes some of the most interesting and useful Perl news on a regular basis. Perl Weekly (http://perlweekly.com/) offers a weekly take on news from the Perl world.

## Development Sites

Best Practical Solutions (http://bestpractical.com/) maintains an installation of their popular request tracking system, RT, for CPAN authors as well as Perl development. Every CPAN distribution has its own RT queue on http://rt.cpan.org/. Perl itself has a ticket queue at http://rt.perl.org/.

The Perl 5 Porters (or *p5p*) mailing list is the focal point of the development of Perl. See http://lists.cpan.org/showlist.cgi?name=perl5-porters.

The Perl Foundation (http://www.perlfoundation.org/) hosts a wiki for all things Perl. See http://www.perlfoundation.org/perl5.

Many Perl hackers use Github (http://github.com/) to host their projects[2]. See especially Gitpan (http://github.com/gitpan/), which hosts Git repositories chronicling the complete history of every distribution on the CPAN.

---

**A Local Git Mirror**

GitPAN receives infrequent updates. As an alternative to hacking CPAN distributions from GitPAN, consider using Yanick Champoux's wonderful `Git::CPAN::Patch` module to create local Git repositories from CPAN distributions.

---

## Events

The Perl community holds countless conferences, workshops, seminars, and meetings. In particular, the community-run YAPC–Yet Another Perl Conference–is a successful, local, low-cost conference model held on multiple continents. See http://yapc.org/.

The Perl Foundation wiki lists other events at http://www.perlfoundation.org/perl5/index.cgi?perl_events.

---

[2]...including the sources of this book at http://github.com/chromatic/modern_perl_book/

Hundreds of local Perl Mongers groups get together frequently for technical talks and social interaction. See http://www.pm.org/.

# IRC

When Perl mongers can't meet in person, many collaborate and chat online through the textual chat system known as IRC. Many of the most popular and useful Perl projects have their own IRC channels, such as *#moose* and *#catalyst*.

The main server for Perl community is irc://irc.perl.org/. Notable channels include *#perl-help*, for general assistance on Perl programming, and *#perl-qa*, devoted to testing and other quality issues. Be aware that the channel *#perl* is a general purpose channel for discussing whatever its participants want to discuss[3].

---

[3] . . . and, as such, it's not primarily a helpdesk.

# CHAPTER 3

# The Perl Language

Like a spoken language, the whole of Perl is a combination of several smaller but interrelated parts. Unlike spoken language, where nuance and tone of voice and intuition allow people to communicate despite slight misunderstandings and fuzzy concepts, computers and source code require precision. You can write effective Perl code without knowing every detail of every language feature, but you must understand how they work together to write Perl code well.

## Names

*Names* (or *identifiers*) are everywhere in Perl programs: you get to choose them for variables, functions, packages, classes, and even filehandles. Valid Perl names all begin with a letter or an underscore and may optionally include any combination of letters, numbers, and underscores. When the utf8 pragma (Unicode and Strings, pp. 30) is in effect, you may use any UTF-8 word characters in identifiers. All of these are valid Perl identifiers:

```
my $name;
my @_private_names;
my %Names_to_Addresses;
sub anAwkwardName3;

# with use utf8; enabled
package Ingy::Döt::Net;
```

These are invalid Perl identifiers:

```
my $invalid name;
my @3;
my %~flags;

package a-lisp-style-name;
```

*Names exist primarily for the benefit of the programmer.* These rules apply only to literal names which appear in your source code, such as sub `fetch_pie` or my `$waffleiron`. Only Perl's parser enforces the rules about identifier names. Perl allows you to refer to entities with names generated at runtime or provided as input to a program. These *symbolic lookups* provide flexibility at the expense of safety.

In particular, invoking functions or methods indirectly or looking up symbols in a namespace lets you bypass Perl's parser. Symbolic lookups can produce confusing code. As Mark Jason Dominus recommends so effectively[1], prefer a hash (Hashes, pp. 68) or nested data structure (Nested Data Structures, pp. 92) over variables named, for example, $recipe1, $recipe2, and so on.

## Variable Names and Sigils

*Variable names* always have a leading *sigil* (a symbol) which indicates the type of the variable's value. *Scalar variables* (Scalars, pp. 59) use the dollar sign ($). *Array variables* (Arrays, pp. 61) use the at sign (@). *Hash variables* (Hashes, pp. 68) use the percent sign (%):

```
my $scalar;
my @array;
my %hash;
```

Sigils allow you to separate variables into different namespaces. It's possible–though confusing–to declare multiple variables of the same name with different types:

```
my ($bad_name, @bad_name, %bad_name);
```

Though Perl won't get confused, people reading this code will.

The sigil of a variable can change depending on what you do with it; the term for this is *variant sigils*. As context determines how many items you expect from an operation or what type of data you expect to get, so the sigil governs how you manipulate the data of a variable. For example, you must use the scalar sigil ($) to access a single element of an array or a hash:

```
my $hash_element  = $hash{ $key };
my $array_element = $array[ $index ]
```

---

[1] http://perl.plover.com/varvarname.html

```
$hash{ $key }      = 'value';
$array[ $index ]   = 'item';
```

The parallel with amount context is important. Using a scalar element of an aggregate as an *lvalue* (the target of an assignment; on the *left* side of the = character) imposes scalar context (Context, pp. 5) on the *rvalue* (the value assigned; on the *right* side of the = character).

Similarly, accessing multiple elements of a hash or an array–an operation known as *slicing*–uses the at symbol (@) and imposes list context[2]:

```
my @hash_elements  = @hash{ @keys };
my @array_elements = @array[ @indexes ];

my %hash;
@hash{ @keys }     = @values;
```

The most reliable way to determine the type of a variable–scalar, array, or hash–is to examine the operations performed on it. Scalars support all basic operations, such as string, numeric, and boolean manipulations. Arrays support indexed access through square brackets. Hashes support keyed access through curly brackets.

## Namespaces

Perl provides a mechanism to group similar functions and variables into their own unique named spaces–*namespaces* (Packages, pp. 80). A namespace is collection of symbols grouped under a globally unique name. Perl allows multi-level namespaces, with names joined by double colons ( : : ), where DessertShop : : IceCream refers to a logical collection of related variables and functions, such as scoop() and pour_hot_fudge().

Within a namespace, you may use the short name of its members. Outside of the namespace, you must refer to a member by its *fully-qualified name*. Within DessertShop::IceCream, add_sprinkles() refers to the same function as does DessertShop::IceCream::add_sprinkles() outside of the namespace.

While standard naming rules apply to package names, user-defined packages all start with uppercase letters by convention. The Perl core reserves lowercase package names for core pragmas (Pragmas, pp. 200), such as strict and warnings. This is a policy enforced primarily by community guidelines.

---

[2]...even if the list itself has zero or one elements

23

All namespaces in Perl are globally visible. When Perl looks up a symbol in DessertShop::IceCream::Freezer, it looks in the main:: symbol table for a symbol representing the DessertShop:: namespace, then in that namespace for the IceCream:: namespace, and so on. Yet Freezer:: is visible from outside of the IceCream:: namespace. Namespaces are all globally accessible. The nesting of the former within the latter is only a storage mechanism, and implies nothing further about relationships between parent and child or sibling packages.

Only a programmer can make *logical* relationships between entities obvious–by choosing good names and organizing them well.

# Variables

A *variable* in Perl is a storage location for a value (Values, pp. 26). While a trivial program can manipulate values directly, most programs work with variables to simplify the logic of the code. A variable represents values; it's easier to explain the Pythagorean theorem in terms of the variables a, b, and c than by intuiting its principle by producing a long list of valid values. This concept may seem basic, but to program effectively, you must learn the art of balancing the generic and reusable with the specific.

## Variable Scopes

Variables are available within your program depending on their scope (Scope, pp. 119). Most of the variables you will encounter have lexical scope (Lexical Scope, pp. 119), or scope governed by the syntax of the program as written. Most lexical scopes are either the contents of blocks delimited by curly braces ({ and }) or entire files. *Files* themselves provide their own lexical scopes, such that the package declaration on its own does not create a new scope:

```
package Store::Toy;

my $discount = 0.10;

package Store::Music;

# $discount still visible
say "Our current discount is $discount!";
```

You may also provide a block to the package declaration[3]. Because this introduces a new block, it also provides a new lexical scope:

```
package Store::Toy
{
    my $discount = 0.10;
}

package Store::Music
{
    # $discount not available
}

package Store::BoardGame;

# $discount still not available
```

## Variable Sigils

The sigil of the variable in a declaration determines the type of the variable: scalar, array, or hash. The sigil used when *accessing* a variable varies depending on what you do to the variable. For example, you declare an array as @values. Access the first element–a single value–of the array with $values[0]. Access a list of values from the array with @values[ @indices ]. As you might expect, the sigil you use determines amount context in an lvalue situation:

```
# imposes lvalue context on some_function()
@values[ @indexes ] = some_function()
```

... or gets coerced in an rvalue situation:

```
# list evaluated to final element in scalar context
my $element = @values[ @indices ]
```

## Anonymous Variables

Perl variables do not *require* names. Names exist to help you, the programmer, keep track of an $apple, @barrels, or %cookie_recipes. Variables created *without* literal names in your source code are *anonymous* variables. The only way to access anonymous variables is by reference (References, pp. 83).

---

[3]As of 5.14.

25

## Variables, Types, and Coercion

This relationship between variable types, sigils, and context is essential to your understanding of Perl.

A Perl variable represents both a value (a dollar cost, available pizza toppings, the names and numbers of guitar stores) and the container which stores that value. Perl's type system deals with *value types* and *container types*. While a variable's *container type*–scalar, array, or hash–cannot change, Perl is flexible about a variable's value type. You may store a string in a variable in one line, append to that variable a number on the next, and reassign a reference to a function (Function References, pp. 89) on the third[4].

Performing an operation on a variable which imposes a specific value type may cause coercion (Coercion, pp. 78) from the variable's existing value type.

For example, the documented way to determine the number of entries in an array is to evaluate that array in scalar context (Context, pp. 5). Because a scalar variable can only ever contain a scalar, assigning an array to a scalar imposes scalar context on the operation, and an array evaluated in scalar context produces the number of elements in the array:

```
my $count = @items;
```

# Values

As you gain experience, you'll discover that the structure of your programs will depend on the way you model your data with variables.

Variables allow the abstract manipulation of data while the values they hold make programs concrete and useful. The more accurate your values, the better your programs. These values are your aunt's name and address, the distance between your office and a golf course on the moon, or the weight of all of the cookies you've eaten in the past year. Within your program, the rules regarding the format of that data are often strict.

Effective programs need effective (simple, fast, efficient, easy to use) ways of representing their data.

## Strings

A *string* is a piece of textual or binary data with no particular formatting or contents. It could be your name, the contents of an image file, or the source code of

---

[4] ...but you'll confuse yourself if you do all of that.

the program itself. A string has meaning in the program only when you give it meaning.

To represent a literal string in your program, surround it with a pair of quoting characters. The most common *string delimiters* are single and double quotes:

```
my $name    = 'Donner Odinson, Bringer of Despair';
my $address = "Room 539, Bilskirnir, Valhalla";
```

Characters in a *single-quoted string* are exactly and only ever what they appear to be, with two exceptions. To include a single quote inside a single-quoted string, escaping it with a leading backslash:

```
my $reminder = 'Don\'t forget to escape '
             . 'the single quote!';
```

If you want a backslash at the *end* of the string, you'll have to escape it as well, to avoid making Perl think you're trying to escape the closing delimiter[5]:

```
my $exception = 'This string ends with a '
              . 'backslash, not a quote: \\';
```

Any other backslash will be part of the string as it appears, unless you have two adjacent backslashes, in which case Perl will believe that you intended to escape the second:

```
is('Modern \ Perl', 'Modern \\ Perl',
    'single quotes backslash escaping');
```

A *double-quoted string* gives you more options. For example, you may encode otherwise invisible whitespace characters in the string:

```
my $tab       = "\t";
my $newline   = "\n";
my $carriage  = "\r";
my $formfeed  = "\f";
my $backspace = "\b";
```

---

[5] Programming language design is full of corner cases like this.

This demonstrates a useful principle: there are multiple possible representations of the same string. You can include a tab within a string by typing the \t escape sequence or by hitting the Tab key on your keyboard. Within Perl's purview, both strings behave the same way, even though the representation of the string may differ in the source code.

A string declaration may cross (and include) newlines, so these two declarations are equivalent:

```
my $escaped = "two\nlines";
my $literal = "two
lines";
is $escaped, $literal, 'equivalent \n and newline';
```

With that said, the escape sequences are often much easier to read than their literal equivalents.

As you manipulate and modify strings, Perl will change their sizes as appropriate; these strings have variable lengths. For example, you can combine multiple strings into a larger string with the *concatenation* operator . :

```
my $kitten = 'Choco' . ' ' . 'Spidermonkey';
```

. . . though this is effectively the same as if you'd initialized the string all at once.

You may also *interpolate* the value of a scalar variable or the values of an array within a double-quoted string, such that the *current* contents of the variable become part of the string as if you'd concatenated them:

```
my $factoid = "$name lives at $address!";

# equivalent to
my $factoid = $name . ' lives at ' . $address . '!';
```

Include a literal double-quote inside a double-quoted string by *escaping* it with a leading backslash:

```
my $quote = "\"Ouch,\", he cried.  \"That hurt!\"";
```

When repeated backslashing becomes unwieldy, use a *quoting operator*, which allows you to choose an alternate string delimiter. The q operator indicates single quoting (no interpolation), while the qq operator provides double quoting behavior

28

(interpolation). The character immediately following the operator determines the characters used to delimit the strings. If the character is the opening character of a balanced pair–such as opening and closing braces–the closing character will be the final delimiter. Otherwise, the character itself will be both the starting and ending delimiter.

```
my $quote     = qq{"Ouch", he said.   "That hurt!"};
my $reminder  = q^Don't escape the single quote!^;
my $complaint = q{It's too early to be awake.};
```

When declaring a complex string with a series of embedded escapes is tedious, use the *heredoc* syntax to assign multiple lines to a string:

```
my $blurb =<<'END_BLURB';

He looked up. "Change is the constant on which they all
can agree.  We instead, born out of time, remain perfect
and perfectly self-aware. We only suffer change as we
pursue it. It is against our nature. We rebel against
that change. Shall we consider them greater for it?"
END_BLURB
```

The <<'END_BLURB' syntax has three parts. The double angle-brackets introduce the heredoc. The quotes determine whether the heredoc follows single- or double-quoted behavior. (The default behavior is double-quoted.) END_BLURB is an arbitrary identifier which the Perl parser uses as the ending delimiter.

Regardless of the indentation of the heredoc declaration itself, the ending delimiter must *start* at the beginning of the line:

```
sub some_function {
    my $ingredients =<<'END_INGREDIENTS';
    Two eggs
    One cup flour
    Two ounces butter
    One-quarter teaspoon salt
    One cup milk
    One drop vanilla
    Season to taste
END_INGREDIENTS
}
```

29

> If the identifier *begins* with whitespace, that same whitespace must be present before the ending delimiter–that is, `<<' END_HEREDOC'>>` needs a leading space before `END_HEREDOC`. Yet if you indent the identifier, Perl will *not* remove equivalent whitespace from the start of each line of the heredoc. Yes, that's less than ideal.

Using a string in a non-string context will induce coercion (Coercion, pp. 78).

## Unicode and Strings

*Unicode* is a system for representing the characters of the world's written languages. While most English text uses a character set of only 127 characters (which requires seven bits of storage and fits nicely into eight-bit bytes), it's naïve to believe that you won't someday need an umlaut.

Perl strings can represent either of two separate but related data types:

Sequences of Unicode characters

Each character has a *codepoint*, a unique number which identifies it in the Unicode character set.

Sequences of octets

Binary data is a sequence of *octets*–8 bit numbers, each of which can represent a number between 0 and 255.

> **Words Matter**
>
> Why *octet* and not *byte*? Assuming that one character fits in one byte will cause you no end of Unicode grief. Separate the idea of memory storage from character representation. Forget that you ever heard of bytes.

Unicode strings and binary strings look superficially similar. Each has a `length()`. Each supports standard string operations such as concatenation, splicing, and regular expression processing (Regular Expressions and Matching, pp. 145). Any string which is not purely binary data is textual data, and thus should be a sequence of Unicode characters.

However, because of how your operating system represents data on disk or from users or over the network–as sequences of octets–Perl can't know if the data you read is an image file or a text document or anything else. By default, Perl treats all incoming data as sequences of octets. It's up to you to add a specific meaning to that data.

## Character Encodings

A Unicode string is a sequence of octets which represents a sequence of characters. A *Unicode encoding* maps octet sequences to characters. Some encodings, such as UTF-8, can encode all of the characters in the Unicode character set. Other encodings represent only a subset of Unicode characters. For example, ASCII encodes plain English text with no accented characters, while Latin-1 can represent text in most languages which use the Latin alphabet.

> **An Evolving Standard**
>
> Perl 5.14 supports the Unicode 6.0 standard, 5.16 the 6.1 standard, and 5.18 the 6.2 standard. See http://unicode.org/versions/.

To avoid most Unicode problems, always decode to and from the appropriate encoding at the inputs and outputs of your program.

## Unicode in Your Filehandles

When you tell Perl that a specific filehandle (Files, pp. 213) should handle data with a specific Unicode encoding, Perl will use an *IO layer* to convert between octets and characters. The *mode* operand of the open builtin allows you to request an IO layer by name. For example, the :utf8 layer decodes UTF-8 data:

```
open my $fh, '<:utf8', $textfile;

my $unicode_string = <$fh>;
```

Use binmode to apply an IO layer to an existing filehandle:

```
binmode $fh, ':utf8';
my $unicode_string = <$fh>;

binmode STDOUT, ':utf8';
say $unicode_string;
```

Without the `utf8` mode, printing certain Unicode strings to a filehandle will result in a warning (`Wide character in %s`), because files contain octets, not Unicode characters.

> **Enable UTF-8 Everywhere**
>
> The `utf8::all` module enables UTF-8 IO layers on all filehandles throughout your program and enables all sorts of other Unicode features. It's very handy, but it's no substitute for (eventually) figuring out what your program needs.

## Unicode in Your Data

The core module `Encode` provides a function named `decode()` to convert a scalar containing octets to Perl's internal version of Unicode strings. The corresponding `encode()` function converts from Perl's internal encoding to the desired encoding:

```
my $from_utf8 = decode('utf8', $data);
my $to_latin1 = encode('iso-8859-1', $string);
```

To handle Unicode properly, you must always *decode* incoming data via a known encoding and *encode* outgoing data to a known encoding. Yes, this means you have to know what kind of data you expect to give and receive, but you should know this anyway. Being specific will help you avoid all kinds of trouble.

## Unicode in Your Programs

You may include Unicode characters in your programs in three ways. The easiest is to use the `utf8` pragma (Pragmas, pp. 200), which tells the Perl parser to interpret the rest of the source code file with the UTF-8 encoding. This allows you to use Unicode characters in strings and identifiers:

```
use utf8;

sub £_to_¥ { ... }

my $yen = £_to_¥('1000£');
```

To *write* this code, your text editor must understand UTF-8 and you must save the file with the appropriate encoding[6].

Within double-quoted strings, you may use the Unicode escape sequence to represent character encodings. The syntax \x{} represents a single character; place the hex form of the character's Unicode number[7] within the curly brackets:

```
my $escaped_thorn = "\x{00FE}";
```

Some Unicode characters have names, and these names are often clearer to read than their numbers even though they're much longer. Use the charnames pragma to enable them and the \N{} escape to refer to them:

```
use charnames ':full';
use Test::More tests => 1;

my $escaped_thorn = "\x{00FE}";
my $named_thorn   = "\N{LATIN SMALL LETTER THORN}";

is $escaped_thorn, $named_thorn,
    'Thorn equivalence check';
```

You may use the \x{} and \N{} forms within regular expressions as well as anywhere else you may legitimately use a string or a character.

## Implicit Conversion

Most Unicode problems in Perl arise from the fact that a string could be either a sequence of octets or a sequence of characters. Perl allows you to combine these types through the use of implicit conversions. When these conversions are wrong, they're rarely *obviously* wrong and they're often *spectacularly* wrong in ways that are difficult to debug.

When Perl concatenates a sequence of octets with a sequence of Unicode characters, it implicitly decodes the octet sequence using the Latin-1 encoding. The resulting string will contain Unicode characters. When you print Unicode characters, Perl will encode the string using UTF-8, because Latin-1 cannot represent the entire set of Unicode characters–Latin-1 is a subset of UTF-8.

---

[6]Again, any two programs which communicate with Unicode data must agree on the encoding of that data.

[7]See http://unicode.org/charts/ for an exhaustive list.

The asymmetry between encodings and octets can lead to Unicode strings encoded as UTF-8 for output and decoded as Latin-1 from input. Worse yet, when the text contains only English characters with no accents, the bug stays hidden, because both encodings use the same representation for every character.

```
my $hello    = "Hello, ";
my $greeting = $hello . $name;
```

If $name contains an English name such as *Alice* you will never notice any problem, because the Latin-1 representation is the same as the UTF-8 representation. If $name contains a name such as *José*, $name can contain several possible values:

- $name contains four Unicode characters.

- $name contains four Latin-1 octets representing four Unicode characters.

- $name contains *five* UTF-8 octets representing four Unicode characters.

The string literal has several possible scenarios:

- It is an ASCII string literal and contains octets.

    ```
    my $hello = "Hello, ";
    ```

- It is a Latin-1 string literal with no explicit encoding and contains octets.

    ```
    my $hello = "¡Hola, ";
    ```

    The string literal contains octets.

- It is a non-ASCII string literal with the utf8 or encoding pragma in effect and contains Unicode characters.

    ```
    use utf8;
    my $hello = "Kuirabá, ";
    ```

If both $hello and $name are Unicode strings, the concatenation will produce another Unicode string.

If both strings are octet streams, Perl will concatenate them into a new octet string. If both values are octets of the same encoding–both Latin-1, for example, the concatenation will work correctly. If the octets do not share an encoding–for example, a concatenation appending UTF-8 data to Latin-1 data–then the resulting sequence of octets makes sense in *neither* encoding. This could happen if the user entered a name as UTF-8 data and the greeting were a Latin-1 string literal, but the program decoded neither.

If only one of the values is a Unicode string, Perl will decode the other as Latin-1 data. If this is not the correct encoding, the resulting Unicode characters will be wrong. For example, if the user input were UTF-8 data and the string literal were a Unicode string, the name would be incorrectly decoded into five Unicode characters to form *JosÃ©* (*sic*) instead of *José* because the UTF-8 data means something else when decoded as Latin-1 data.

If your head is spinning, you're not alone. Always decode on input and encode on output.

See `perldoc perluniintro` for a far more detailed explanation of Unicode, encodings, and how to manage incoming and outgoing data in a Unicode world[8] and his "Perl Unicode Cookbook" series on Perl.com http://www.perl.com/pub/2012/04/perlunicook-standard-preamble.html.

---

Perl 5.12 added a feature, `unicode_strings`, which enables Unicode semantics for all string operations within its scope. Perl 5.14 improved this feature and Perl 5.16 completed it. If you work with Unicode in Perl, you need to use at least Perl 5.14 and, ideally, Perl 5.18.

---

# Numbers

Perl supports numbers as both integers and floating-point values. You may represent them with scientific notation as well as in binary, octal, and hexadecimal forms:

```
my $integer   = 42;
my $float     = 0.007;
my $sci_float = 1.02e14;
my $binary    = 0b101010;
my $octal     = 052;
my $hex       = 0x20;
```

---

[8]For *far* more detail about managing Unicode effectively throughout your programs, see Tom Christiansen's answer to "Why does Modern Perl avoid UTF-8 by default?" http://stackoverflow.com/questions/6162484/why-does-modern-perl-avoid-utf-8-by-default/6163129#6163129

The emboldened characters are the numeric prefixes for binary, octal, and hex notation respectively. Be aware that a leading zero on an integer *always* indicates octal mode.

> ### When 1.99 + 1.99 is 4
>
> Even though you can write floating-point values explicitly with perfect accuracy, Perl–like most programming languages–represents them internally in a binary format. This representation is sometimes imprecise in specific ways; consult `perldoc perlnumber` for more details.

You may *not* use commas to separate thousands in numeric literals, lest the parser interpret the commas as the comma operator. Instead, use underscores within the number. The parser will treat them as invisible characters. Thus all of these are equivalent, though the second might be the most readable:

```
my $billion = 1000000000;
my $billion = 1_000_000_000;
my $billion = 10_0_00_00_0_0_0;
```

Because of coercion (Coercion, pp. 78), Perl programmers rarely have to worry about converting data from outside the program to numbers. Perl will treat anything which looks like a number *as* a number when evaluated in a numeric context. In the rare circumstances where *you* need to know if something looks like a number without evaluating it in a numeric context, use the `looks_like_number` function from the core module `Scalar::Util`. This function returns a true value if Perl will consider the given argument numeric.

The `Regexp::Common` module from the CPAN provides several well-tested regular expressions to identify more specific *types* of numeric values such as whole numbers, integers, and floating-point values.

## Undef

Perl's `undef` value represents an unassigned, undefined, and unknown value. Declared but undefined scalar variables contain `undef`:

```
my $name = undef;    # unnecessary assignment
my $rank;            # also contains undef
```

36

undef evaluates to false in boolean a context. Evaluating undef in a string context–
such as interpolating it into a string:

```
my $undefined;
my $defined = $undefined . '... and so forth';
```

...produces an uninitialized value warning:

```
Use of uninitialized value $undefined in
concatenation (.) or string...
```

The defined builtin returns a true value if its operand evaluates to a defined value
(that is, anything other than undef):

```
my $status = 'suffering from a cold';

say defined $status;   # 1, which is a true value
say defined undef;     # empty string; a false value
```

## The Empty List

When used on the right-hand side of an assignment, the () construct represents an
empty list. In scalar context, this evaluates to undef. In list context, it is an empty
list. When used on the left-hand side of an assignment, the () construct imposes
list context. Why would you ever do this? To count the number of elements returned from an expression in list context without using a temporary variable, use
the idiom (Idioms, pp. 247):

```
my $count = () = get_clown_hats();
```

Because of the right associativity (Associativity, pp. 100) of the assignment operator, Perl first evaluates the second assignment by calling get_clown_hats() in
list context. This produces a list.

Assignment to the empty list throws away all of the values of the list, but that
assignment takes place in scalar context, which evaluates to the number of items
on the right hand side of the assignment. As a result, $count contains the number
of elements in the list returned from get_clown_hats().

Sound complicated? It can confuse new programmers, but with practice, you'll see
how Perl's fundamental design features fit together.

37

## Lists

A list is a comma-separated group of one or more expressions. Lists may occur verbatim in source code as values:

```perl
my @first_fibs = (1, 1, 2, 3, 5, 8, 13, 21);
```

... as targets of assignments:

```perl
my ($package, $filename, $line) = caller();
```

... or as lists of expressions:

```perl
say name(), ' => ', age();
```

Parentheses do not *create* lists. The comma operator creates lists. Where present, the parentheses in these examples group expressions to change their *precedence* (Precedence, pp. 99).

Use the range operator to create lists of literals in a compact form[9]:

```perl
my @chars = 'a' .. 'z';
my @count = 13 .. 27;
```

Use the qw() operator to split a literal string on whitespace to produce a list of strings[10]:

```perl
my @stooges = qw( Larry Curly Moe Shemp Joey Kenny );
```

> **No Comment Please**
>
> Perl will emit a warning if a qw() contains a comma or the comment character (#), because not only are such characters rare in a qw(), their presence is often a mistake.

---

[9]See? Lists but no parentheses!

[10]Parentheses, but you could use any delimiter, such as qw!!.

Lists can (and often do) occur as the results of expressions, but these lists do not appear literally in source code.

Lists and arrays are not interchangeable in Perl. You may store a list in an array and you may coerce an array to a list, but lists and arrays are separate concepts. Lists are values. Arrays are containers. For example, indexing into a list always occurs in list context. Indexing into an array can occur in scalar context (for a single element) or list context (for a slice):

```
# don't worry about the details right now
sub context
{
    my $context = wantarray();

    say defined $context
        ? $context
            ? 'list'
            : 'scalar'
        : 'void';
    return 0;
}

my @list_slice  = (1, 2, 3)[context()];
my @array_slice = @list_slice[context()];
my $array_index = $array_slice[context()];

say context(); # list context
context();     # void context
```

# Control Flow

Perl's basic *control flow* is straightforward. Program execution starts at the beginning (the first line of the file executed) and continues to the end:

```
say 'At start';
say 'In middle';
say 'At end';
```

Perl's *control flow directives* change the order of execution–that is, what happens next in the program.

## Branching Directives

The `if` directive performs the associated action only when its conditional expression evaluates to a *true* value:

```
say 'Hello, Bob!' if $name eq 'Bob';
```

This postfix form is useful for simple expressions. Its block form groups multiple expressions into a unit which evaluates to a single boolean value:

```
if ($name eq 'Bob')
{
    say 'Hello, Bob!';
    found_bob();
}
```

While the block form requires parentheses around its condition, the postfix form does not.

The conditional expression may consist of multiple subexpressions, as long as it evaluates to something which can be coerced to a boolean value:

```
if ($name eq 'Bob' && not greeted_bob())
{
    say 'Hello, Bob!';
    found_bob();
}
```

In the postfix form, adding parentheses can clarify the intent of the code at the expense of visual cleanliness:

```
greet_bob() if ($name eq 'Bob' && not greeted_bob());
```

The `unless` directive is the negated form of `if`. Perl will perform the action when the conditional expression evaluates to a *false* value:

```
say "You're not Bob!" unless $name eq 'Bob';
```

Like `if`, `unless` also has a block form, though many programmers avoid it due to its potential for confusion:

```
unless (is_leap_year() and is_full_moon())
{
    frolic();
    gambol();
}
```

unless works very well for postfix conditionals, especially parameter validation in functions (Postfix Parameter Validation, pp. 253):

```
sub frolic
{
    # do nothing without parameters
    return unless @_;

    for my $chant (@_) { ... }
}
```

The block forms of if and unless both support the else directive, which provides code to run when the conditional expression does not evaluate to the appropriate true or false value:

```
if ($name eq 'Bob')
{
    say 'Hi, Bob!';
    greet_user();
}
else
{
    say "I don't know you.";
    shun_user();
}
```

else blocks allow you to rewrite if and unless conditionals in terms of each other:

```
unless ($name eq 'Bob')
{
    say "I don't know you.";
    shun_user();
}
```

```
else
{
    say 'Hi, Bob!';
    greet_user();
}
```

However, the implied double negative of using unless with an else block can be confusing. This example may be the only place you ever see it.

Just as Perl provides both if and unless to allow you to phrase your conditionals in the most readable way, Perl has both positive and negative conditional operators:

```
if ($name ne 'Bob')
{
    say "I don't know you.";
    shun_user();
}
else
{
    say 'Hi, Bob!';
    greet_user();
}
```

... though the double negative implied by the presence of the else block may be difficult to read.

If you have lots of conditions to check–and if they're mutually exclusive–use one or more elsif directives:

```
if ($name eq 'Bob')
{
    say 'Hi, Bob!';
    greet_user();
}
elsif ($name eq 'Jim')
{
    say 'Hi, Jim!';
    greet_user();
}
else
{
```

```
    say "You're not my uncle.";
    shun_user();
}
```

An unless chain may also use an elsif block[11]. There is no elseunless.
Writing else if is a syntax error[12]:

```
if ($name eq 'Rick')
{
    say 'Hi, cousin!';
}

# warning; syntax error
else if ($name eq 'Kristen')
{
    say 'Hi, cousin-in-law!';
}
```

## The Ternary Conditional Operator

The *ternary conditional* operator evaluates a conditional expression and evaluates
to one of two alternatives:

```
my $time_suffix = after_noon($time)
                ? 'afternoon'
                : 'morning';
```

The conditional expression precedes the question mark character (?) and the colon
character (:) separates the alternatives. The alternatives are expressions of arbitrary complexity–including other ternary conditional expressions.

---

An interesting, though obscure, idiom is to use the ternary conditional to select
between alternative *variables*, not only values:

```
push @{ rand() > 0.5 ? \@red_team : \@blue_team },
    Player->new;
```

Again, weigh the benefits of clarity versus the benefits of conciseness.

---

[11]Good luck deciphering that!

[12]Larry prefers elsif for aesthetic reasons, as well the prior art of the Ada programming language.

## Short Circuiting

Perl exhibits *short-circuiting* behavior when it encounters complex conditional expressions. When Perl can determine that a complex expression would succeed or fail as a whole without evaluating every subexpression, it will not evaluate subsequent subexpressions. This is most obvious with an example:

```
say 'Both true!' if ok( 1, 'subexpression one' )
                && ok( 1, 'subexpression two' );

done_testing();
```

The return value of ok() (Testing, pp. 203) is the boolean value produced by the first argument, so the example prints:

```
ok 1 - subexpression one
ok 2 - subexpression two
Both true!
```

When the first subexpression–the first call to ok–evaluates to a true value, Perl must evaluate the second subexpression. If the first subexpression had evaluated to a false value, there would be no need to check subsequent subexpressions, as the entire expression could not succeed:

```
say 'Both true!' if ok( 0, 'subexpression one' )
                && ok( 1, 'subexpression two' );
```

This example prints:

```
not ok 1 - subexpression one
```

Even though the second subexpression would obviously succeed, Perl never evaluates it. The same short-circuiting behavior is evident for logical-or operations:

```
say 'Either true!' if ok( 1, 'subexpression one' )
                 || ok( 1, 'subexpression two' );
```

This example prints:

```
ok 1 - subexpression one
Either true!
```

With the success of the first subexpression, Perl can avoid evaluating the second subexpression. If the first subexpression were false, the result of evaluating the second subexpression would dictate the result of evaluating the entire expression.

Besides allowing you to avoid potentially expensive computations, short circuiting can help you to avoid errors and warnings, as in the case where using an undefined value might raise a warning:

```
my $bbq;
if (defined $bbq and $bbq eq 'brisket') { ... }
```

## Context for Conditional Directives

The conditional directives–if, unless, and the ternary conditional operator–all evaluate an expression in boolean context (Context, pp. 5). As comparison operators such as eq, ==, ne, and != all produce boolean results when evaluated, Perl coerces the results of other expressions–including variables and values–into boolean forms.

Perl has no single true value nor a single false value. Any number which evaluates to 0 is false. This includes 0, 0.0, 0e0, 0x0, and so on. The empty string (' ') and '0' evaluate to a false value, but the strings '0.0', '0e0', and so on do not. The idiom '0 but true' evaluates to 0 in numeric context but true in boolean context, thanks to its string contents.

Both the empty list and undef evaluate to a false value. Empty arrays and hashes return the number 0 in scalar context, so they evaluate to a false value in boolean context. An array which contains a single element–even undef–evaluates to true in boolean context. A hash which contains any elements–even a key and a value of undef–evaluates to a true value in boolean context.

---

**Greater Control Over Context**

The Want module from the CPAN allows you to detect boolean context within your own functions. The core overloading pragma (Overloading, pp. 240) allows you to specify what your own data types produce when evaluated in various contexts.

---

## Looping Directives

Perl provides several directives for looping and iteration. The *foreach*-style loop evaluates an expression which produces a list and executes a statement or block until it has exhausted that list:

```
foreach (1 .. 10)
{
    say "$_ * $_ = ", $_ * $_;
}
```

This example uses the range operator to produce a list of integers from one to ten inclusive. The `foreach` directive loops over them, setting the topic variable `$_` (The Default Scalar Variable, pp. 9) to each in turn. Perl executes the block for each integer and, as a result, prints the squares of the integers.

> **foreach versus for**
>
> Many Perl programmers refer to iteration as `foreach` loops, but Perl treats the names `foreach` and `for` interchangeably. The parenthesized expression determines the type and behavior of the loop; the keyword does not.

Like `if` and `unless`, this loop has a postfix form:

```
say "$_ * $_ = ", $_ * $_ for 1 .. 10;
```

A `for` loop may use a named variable instead of the topic:

```
for my $i (1 .. 10)
{
    say "$i * $i = ", $i * $i;
}
```

When a `for` loop uses an iterator variable, the variable scope is *within* the loop. Perl will set this lexical to the value of each item in the iteration. Perl will not modify the topic variable (`$_`). If you have declared a lexical `$i` in an outer scope, its value will persist outside the loop:

```
my $i = 'cow';

for my $i (1 .. 10)
{
    say "$i * $i = ", $i * $i;
```

```
}

is( $i, 'cow', 'Value preserved in outer scope' );
```

This localization occurs even if you do not redeclare the iteration variable as a lexical[13]:

```
my $i = 'horse';

for $i (1 .. 10)
{
    say "$i * $i = ", $i * $i;
}

is( $i, 'horse', 'Value preserved in outer scope' );
```

## Iteration and Aliasing

The for loop *aliases* the iterator variable to the values in the iteration such that any modifications to the value of the iterator modifies the iterated value in place:

```
my @nums = 1 .. 10;

$_ **= 2 for @nums;

is( $nums[0], 1, '1 * 1 is 1' );
is( $nums[1], 4, '2 * 2 is 4' );

...

is( $nums[9], 100, '10 * 10 is 100' );
```

This aliasing also works with the block style for loop:

```
for my $num (@nums)
{
    $num **= 2;
}
```

---

[13] ... but *do* declare your iteration variables as lexicals to reduce their scope.

...as well as iteration with the topic variable:

```
for (@nums)
{
    $_ **= 2;
}
```

You cannot use aliasing to modify *constant* values, however. Perl will produce an exception about modification of read-only values.

```
$_++ and say for qw( Huex Dewex Louid );
```

You may occasionally see the use of **for** with a single scalar variable:

```
for ($user_input)
{
    s/\A\s+//;       # trim leading whitespace
    s/\s+\z//;       # trim trailing whitespace

    $_ = quotemeta;  # escape non-word characters
}
```

This idiom (Idioms, pp. 247) uses the iteration operator for its side effect of aliasing $_. Usually it's clearer to operate on the named variable itself.

## Iteration and Scoping

The topic variable's iterator scoping has a subtle gotcha. Consider a function `topic_mangler()` which modifies $_ on purpose. If code iterating over a list called `topic_mangler()` without protecting $_, you'd have to spend some time debugging the effects:

```
for (@values)
{
    topic_mangler();
}

sub topic_mangler
{
    s/foo/bar/;
}
```

Yes, the substitution in `topic_mangler()` will modify elements of `@values` in place. If you *must* use `$_` rather than a named variable, use the topic aliasing behavior of `for`:

```
sub topic_mangler
{
    # was $_ = shift;
    for (shift)
    {
        s/foo/bar/;
        s/baz/quux/;
        return $_;
    }
}
```

Alternately, use a named iteration variable in the `for` loop. That's almost always the right advice.

## The C-Style For Loop

The C-style *for loop* requires you to manage the conditions of iteration:

```
for (my $i = 0; $i <= 10; $i += 2)
{
    say "$i * $i = ", $i * $i;
}
```

You must explicitly assign to an iteration variable in the looping construct, as this loop performs neither aliasing nor assignment to the topic variable. While any variable declared in the loop construct is scoped to the lexical block of the loop, Perl will not limit the lexical scope of a variable declared outside of the loop construct:

```
my $i = 'pig';

for ($i = 0; $i <= 10; $i += 2)
{
    say "$i * $i = ", $i * $i;
}

isnt( $i, 'pig', '$i overwritten with a number' );
```

49

The looping construct may have three subexpressions. The first subexpression–the initialization section–executes only once, before the loop body executes. Perl evaluates the second subexpression–the conditional comparison–before each iteration of the loop body. When this evaluates to a true value, iteration proceeds. When it evaluates to a false value, iteration stops. The final subexpression executes after each iteration of the loop body.

```
for (
    # loop initialization subexpression
    say 'Initializing', my $i = 0;

    # conditional comparison subexpression
    say "Iteration: $i" and $i < 10;

    # iteration ending subexpression
    say 'Incrementing ' . $i++
)
{
    say "$i * $i = ", $i * $i;
}
```

Note the lack of a semicolon after the final subexpression as well as the use of the comma operator and low-precedence and; this syntax is surprisingly finicky. When possible, prefer the foreach-style loop to the for loop.

All three subexpressions are optional. One infinite for loop is:

```
for (;;) { ... }
```

## While and Until

A *while* loop continues until the loop conditional expression evaluates to a boolean false value. An idiomatic infinite loop is:

```
while (1) { ... }
```

Unlike the iteration foreach-style loop, the while loop's condition has no side effects. If @values has one or more elements, this code is also an infinite loop, because every iteration will evaluate @values in scalar context to a non-zero value and iteration will continue:

```perl
while (@values)
{
    say $values[0];
}
```

To prevent such an infinite while loop, use a *destructive update* of the @values array by modifying the array within each iteration:

```perl
while (@values)
{
    my $value = shift @values;
    say $value;
}
```

Modifying @values inside of the while condition check also works, but it has some subtleties related to the truthiness of each value.

```perl
while (my $value = shift @values)
{
    say $value;
}
```

This loop will exit as soon as it reaches an element that evaluates to a false value, not necessarily when it has exhausted the array. That may be the desired behavior, but it probably deserves a comment to explain why.

The *until* loop reverses the sense of the test of the while loop. Iteration continues while the loop conditional expression evaluates to a false value:

```perl
until ($finished_running)
{
    . . .
}
```

The canonical use of the while loop is to iterate over input from a filehandle:

```perl
while (<$fh>)
{
    # remove newlines
    chomp;
    . . .
}
```

Perl interprets this while loop as if you had written:

```
while (defined($_ = <$fh>))
{
    # remove newlines
    chomp;
    ...
}
```

Without the implicit defined, any line read from the filehandle which evaluated to a false value in a scalar context–a blank line or a line which contained only the character 0–would end the loop. The readline (<>) operator returns an undefined value only when it has reached the end of the file.

Both while and until have postfix forms, such as the infinite loop 1 while 1;. Any single expression is suitable for a postfix while or until, including the classic "Hello, world!" example from 8-bit computers of the early 1980s:

```
print "Hello, world!  " while 1;
```

Infinite loops are more useful than they seem, especially for event loops in GUI programs, program interpreters, or network servers:

```
$server->dispatch_results until $should_shutdown;
```

Use a do block to group several expressions into a single unit:

```
do
{
    say 'What is your name?';
    my $name = <>;
    chomp $name;
    say "Hello, $name!" if $name;
} until (eof);
```

A do block parses as a single expression which may contain several expressions. Unlike the while loop's block form, the do block with a postfix while or until will execute its body *at least* once. This construct is less common than the other loop forms, but no less powerful.

## Loops within Loops

You may nest loops within other loops:

```
for my $suit (@suits)
{
    for my $values (@card_values) { ... }
}
```

When you do this, declare your iteration variables! The potential for confusion with the topic variable and its scope is too great otherwise.

Novices commonly exhaust filehandles accidentally while nesting foreach and while loops:

```
use autodie 'open';
open my $fh, '<', $some_file;

for my $prefix (@prefixes)
{
    # DO NOT USE; buggy code
    while (<$fh>)
    {
        say $prefix, $_;
    }
}
```

Opening the filehandle outside of the for loop leaves the file position unchanged between each iteration of the for loop. On its second iteration, the while loop will have nothing to read and will not iterate. You can solve this problem in many ways; re-open the file inside the for loop (wasteful but simple), slurp the entire file into memory (works best with small files), or seek the filehandle back to the beginning of the file for each iteration:

```
for my $prefix (@prefixes)
{
    while (<$fh>)
    {
        say $prefix, $_;
    }

    seek $fh, 0, 0;
}
```

## Loop Control

Sometimes you need to break out of a loop before you have exhausted the iteration conditions. Perl's standard control mechanisms–exceptions and `return`–work, but you may also use *loop control* statements.

The *next* statement restarts the loop at its next iteration. Use it when you've done all you need to in the current iteration. To loop over lines in a file and skip everything that starts with the comment character #:

```
while (<$fh>)
{
    next if /\A#/;
    ...
}
```

---

**Multiple Exits versus Nested Ifs**

Compare the use of `next` with the alternative: wrapping the rest of the body of the block in an `if`. Now consider what happens if you have multiple conditions which could cause you to skip a line. Loop control modifiers with postfix conditionals can make your code much more readable.

---

The *last* statement ends the loop immediately. To finish processing a file once you've seen the ending token, write:

```
while (<$fh>)
{
    next if /\A#/;
    last if /\A__END__/
    ...
}
```

The *redo* statement restarts the current iteration without evaluating the conditional again. This can be useful in those few cases where you want to modify the line you've read in place, then start processing over from the beginning without clobbering it with another line. To implement a silly file parser that joins lines which end with a backslash:

```
while (my $line = <$fh>)
{
    chomp $line;

    # match backslash at the end of a line
    if ($line =~ s{\\$}{})
    {
        $line .= <$fh>;
        chomp $line;
        redo;
    }

    . . .
}
```

Using loop control statements in nested loops can be confusing. If you cannot avoid nested loops–by extracting inner loops into named functions–use a *loop label* to clarify:

```
LINE:
while (<$fh>)
{
    chomp;

    PREFIX:
    for my $prefix (@prefixes)
    {
        next LINE unless $prefix;
        say "$prefix: $_";
        # next PREFIX is implicit here
    }
}
```

## Continue

The continue construct behaves like the third subexpression of a for loop; Perl executes any continue block before subsequent iterations of a loop, whether due to normal loop repetition or premature re-iteration from next[14]. You may use it

---

[14]The Perl equivalent to C's continue is next.

with a while, until, when, or for loop. Examples of continue are rare, but it's useful any time you want to guarantee that something occurs with every iteration of the loop, regardless of how that iteration ends:

```
while ($i < 10 )
{
    next unless $i % 2;
    say $i;
}
continue
{
    say 'Continuing...';
    $i++;
}
```

Be aware that a continue block does *not* execute when control flow leaves a loop due to last or redo.

## Switch Statements

Perl 5.10 introduced a new construct named given as a Perlish switch statement. It didn't quite work out; given is still experimental, but it's less buggy in 5.18 than it was in any previous version of Perl. That's a nice way of saying "don't use it unless you know what you're doing."

If you need a switch statement, use for to alias the topic variable ($_) and when to match it against simple expressions with smart match (Smart Matching, pp. 161) semantics. To write the Rock, Paper, Scissors[15] game:

```
my @options  = ( \&rock, \&paper, \&scissors );
my $confused = "I don't understand your move.";

do
{
    say "Rock, Paper, Scissors!  Pick one: ";
    chomp( my $user = <STDIN> );
    my $computer_match = $options[ rand @options ];
    $computer_match->( lc( $user ) );
} until (eof);
```

---

[15] Adding Spock and Lizard is an exercise for the reader.

```perl
sub rock
{
    print "I chose rock.  ";

    for (shift)
    {
        when (/paper/)    { say 'You win!' };
        when (/rock/)     { say 'We tie!'  };
        when (/scissors/) { say 'I win!'   };
        default           { say $confused  };
    }
}

sub paper
{
    print "I chose paper.  ";

    for (shift)
    {
        when (/paper/)    { say 'We tie!'  };
        when (/rock/)     { say 'I win!'   };
        when (/scissors/) { say 'You win!' };
        default           { say $confused  };
    }
}

sub scissors
{
    print "I chose scissors.  ";

    for (shift)
    {
        when (/paper/)    { say 'I win!'   };
        when (/rock/)     { say 'You win!' };
        when (/scissors/) { say 'We tie!'  };
        default           { say $confused  };
    }
}
```

Perl executes the default rule when none of the other conditions match.

57

> ### Simplified Dispatch with Multimethods
>
> The CPAN module MooseX::MultiMethods provides another technique to simplify this code.

## Tailcalls

A *tailcall* occurs when the last expression within a function is a call to another function. The outer function's return value becomes the inner function's return value:

```
sub log_and_greet_person
{
    my $name = shift;
    log( "Greeting $name" );

    return greet_person( $name );
}
```

Returning from greet_person() directly to the caller of log_and_greet_-person() is more efficient than returning *to* log_and_greet_person() and then *from* log_and_greet_person(). Returning directly *from* greet_person() to the caller of log_and_greet_person() is a *tailcall optimization*.

Heavily recursive code (Recursion, pp. 115)–especially mutually recursive code–can consume a lot of memory. Tailcalls reduce the memory needed for internal bookkeeping of control flow and can make expensive algorithms cheaper. Unfortunately, Perl does not automatically perform this optimization, so you have to do it yourself when it's necessary.

The builtin goto operator has a form which calls a function as if the current function were never called, essentially erasing the bookkeeping for the new function call. The ugly syntax confuses people who've heard "Never use goto", but it works:

```
sub log_and_greet_person
{
    my ($name) = @_;
    log( "Greeting $name" );
```

```
        goto &greet_person;
}
```

This example has two important characteristics. First, goto &function_name or goto &$function_reference requires the use of the function sigil (&) so that the parser knows to perform a tailcall instead of jumping to a label. Second, this form of function call passes the contents of @_ implicitly to the called function. You may modify @_ to change the passed arguments if you desire.

This technique is relatively rare; it's most useful when you want to hijack control flow to get out of the way of other functions inspecting caller (such as when you're implementing special logging or some sort of debugging feature), or when using an algorithm which requires a lot of recursion. Remember it if you need it, but feel free not to use it.

# Scalars

Perl's fundamental data type is the *scalar*: a single, discrete value. That value may be a string, an integer, a floating point value, a filehandle, or a reference— but it is always a single value. Scalars may be lexical, package, or global (Global Variables, pp. 255) variables. You may only declare lexical or package variables. The names of scalar variables must conform to standard variable naming guidelines (Names, pp. 21). Scalar variables always use the leading dollar-sign ($) sigil (Variable Sigils, pp. 25).

---

**Variant Sigils and Context**

Scalar values and scalar context have a deep connection; assigning to a scalar imposes scalar context. Using the scalar sigil with an aggregate variable imposes scalar context to access a single element of the hash or array.

---

## Scalars and Types

A scalar variable can contain any type of scalar value without special conversions, coercions, or casts. The type of value stored in a scalar variable, once assigned, can change arbitrarily:

```
my $value;
$value = 123.456;
```

```
$value = 77;
$value = "I am Chuck's big toe.";
$value = Store::IceCream->new;
```

Even though this code is *legal*, changing the type of data stored in a scalar is confusing.

This flexibility of type often leads to value coercion (Coercion, pp. 78). For example, you may treat the contents of a scalar as a string, even if you didn't explicitly assign it a string:

```
my $zip_code       = 97123;
my $city_state_zip = 'Hillsboro, Oregon' . ' ' . $zip_cod
```

You may also use mathematical operations on strings:

```
my $call_sign = 'KBMIU';

# update sign in place and return new value
my $next_sign = ++$call_sign;

# return old value, then update sign
my $curr_sign = $call_sign++;

# but does not work as:
my $new_sign  = $call_sign + 1;
```

> ### One-Way Increment Magic
>
> This magical string increment behavior has no corresponding magical decrement behavior. You can't restore the previous string value by writing `$call_sign--`.

This string increment operation turns a into b and z into aa, respecting character set and case. While ZZ9 becomes AAA0, ZZ09 becomes ZZ10–numbers wrap around while there are more significant places to increment, as on a vehicle odometer.

Evaluating a reference (References, pp. 83) in string context produces a string. Evaluating a reference in numeric context produces a number. Neither operation modifies the reference in place, but you cannot recreate the reference from either result:

```
my $authors      = [qw( Pratchett Vinge Conway )];
my $stringy_ref = ''  . $authors;
my $numeric_ref =  0 + $authors;
```

$authors is still useful as a reference, but $stringy_ref is a string with no connection to the reference and $numeric_ref is a number with no connection to the reference.

To allow coercion without data loss, Perl scalars can contain both numeric and string components. The internal data structure which represents a scalar in Perl has a numeric slot and a string slot. Accessing a string in a numeric context produces a scalar with both string and numeric values. The dualvar() function within the core Scalar::Util module allows you to manipulate both values directly within a single scalar.

Scalars do not contain a separate slot for boolean values. In boolean context, the empty strings ('') and '0' evaluate to false values. All other strings evaluate to true values. In boolean context, numbers which evaluate to zero (0, 0.0, and 0e0) evaluate to false values. All other numbers are evaluate to true values.

> **What is Truth?**
>
> Be careful that the *strings* '0.0' and '0e0' evaluate to true values. This is one place where Perl makes a distinction between what *looks like* a number and what really is a number.

One other value is always a false value: undef.

# Arrays

Perl *arrays* are *first-class* data structures–the language supports them as a built-in data type–which store zero or more scalars. You can access individual members of the array by integer indexes, and you can add or remove elements at will. Arrays grow or shrink as you manipulate them.

The @ sigil denotes an array. To declare an array:

```
my @items;
```

## Array Elements

Use the scalar sigil to *access* an individual element of an array. $cats[0] is an unambiguous use of the @cats array, because postfix (Fixity, pp. 101) square brackets ([]) always mean indexed access to an array.

The first element of an array is at the zeroth index:

```
# @cats contains a list of Cat objects
my $first_cat = $cats[0];
```

The last index of an array depends on the number of elements in the array. An array in scalar context (due to scalar assignment, string concatenation, addition, or boolean context) evaluates to the number of elements in the array:

```
# scalar assignment
my $num_cats = @cats;

# string concatenation
say 'I have ' . @cats . ' cats!';

# addition
my $num_animals = @cats + @dogs + @fish;

# boolean context
say 'Yep, a cat owner!' if @cats;
```

To get the *index* of the final element of an array, subtract one from the number of elements of the array (because array indexes start at 0) or use the unwieldy $#cats syntax:

```
my $first_index = 0;
my $last_index  = @cats - 1;
# or
# my $last_index = $#cats;

say    "My first cat has an index ·of $first_index, "
    . "and my last cat has an index of $last_index."
```

When you care more about the relative position of an element in the array, use a negative array index. The last element of an array is available at the index -1. The second to last element of the array is available at index -2, and so on:

```
my $last_cat          = $cats[-1];
my $second_to_last_cat = $cats[-2];
```

$# has another use: resize an array in place by *assigning* to $#array. Remember that Perl arrays are mutable. They expand or contract as necessary. When you shrink an array, Perl will discard values which do not fit in the resized array. When you expand an array, Perl will fill the expanded positions with undef.

## Array Assignment

Assign to individual positions in an array directly by index:

```
my @cats;
$cats[3] = 'Jack';
$cats[2] = 'Tuxedo';
$cats[0] = 'Daisy';
$cats[1] = 'Petunia';
$cats[4] = 'Brad';
$cats[5] = 'Choco';
```

If you assign to an index beyond the array's current bound, Perl will extend the array to account for the new size and will fill in all intermediary positions with undef. After the first assignment, the array will contain undef at positions 0, 1, and 2 and Jack at position 3.

As an assignment shortcut, initialize an array from a list:

```
my @cats = ( 'Daisy', 'Petunia', 'Tuxedo', ... );
```

...but remember that these parentheses *do not* create a list. Without parentheses, this would assign Daisy as the first and only element of the array, due to operator precedence (Precedence, pp. 99). Petunia, Tuxedo, and all of the other cats would be evaluated in void context and Perl would complain[16].

You may assign any expression which produces a list in list context to an array:

```
my @cats     = get_cat_list();
my @timeinfo = localtime();
my @nums     = 1 .. 10;
```

---

[16] So would the cats, Petunia especially.

Assigning to a scalar element of an array imposes scalar context, while assigning to the array as a whole imposes list context.

To clear an array, assign an empty list:

```
my @dates = ( 1969, 2001, 2010, 2051, 1787 );
...
@dates    = ();
```

This is one of the only cases where parentheses *do* indicate a list; without something to mark a list, Perl and readers of the code would get confused.

> **Arrays Start Empty**
>
> my @items = (); is a longer and noisier version of my @items. Freshly-declared arrays start out empty.

## Array Operations

Sometimes an array is more convenient as an ordered, mutable collection of items than as a mapping of indices to values. Perl provides several operations to manipulate array elements without using indices.

The push and pop operators add and remove elements from the tail of an array, respectively:

```
my @meals;

# what is there to eat?
push @meals, qw( hamburgers pizza lasagna turnip );

# ... but your nephew hates vegetables
pop @meals;
```

You may push a list of values onto an array, but you may only pop one at a time. push returns the new number of elements in the array. pop returns the removed element.

Because push operates on a list, you can easily append the elements of one multiple arrays with:

```
push @meals, @breakfast, @lunch, @dinner;
```

Similarly, unshift and shift add elements to and remove an element from the start of an array, respectively:

```
# expand our culinary horizons
unshift @meals, qw( tofu spanakopita taquitos );

# rethink that whole soy idea
shift @meals;
```

unshift prepends a list of elements to the start of the array and returns the new number of elements in the array. shift removes and returns the first element of the array.

Few programs use the return values of push and unshift.

The splice operator removes and replaces elements from an array given an offset, a length of a list slice, and replacement elements. Both replacing and removing are optional; you may omit either behavior. The perlfunc description of splice demonstrates its equivalences with push, pop, shift, and unshift. One effective use is removal of two elements from an array:

```
my ($winner, $runnerup) = splice @finalists, 0, 2;

# or
my $winner              = shift @finalists;
my $runnerup            = shift @finalists;
```

The each operator allows you to iterate over an array by index and value:

```
while (my ($index, $value) = each @bookshelf)
{
    say "#$index: $value";
    ...
}
```

## Array Slices

The *array slice* construct allows you to access elements of an array in list context. Unlike scalar access of an array element, this indexing operation takes a list of zero or more indices and uses the array sigil (@):

```
my @youngest_cats = @cats[-1, -2];
my @oldest_cats   = @cats[0 .. 2];
my @selected_cats = @cats[ @indexes ];
```

Array slices are useful for assignment:

```
@users[ @replace_indices ] = @replace_users;
```

The only syntactic difference between an array slice of one element and the scalar access of an array element is the leading sigil. The *semantic* difference is greater: an array slice always imposes list context. An array slice evaluated in scalar context will produce a warning:

```
Scalar value @cats[1] better written as $cats[1]...
```

An array slice imposes list context on the expression used as its index:

```
# function called in list context
my @hungry_cats = @cats[ get_cat_indices() ];
```

A slice can contain zero or more elements–including one:

```
# single-element array slice; list context
@cats[-1] = get_more_cats();

# single-element array access; scalar context
$cats[-1] = get_more_cats();
```

## Arrays and Context

In list context, arrays flatten into lists. If you pass multiple arrays to a normal function, they will flatten into a single list:

```
my @cats = qw( Daisy Petunia Tuxedo Brad Jack Choco );
my @dogs = qw( Rodney Lucky Rosie );

take_pets_to_vet( @cats, @dogs );

sub take_pets_to_vet
{
    # BUGGY: do not use!
    my (@cats, @dogs) = @_;
    ...
}
```

Within the function, @_ will contain nine elements, not two, because list assignment to arrays is *greedy*. An array will consume as many elements from the list as possible. After the assignment, @cats will contain *every* argument passed to the function. @dogs will be empty[17].

This flattening behavior sometimes confuses novices who attempt to create nested arrays:

```
# creates a single array, not an array of arrays
my @numbers = (1 .. 10, (11 .. 20, (21 .. 30)));
```

... but this code is effectively the same as either:

```
# parentheses do not create lists
my @numbers = ( 1 .. 10, 11 .. 20, 21 .. 30 );

# creates a single array, not an array of arrays
my @numbers = 1 .. 30;
```

... because parentheses merely group expressions. They do not *create* lists. To avoid this flattening behavior, use array references (Array References, pp. 86).

## Array Interpolation

Arrays interpolate in strings as lists of the stringifications of each item separated by the current value of the magic global $". The default value of this variable is a single space. Its *English.pm* mnemonic is $LIST_SEPARATOR. Thus:

```
my @alphabet = 'a' .. 'z';
say "[@alphabet]";
[a b c d e f g h i j k l m
 n o p q r s t u v w x y z]
```

Localize $" with a delimiter to ease your debugging[18]:

```
# what's in this array again?
local $" = ')(';
say "(@sweet_treats)";
(pie) (cake) (doughnuts) (cookies) (cinnamon roll)
```

---

[17] ... but Rosie thinks she's a cat, so it's not all bad.

[18] Credit goes to Mark Jason Dominus for this technique.

# Hashes

A *hash* is a first-class Perl data structure which associates string keys with scalar values. Just as the name of a variable corresponds to something which holds a value, so does a hash key refer to something which contains a value. Think of a hash like a contact list: use the names of your friends to look up their phone numbers. Other languages call hashes *tables*, *associative arrays*, *dictionaries*, or *maps*.

Hashes have two important properties: they store one scalar per unique key and they provide no specific ordering of keys. Keep that latter property in mind. Though it has always been true in Perl, it's very, very true in Perl 5.18.

## Declaring Hashes

Hashes use the % sigil. Declare a lexical hash with:

```
my %favorite_flavors;
```

A hash starts out empty. You could write my `%favorite_flavors = ();`, but that's redundant.

Hashes use the scalar sigil $ when accessing individual elements and curly braces { } for keyed access:

```
my %favorite_flavors;
$favorite_flavors{Gabi}    = 'Dark chocolate raspberry';
$favorite_flavors{Annette} = 'French vanilla';
```

Assign a list of keys and values to a hash in a single expression:

```
my %favorite_flavors = (
    'Gabi',    'Dark chocolate raspberry',
    'Annette', 'French vanilla',
);
```

Hashes store pairs of keys and values. Perl will warn you if you assign an odd number of elements to a hash. Idiomatic Perl often uses the *fat comma* operator (=>) to associate values with keys, as it makes the pairing more visible:

```
my %favorite_flavors = (
    Gabi    => 'Dark chocolate raspberry',
    Annette => 'French vanilla',
);
```

The fat comma operator acts like the regular comma *and* also automatically quotes the previous bareword (Barewords, pp. 259). The `strict` pragma will not warn about such a bareword–and if you have a function with the same name as a hash key, the fat comma will *not* call the function:

```
sub name { 'Leonardo' }

my %address = (
    name => '1123 Fib Place'
);
```

The key of this hash will be `name` and not `Leonardo`. To call the function, make the function call explicit:

```
my %address = (
    name() => '1123 Fib Place'
);
```

Assign an empty list to empty a hash[19]:

```
%favorite_flavors = ();
```

## Hash Indexing

To access an individual hash value, use a key (a *keyed access* operation):to

```
my $address = $addresses{$name};
```

In this example, `$name` contains a string which is also a key of the hash. As with accessing an individual element of an array, the hash's sigil has changed from % to $ to indicate keyed access to a scalar value.

You may also use string literals as hash keys. Perl quotes barewords automatically according to the same rules as fat commas:

```
# auto-quoted
my $address = $addresses{Victor};

# needs quoting; not a valid bareword
```

---

[19] You may occasionally see `undef %hash`, but that's a little ugly.

69

```
my $address = $addresses{'Sue-Linn'};

# function call needs disambiguation
my $address = $addresses{get_name()};
```

---

**Don't Quote Me**

Novices often always quote string literal hash keys, but experienced developers elide the quotes whenever possible. If you code this way, you can use the rare presence of quotes to indicate that you're doing something different.

---

Even Perl builtins get the autoquoting treatment:

```
my %addresses =
(
    Leonardo => '1123 Fib Place',
    Utako    => 'Cantor Hotel, Room 1',
);

sub get_address_from_name
{
    return $addresses{+shift};
}
```

The unary plus (Unary Coercions, pp. 255) turns what would be a bareword (shift) subject to autoquoting rules into an expression. As this implies, you can use an arbitrary expression–not only a function call–as the key of a hash:

```
# don't actually do this though
my $address = $addresses{reverse 'odranoeL'};

# interpolation is fine
my $address = $addresses{"$first_name $last_name"};

# so are method calls
my $address = $addresses{ $user->name };
```

Hash keys can only be strings. Anything that evaluates to a string is an acceptable hash key. Perl will go so far as to coerce (Coercion, pp. 78) any non-string into a string. For example, if you use an object as a hash key, you'll get the stringified version of that object instead of the object itself:

```
for my $isbn (@isbns)
{
    my $book = Book->fetch_by_isbn( $isbn );

    # unlikely to do what you want
    $books{$book} = $book->price;
}
```

## Hash Key Existence

The `exists` operator returns a boolean value to indicate whether a hash contains the given key:

```
my %addresses =
(
    Leonardo => '1123 Fib Place',
    Utako    => 'Cantor Hotel, Room 1',
);

say "Have Leonardo's address"
    if exists $addresses{Leonardo};
say "Have Warnie's address"
    if exists $addresses{Warnie};
```

Using `exists` instead of accessing the hash key directly avoids two problems. First, it does not check the boolean nature of the hash *value*; a hash key may exist with a value even if that value evaluates to a boolean false (including `undef`):

```
my  %false_key_value = ( 0 => '' );
ok( %false_key_value,
      'hash containing false key & value
        should evaluate to a true value' );
```

Second, `exists` avoids autovivification (Autovivification, pp. 94) within nested data structures (Nested Data Structures, pp. 92).

If a hash key exists, its value may be `undef`. Check that with `defined`:

```
$addresses{Leibniz} = undef;

say "Gottfried lives at $addresses{Leibniz}"
    if exists   $addresses{Leibniz}
    && defined $addresses{Leibniz};
```

## Accessing Hash Keys and Values

Hashes are aggregate variables, but their pairwise nature is unique. Perl allows you to iterate over the keys of a hash, over the values of a hash, or over pairs of keys and values. The keys operator produces a list of hash keys:

```
for my $addressee (keys %addresses)
{
    say "Found an address for $addressee!";
}
```

The values operator produces a list of hash values:

```
for my $address (values %addresses)
{
    say "Someone lives at $address";
}
```

The each operator produces a list of two-element lists of the key and the value:

```
while (my ($addressee, $address) = each %addresses)
{
    say "$addressee lives at $address";
}
```

Unlike arrays, there is no obvious ordering to these lists. The ordering depends on the internal implementation of the hash, the particular version of Perl you are using, the size of the hash, and a random factor. Even so, the order of hash items is consistent between keys, values, and each. Modifying the hash may change the order, but you can rely on that order if the hash remains the same. However, even if two hashes have the *same* keys and values, you cannot rely on the iteration order between those hashes being the same. They may have been constructed differently or have had elements removed. In Perl 5.18, even if they were constructed the same way, you cannot depend on the same iteration order between them.

Each hash has only a *single* iterator for the each operator. You cannot reliably iterate over a hash with each more than once; if you begin a new iteration while another is in progress, the former will end prematurely and the latter will begin partway through the hash. During such iteration, beware not to call any function which may itself try to iterate over the hash with each.

In practice this occurs rarely. Reset a hash's iterator with keys or values in void context when you need it:

```
# reset hash iterator
keys %addresses;

while (my ($addressee, $address) = each %addresses)
{
    . . .
}
```

## Hash Slices

A *hash slice* is a list of keys or values of a hash indexed in a single operation. To initialize multiple elements of a hash at once:

```
# %cats already contains elements
@cats{qw( Jack Brad Mars Grumpy )} = (1) x 4;
```

This is equivalent to the initialization:

```
my %cats = map { $_ => 1 }
            qw( Jack Brad Mars Grumpy );
```

...except that the hash slice initialization does not *replace* the existing contents of the hash.

Hash slices also allow you to retrieve multiple values from a hash in a single operation. As with array slices, the sigil of the hash changes to @ to indicate list context. The use of the curly braces indicates keyed access and makes the fact that you're working with a hash unambiguous:

```
my @buyer_addresses = @addresses{ @buyers };
```

Hash slices make it easy to merge two hashes:

73

```
my %addresses        = ( ... );
my %canada_addresses = ( ... );

@addresses{ keys    %canada_addresses }
          = values %canada_addresses;
```

This is equivalent to looping over the contents of %canada_addresses manually, but is much shorter. Note that this relies on the iteration order of the hash remaining consistent between keys and values. Perl guarantees this, but only because these operations occur on the same hash and because nothing modifies the hash between the keys and values operations.

What if the same key occurs in both hashes? The hash slice approach always *overwrites* existing key/value pairs in %addresses. If you want other behavior, looping is more appropriate.

## The Empty Hash

An empty hash contains no keys or values. It evaluates to a false value in a boolean context. A hash which contains at least one key/value pair evaluates to a true value in boolean context even if all of the keys or all of the values or both would themselves evaluate to boolean false values.

```
use Test::More;

my %empty;
ok( ! %empty, 'empty hash should evaluate false' );

my %false_key = ( 0 => 'true value' );
ok( %false_key, 'hash containing false key
                  should evaluate to true' );

my %false_value = ( 'true key' => 0 );
ok( %false_value, 'hash containing false value
                    should evaluate to true' );

done_testing();
```

In scalar context, a hash evaluates to a string which represents the ratio of full buckets in the hash–internal details about the hash implementation that you can safely ignore. (In a boolean scalar context, this ratio evaluates to a false value, so remember *that* instead of the ratio details.)

In list context, a hash evaluates to a list of key/value pairs similar to the list produced by the `each` operator. However, you *cannot* iterate over this list the same way you can iterate over the list produced by `each`. This loop will never terminate:

```
# infinite loop for non-empty hashes
while (my ($key, $value) = %hash)
{
    ...
}
```

You *can* loop over the list of keys and values with a `for` loop, but the iterator variable will get a key on one iteration and its value on the next, because Perl will flatten the hash into a single list of interleaved keys and values.

## Hash Idioms

Because each key exists only once in a hash, assigning the same key to a hash multiple times stores only the most recent value associated with that key. This behavior has advantages! For example, to find unique elements of a listlist :

```
my %uniq;
undef @uniq{ @items };
my @uniques = keys %uniq;
```

Using `undef` with a hash slice sets the values of the hash to `undef`. This idiom is the cheapest way to perform set operations with a hash.

Hashes are also useful for counting elements, such as IP addresses in a log file:

```
my %ip_addresses;

while (my $line = <$logfile>)
{
    chomp $line;
    my ($ip, $resource) = analyze_line( $line );
    $ip_addresses{$ip}++;
    ...
}
```

The initial value of a hash value is `undef`. The postincrement operator (++) treats that as zero. This in-place modification of the value increments an existing value for that key. If no value exists for that key, Perl creates a value (undef) and immediately increments it to one, as the numification of undef produces the value 0.

This strategy provides a useful caching mechanism to store the result of an expensive operation with little overhead:

```
{
    my %user_cache;

    sub fetch_user
    {
        my $id = shift;
        $user_cache{$id} //= create_user($id);
        return $user_cache{$id};
    }
}
```

This *orcish maneuver*[20] returns the value from the hash, if it exists. Otherwise, it calculates, caches, and returns the value. The defined-or assignment operator (//=) evaluates its left operand. If that operand is not defined, the operator assigns to the lvalue the value of its right operand. In other words, if there's no value in the hash for the given key, this function will call create_user() with the key and update the hash.

Perl 5.10 introduced the defined-or and defined-or assignment operators. Prior to 5.10, most code used the boolean-or assignment operator (||=) for this purpose. Unfortunately, some valid values evaluate to a false value in boolean context, so evaluating the *definedness* of values is almost always more accurate. This lazy orcish maneuver tests for the definedness of the cached value, not truthiness. You may still see code with the pre-5.10 behavior. When you do, consider whether the defined-or operator makes more sense.

If your function takes several arguments, use a slurpy hash (Slurping, pp. 110) to gather key/value pairs into a single hash as named function arguments:

```
sub make_sundae
{
    my %parameters = @_;
    ...
```

---

[20]Or-cache, if you like puns spelled out.

```
}

make_sundae( flavor  => 'Lemon Burst',
             topping => 'cookie bits' );
```

This approach allows you to set default values:

```
sub make_sundae
{
    my %parameters             = @_;
    $parameters{flavor}    //= 'Vanilla';
    $parameters{topping}   //= 'fudge';
    $parameters{sprinkles} //= 100;
    ...
}
```

... or include them in the hash initialization, as latter assignments take precedence over earlier assignments:

```
sub make_sundae
{
    my %parameters =
    (
        flavor   => 'Vanilla',
        topping  => 'fudge',
        sprinkles => 100,
        @_,
    );
    ...
}
```

## Locking Hashes

As hash keys are barewords, they offer little typo protection compared to the function and variable name protection offered by the strict pragma. The little-used core module Hash::Util can make hashes safer.

To prevent someone from accidentally adding a hash key you did not intend (whether as a typo or from untrusted user input), use the lock_keys() function to restrict the hash to its current set of keys. Any attempt to add a new key to the hash will raise an exception. Similarly you can lock or unlock the existing value

77

for a given key in the hash (`lock_value()` and `unlock_value()`) and make or unmake the entire hash read-only with `lock_hash()` and `unlock_hash()`.

This is lax security; anyone can use the appropriate unlocking functions to work around the locking. Yet it does protect against typos and other accidental behavior.

# Coercion

Throughout its lifetime, a Perl variable may contain values of different types–strings, integers, rational numbers, and more. Rather than attaching type information to variables, Perl relies on the context provided by operators (Numeric, String, and Boolean Context, pp. 8) to determine how to handle values. By design, Perl attempts to do what you mean[21], though you must be specific about your intentions. If you treat a variable which happens to contain a number as a string, Perl will do its best to *coerce* that number into a string.

## Boolean Coercion

Boolean coercion occurs when you test the *truthiness* of a value, such as in an `if` or `while` condition. Numeric 0, `undef`, the empty string, and the string `'0'` all evaluate as false values. All other values–including strings which may be *numerically* equal to zero (such as `'0.0'`, `'0e'`, and `'0 but true'`)–evaluate as true values.

When a scalar has *both* string and numeric components (Dualvars, pp. 80), Perl prefers to check the string component for boolean truth. `'0 but true'` evaluates to zero numerically, but it is not an empty string, and so it evaluates to a true value in boolean context.

## String Coercion

String coercion occurs when using string operators such as comparisons (`eq` and `cmp`), concatenation, `split`, `substr`, and regular expressions, as well as when using a value or an expression as a hash key. The undefined value stringifies to an empty string, but produces a "use of uninitialized value" warning. Numbers *stringify* to strings containing their values, so the value 10 stringifies to the string 10. You can even `split` a number into individual digits with:

```
my @digits = split '', 1234567890;
```

---

[21]Called *DWIM* for *do what I mean* or *dwimmery*.

78

# Numeric Coercion

Numeric coercion occurs when using numeric comparison operators (such as ==
and <=>), when performing mathematic operations, and when using a value or
expression as an array or list index. The undefined value *numifies* to zero and
produces a "Use of uninitialized value" warning. Strings which do not begin with
numeric portions also numify to zero and produce an "Argument isn't numeric"
warning. Strings which begin with characters allowed in numeric literals numify to
those values and produce no warnings, such that 10 leptons leaping numifies
to 10 and 6.022e23 moles marauding numifies to 6.022e23.

The core module Scalar::Util contains a looks_like_number() function
which uses the same parsing rules as the Perl grammar to extract a number from a
string.

---

**Mathematicians Rejoice**

The strings Inf and Infinity represent the infinite value and behave as
numbers. The string NaN represents the concept "not a number". Numifying them produces no "Argument isn't numeric" warning. Beware that
Perl's ideas of infinity and not a number may not match your platform's
ideas; these notions aren't always portable across operating systems. Perl
is consistent even if the rest of the universe isn't.

---

# Reference Coercion

Using a dereferencing operation on a non-reference turns that value *into* a reference. This process of autovivification (Autovivification, pp. 94) is handy when
manipulating nested data structures (Nested Data Structures, pp. 92):

```
my %users;

$users{Brad}{id} = 228;
$users{Jack}{id} = 229;
```

Although the hash never contained values for Brad and Jack, Perl helpfully created hash references for them, then assigned each a key/value pair keyed on id.

# Cached Coercions

Perl's internal representation of values stores both string and numeric values.
Stringifying a numeric value does not *replace* the numeric value. Instead, it *adds*

a stringified value to the internal representation, which then contains *both* components. Similarly, numifying a string value populates the numeric component while leaving the string component untouched.

Certain Perl operations prefer to use one component of a value over another—boolean checks prefer strings, for example. If a value has a cached representation in a form you do not expect, relying on an implicit conversion may produce surprising results. You almost never need to be explicit about what you expect[22], but knowing that this caching occurs may someday help you diagnose an odd situation.

## Dualvars

The multi-component nature of Perl values is available to users in the form of *dualvars*. The core module `Scalar::Util` provides a function `dualvar()` which allows you to bypass Perl coercion and manipulate the string and numeric components of a value separately:

```
use Scalar::Util 'dualvar';
my $false_name = dualvar 0, 'Sparkles & Blue';

say 'Boolean true!'  if        !! $false_name;
say 'Numeric false!' unless  0 + $false_name;
say 'String true!'   if       '' . $false_name;
```

# Packages

A Perl *namespace* associates and encapsulates various named entities within a named category. It's like your family name or a brand name. Unlike a real-world name, a namespace implies no direct relationship between entities. Such relationships may exist, but they do not have to.

A *package* in Perl is a collection of code in a single namespace. The distinction is subtle: the package represents the source code and the namespace represents the entity created when Perl parses that code.

The `package` builtin declares a package and a namespace:

```
package MyCode;

our @boxes;
```

---

[22] Your author can recall doing so twice in fifteen years of programming Perl.

```
sub add_box { ... }
```

All global variables and functions declared or referred to after the package declaration refer to symbols within the MyCode namespace. You can refer to the @boxes variable from the main namespace only by its *fully qualified* name of @MyCode::boxes. A fully qualified name includes a complete package name, so you can call the add_box() function only by MyCode::add_box().

The scope of a package continues until the next package declaration or the end of the file, whichever comes first. With package, you may provide a block which explicitly delineates the scope of the declaration:

```
package Pinball::Wizard
{
    our $VERSION = 1969;
}
```

The default package is the main package. Without a package declaration, the current package is main. This rule applies to one-liners, standalone programs, and even *.pm* files.

Besides a name, a package has a version and three implicit methods, import() (Importing, pp. 111), unimport(), and VERSION(). VERSION() returns the package's version number. This number is a series of numbers contained in a package global named $VERSION. By rough convention, versions are a series of integers separated by dots, as in 1.23 or 1.1.10.

Perl includes a stricter syntax for version numbers, as documented in perldoc version::Internals. These version numbers must have a leading v character and at least three integer components separated by periods:

```
package MyCode v1.2.1;
```

Combined with the block form of a package declaration, you can write:

```
package Pinball::Wizard v1969.3.7 { ... }
```

This syntax is still rare, though. You're more likely to see the pre-5.14 version:

```
package MyCode;

our $VERSION = 1.21;
```

Every package inherits a VERSION() method from the UNIVERSAL base class. You may override VERSION(), though there are few reasons to do so. This method returns the value of $VERSION:

```
my $version = Some::Plugin->VERSION;
```

If you provide a version number as an argument, this method will throw an exception unless the version of the module is equal to or greater than the argument:

```
# require at least 2.1
Some::Plugin->VERSION( 2.1 );

die "Your plugin $version is too old"
    unless $version > 2;
```

## Packages and Namespaces

Every package declaration creates a new namespace, if necessary, and causes the parser to put all subsequent package global symbols (global variables and functions) into that namespace.

Perl has *open namespaces*. You can add functions or variables to a namespace at any point, either with a new package declaration:

```
package Pack
{
    sub first_sub { ... }
}

Pack::first_sub();

package Pack
{
    sub second_sub { ... }
}

Pack::second_sub();
```

... or by fully qualifying function names at the point of declaration:

```
# implicit
package main;
```

```
sub Pack::third_sub { ... }
```

You can add to a package at any point during compilation or runtime, regardless of the current file, though building up a package from multiple separate declarations (in multiple files!) can make code difficult to spelunk.

Namespaces can have as many levels as your organizational scheme requires, though namespaces are not hierarchical. The only relationship between packages is semantic, not technical. Many projects and businesses create their own top-level namespaces. This reduces the possibility of global conflicts and helps to organize code on disk. For example:

- StrangeMonkey is the project name

- StrangeMonkey::UI organizes user interface code

- StrangeMonkey::Persistence organizes data management code

- StrangeMonkey::Test organizes testing code for the project

...and so on. This is a convention, but it's a useful one.

# References

Perl usually does what you expect, even if what you expect is subtle. Consider what happens when you pass values to functions:

```
sub reverse_greeting
{
    my $name = reverse shift;
    return "Hello, $name!";
}

my $name = 'Chuck';
say reverse_greeting( $name );
say $name;
```

Outside of the function, $name contains Chuck, even though the value passed into the function gets reversed into kcuhC. You probably expected that. The value of $name outside the function is separate from the $name inside the function. Modifying one has no effect on the other.

Consider the alternative. If you had to make copies of every value before anything could possibly change them out from under you, you'd have to write lots of extra defensive code.

Sometimes it's useful to modify values in place. If you want to pass a hash full of data to a function to modify it, creating and returning a new hash for each change could be tedious (to say nothing of inefficient).

Perl provides a mechanism by which to refer to a value without making a copy. Any changes made to that *reference* will update the value in place, such that *all* references to that value see the modified value. A reference is a first-class scalar data type which refers to another first-class data type.

## Scalar References

The reference operator is the backslash (\). In scalar context, it creates a single reference which refers to another value. In list context, it creates a list of references. To take a reference to $name:

```perl
my $name     = 'Larry';
my $name_ref = \$name;
```

You must *dereference* a reference to evaluate the value to which it refers. Dereferencing requires you to add an extra sigil for each level of dereferencing:

```perl
sub reverse_in_place
{
    my $name_ref = shift;
    $$name_ref   = reverse $$name_ref;
}

my $name = 'Blabby';
reverse_in_place( \$name );
say $name;
```

The double scalar sigil ($$) dereferences a scalar reference.

While in @_, parameters behave as *aliases* to caller variables[23], so you can modify them in place:

---

[23]Remember that for loops produce a similar aliasing behavior (Iteration and Aliasing, pp. 47).

```
sub reverse_value_in_place
{
    $_[0] = reverse $_[0];
}

my $name = 'allizocohC';
reverse_value_in_place( $name );
say $name;
```

You usually don't want to modify values this way–callers rarely expect it, for example. Assigning parameters to lexicals within your functions removes this aliasing behavior.

---

**Saving Memory with References**

Modifying a value in place, or returning a reference to a scalar can save
memory. Because Perl copies values on assignment, you could end up
with multiple copies of a large string. Passing around references means
that Perl will only copy the references–a far cheaper operation. Before
you modify your code to pass only references, however, measure to see if
this will make a difference.

---

Complex references may require a curly-brace block to disambiguate portions of
the expression. You may *always* use this syntax, though sometimes it clarifies and
other times it obscures:

```
sub reverse_in_place
{
    my $name_ref   = shift;
    ${ $name_ref } = reverse ${ $name_ref };
}
```

If you forget to dereference a scalar reference, Perl will likely coerce the reference into a string value of the form SCALAR(0x93339e8) or a numeric value like
0x93339e8. This value indicates the type of reference (in this case, SCALAR) and
the location in memory of the reference[24].

---

[24]...not that that is useful for anything beyond distinguishing between references.

> ### References Aren't Pointers
>
> Perl does not offer native access to memory locations. The address of the
> reference is a value used as an identifier. Unlike pointers in a language
> such as C, you cannot modify the address of a reference or treat it as
> an address into memory. These addresses are only *mostly* unique because
> Perl may reuse storage locations as it reclaims unused memory.

## Array References

*Array references* are useful in several circumstances:

- To pass and return arrays from functions without list flattening

- To create multi-dimensional data structures

- To avoid unnecessary array copying

- To hold anonymous data structures

Use the reference operator to create a reference to a declared array:

```
my @cards     = qw( K Q J 10 9 8 7 6 5 4 3 2 A );
my $cards_ref = \@cards;
```

Any modifications made through $cards_ref will modify @cards and vice versa.
You may access the entire array as a whole with the @ sigil, whether to flatten the
array into a list (list context) or count its elements (scalar context):

```
my $card_count = @$cards_ref;
my @card_copy  = @$cards_ref;
```

Access individual elements by using the dereferencing arrow (->):

```
my $first_card = $cards_ref->[0];
my $last_card  = $cards_ref->[-1];
```

The arrow is necessary to distinguish between a scalar named $cards_ref and
an array named @cards_ref. Note the use of the scalar sigil (Variable Sigils, pp.
25) to access a single element.

> **Doubling Sigils**
>
> An alternate syntax prepends another scalar sigil to the array reference. It's shorter but uglier to write `my $first_card = $$cards_ref[0];`.

Use the curly-brace dereferencing syntax to slice (Array Slices, pp. 65) an array reference:

```
my @high_cards = @{ $cards_ref }[0 .. 2, -1];
```

You *may* omit the curly braces, but their grouping often improves readability.

To create an anonymous array–without using a declared array–surround a list of values or a list-producing expression with square brackets:

```
my $suits_ref = [qw( Monkeys Robots Dinos Cheese )];
```

This array reference behaves the same as named array references, except that the anonymous array brackets *always* create a new reference. Taking a reference to a named array in its scope always refers to the *same* array. For example:

```
my @meals      = qw( soup sandwiches pizza );
my $sunday_ref = \@meals;
my $monday_ref = \@meals;

push @meals, 'ice cream sundae';
```

...both $sunday_ref and $monday_ref now contain a dessert, while:

```
my @meals      = qw( soup sandwiches pizza );
my $sunday_ref = [ @meals ];
my $monday_ref = [ @meals ];

push @meals, 'berry pie';
```

...neither $sunday_ref nor $monday_ref contains a dessert. Within the square braces used to create the anonymous array, list context flattens the @meals array into a list unconnected to @meals.

87

## Hash References

Use the reference operator on a named hash to create a *hash reference*:

```perl
my %colors = (
    blue   => 'azul',
    gold   => 'dorado',
    red    => 'rojo',
    yellow => 'amarillo',
    purple => 'morado',
);

my $colors_ref = \%colors;
```

Access the keys or values of the hash by prepending the reference with the hash sigil %:

```perl
my @english_colors = keys   %$colors_ref;
my @spanish_colors = values %$colors_ref;
```

Access individual values of the hash (to store, delete, check the existence of, or retrieve) by using the dereferencing arrow or double sigils:

```perl
sub translate_to_spanish
{
    my $color = shift;
    return $colors_ref->{$color};
    # or return $$colors_ref{$color};
}
```

Use the array sigil (@) and disambiguation braces to slice a hash reference:

```perl
my @colors  = qw( red blue green );
my @colores = @{ $colors_ref }{@colors};
```

Create anonymous hashes in place with curly braces:

```perl
my $food_ref = {
    'birthday cake' => 'la torta de cumpleaños',
    candy           => 'dulces',
    cupcake         => 'bizcochito',
    'ice cream'     => 'helado',
};
```

As with anonymous arrays, anonymous hashes create a new anonymous hash on every execution.

---

**Watch Those Braces!**

The common novice error of assigning an anonymous hash to a standard hash produces a warning about an odd number of elements in the hash. Use parentheses for a named hash and curly brackets for an anonymous hash.

---

## Function References

Perl supports *first-class functions* in that a function is a data type just as is an array or hash. In other words, Perl supports *function references*. This enables many advanced features (Closures, pp. 130). Create a function reference by using the reference operator and the function sigil (&) on the name of a function:

```
sub bake_cake { say 'Baking a wonderful cake!' };

my $cake_ref = \&bake_cake;
```

Without the *function sigil* (&), you will take a reference to the function's return value or values.

Create anonymous functions with the bare sub keyword:

```
my $pie_ref = sub { say 'Making a delicious pie!' };
```

The use of the sub builtin *without* a name compiles the function but does not install it in the current namespace. The only way to access this function is via the reference returned from sub. Invoke the function reference with the dereferencing arrow:

```
$cake_ref->();
$pie_ref->();
```

---

> ### Perl 4 Function Calls
>
> An alternate invocation syntax for function references uses the function
> sigil (&) instead of the dereferencing arrow. Avoid this syntax; it has subtle
> implications for parsing and argument passing.

Think of the empty parentheses as denoting an invocation dereferencing operation in the same way that square brackets indicate an indexed (array) lookup and curly brackets a keyed (hash) lookup. Pass arguments to the function within the parentheses:

```
$bake_something_ref->( 'cupcakes' );
```

You may also use function references as methods with objects (Moose, pp. 165). This is useful when you've already looked up the method (Reflection, pp. 187):

```
my $clean = $robot_maid->can( 'cleanup' );
$robot_maid->$clean( $kitchen );
```

## Filehandle References

When you use open's (and opendir's) lexical filehandle form, you deal with filehandle references. Internally, these filehandles are objects of the class IO::File. You can call methods on them directly:

```
use autodie 'open';

open my $out_fh, '>', 'output_file.txt';
$out_fh->say( 'Have some text!' );
```

Old code might use IO::Handle;. Older code may take references to typeglobs:

```
local *FH;
open FH, "> $file" or die "Can't write '$file': $!";
my $fh = \*FH;
```

This idiom predates lexical filehandles[25]. You may still use the reference operator on typeglobs to take references to package-global filehandles such as STDIN, STDOUT, STDERR, or DATA–but these are all global names anyhow.

---

[25]Introduced with Perl 5.6.0 in March 2000, so this code is stuck in the previous millennium.

Prefer lexical filehandles when possible. With the benefit of explicit scoping, lexical filehandles allow you to manage the lifespan of filehandles as a feature of Perl's memory management.

## Reference Counts

Perl uses a memory management technique known as *reference counting*. Every Perl value has an attached counter. Perl increases this counter every time something takes a reference to the value, whether implicitly or explicitly. Perl decreases that counter every time a reference goes away. When the counter reaches zero, Perl knows it can safely recycle that value. Consider the filehandle opened in this inner scope:

```
say 'file not open';

{
    open my $fh, '>', 'inner_scope.txt';
    $fh->say( 'file open here' );
}

say 'file closed here';
```

Within the inner block in the example, there's one $fh. (Multiple lines in the source code mention it, but there's only one variable, the one named $fh.) $fh is only in scope in the block. Its value never leaves the block. When execution reaches the end of the block, Perl recycles the variable $fh and decreases the reference count of the filehandle referred to by $fh. The filehandle's reference count reaches zero, so Perl recycles it to reclaim memory, and calls close() implicitly.

You don't have to understand the details of how all of this works. You only need to understand that your actions in taking references and passing them around affect how Perl manages memory (see Circular References, pp. 96).

## References and Functions

When you use references as arguments to functions, document your intent carefully. Modifying the values of a reference from within a function may surprise the calling code, which never expected anything else to modify its data. To modify the contents of a reference without affecting the reference itself, copy its values to a new variable:

```
my @new_array = @{ $array_ref };
my %new_hash  = %{ $hash_ref  };
```

This is only necessary in a few cases, but explicit cloning helps avoid nasty surprises for the calling code. If you use nested data structures or other complex references, consider the use of the core module `Storable` and its `dclone` (*deep cloning*) function.

# Nested Data Structures

Perl's aggregate data types–arrays and hashes–allow you to store scalars indexed by integer or string keys. Note the word scalar. If you try to store an array in an array, Perl's automatic list flattening will make everything into a single array:

```
my @counts = qw( eenie miney moe   );
my @ducks  = qw( huey  dewey louie );
my @game   = qw( duck  duck  goose );

my @famous_triplets = (
    @counts, @ducks, @game
);
```

Perl's solution to this is references (References, pp. 83), which are special scalars that can refer to other variables (scalars, arrays, and hashes). Nested data structures in Perl, such as an array of arrays or a hash of hashes, are possible through the use of references. References are useful and you need to understand them, but you don't have to like their syntax–they're one of Perl's uglier features.

Use the reference operator, \, to produce a reference to a named variable:

```
my @famous_triplets = (
    \@counts, \@ducks, \@game
);
```

... or the anonymous reference declaration syntax to avoid the use of named variables:

```
my @famous_triplets = (
    [qw( eenie miney moe   )],
    [qw( huey  dewey louie )],
    [qw( duck  duck  goose )],
);

my %meals = (
```

```
breakfast => { entree => 'eggs',
               side   => 'hash browns'  },
lunch     => { entree => 'panini',
               side   => 'apple'        },
dinner    => { entree => 'steak',
               side   => 'avocado salad' },
);
```

---

**Commas are Free**

Perl allows an optional trailing comma after the last element of a list. This makes it easy to add more elements in the future.

---

Use Perl's reference syntax to access elements in nested data structures. The sigil denotes the amount of data to retrieve. The dereferencing arrow indicates that the value of one portion of the data structure is a reference:

```
my $last_nephew = $famous_triplets[1]->[2];
my $meal_side   = $meals{breakfast}->{side};
```

The only way to nest a multi-level data structure is through references, so the arrow in the previous examples is superfluous. You may omit it for clarity, except for invoking function references:

```
my $nephew = $famous_triplets[1][2];
my $meal   = $meals{breakfast}{side};

$actions{generous}{buy_food}->( $nephew, $meal );
```

Use disambiguation blocks to access components of nested data structures as if they were first-class arrays or hashes:

```
my $nephew_count  = @{ $famous_triplets[1] };
my $dinner_courses = keys %{ $meals{dinner} };
```

...or to slice a nested data structure:

```
my ($entree, $side) =
  @{ $meals{breakfast} }{ qw( entree side ) };
```

93

Whitespace helps, but does not entirely eliminate the noise of this construct. Sometimes a temporary variable provides more clarity:

```
my $meal_ref       = $meals{breakfast};
my ($entree, $side) = @$meal_ref{qw( entree side )};
```

...or use `for`'s implicit aliasing to avoid the use of an intermediate reference:

```
my ($entree, $side) = @{ $_ }{qw( entree side )}
                      for $meals{breakfast};
```

`perldoc perldsc`, the data structures cookbook, gives copious examples of how to use Perl's various data structures.

## Autovivification

When you attempt to write to a component of a nested data structure, Perl will create the path through the data structure to the destination as necessary:

```
my @aoaoaoa;
$aoaoaoa[0][0][0][0] = 'nested deeply';
```

After the second line of code, this array of arrays of arrays of arrays contains an array reference in an array reference in an array reference in an array reference. Each array reference contains one element.

Similarly, when you ask Perl to treat an undefined value as if it were a hash reference, Perl will turn that undefined value into a hash reference:

```
my %hohoh;
$hohoh{Robot}{Santa} = 'mostly harmful';
```

This behavior is *autovivification*. While it reduces the initialization code of nested data structures, it cannot distinguish between the honest intent to create missing elements in nested data structures or an accidental typo.

You may wonder at the contradiction between taking advantage of autovivification while enabling `strictures`. The question is one of balance. Is it more convenient to catch errors which change the behavior of your program at the expense of disabling error checks for a few well-encapsulated symbolic references? Is it more convenient to allow data structures to grow or safer to require a fixed size and an allowed set of keys?

> **Controlling Autovivification**
>
> The autovivification pragma (Pragmas, pp. 200) from the CPAN lets you disable autovivification in a lexical scope for specific types of operations.

The answers depend on your project. During early development, allow yourself the freedom to experiment. While testing and deploying, consider an increase of strictness to prevent unwanted side effects. Thanks to the lexical scoping of the strict and autovivification pragmas, you can enable these behaviors where and as necessary.

You *can* verify your expectations before dereferencing each level of a complex data structure, but the resulting code is often lengthy and tedious. It's better to avoid deeply nested data structures by revising your data model to provide better encapsulation.

## Debugging Nested Data Structures

The complexity of Perl's dereferencing syntax combined with the potential for confusion with multiple levels of references can make debugging nested data structures difficult. Two good visualization tools exist.

The core module Data::Dumper converts values of arbitrary complexity into strings of Perl code:

```
use Data::Dumper;

print Dumper( $my_complex_structure );
```

Use this when you need to figure out what a data structure contains, what you should access, and what you accessed instead. Data::Dumper can dump objects as well as function references (if you set $Data::Dumper::Deparse to a true value).

While Data::Dumper is a core module and prints Perl code, its output is verbose. Some developers prefer the use of the YAML::XS or JSON modules for debugging. They do not produce Perl code, but their outputs can be much clearer to read and to understand.

## Circular References

Perl's memory management system of reference counting (Reference Counts, pp. 91) has one drawback. Two references which point to each other (directly or indirectly) form a *circular reference* that Perl cannot destroy on its own. Consider a biological model, where each entity has two parents and zero or more children:

```
my $alice  = { mother => '',     father => ''      };
my $robin  = { mother => '',     father => ''      };
my $cianne = { mother => $alice, father => $robin };

push @{ $alice->{children} }, $cianne;
push @{ $robin->{children} }, $cianne;
```

Both $alice and $robin contain an array reference which contains $cianne. Because $cianne is a hash reference which contains $alice and $robin, Perl will never decrease the reference count of any of these three people to zero. It doesn't recognize that these circular references exist, and it can't manage the lifespan of these entities.

Either break the reference count manually yourself (by clearing the children of $alice and $robin or the parents of $cianne), or use *weak references*. A weak reference is a reference which does not increase the reference count of its referent. Use the core module Scalar::Util's weaken() function to weaken a reference:

```
use Scalar::Util 'weaken';

my $alice  = { mother => '',     father => ''      };
my $robin  = { mother => '',     father => ''      };
my $cianne = { mother => $alice, father => $robin };

push @{ $alice->{children} }, $cianne;
push @{ $robin->{children} }, $cianne;

weaken( $cianne->{mother} );
weaken( $cianne->{father} );
```

$cianne will retain usable references to $alice and $robin, but those weak references do not count toward the number of remaining references to the parents. If the reference count of $alice reaches zero, Perl's garbage collector will reclaim her record, even though $cianne has a weak reference to $alice. Be aware that, when $alice gets reclaimed, $cianne's reference to $alice will be set to undef.

Most data structures do not need weak references, but when they're necessary, they're invaluable.

## Alternatives to Nested Data Structures

While Perl is content to process data structures nested as deeply as you can imagine, the human cost of understanding these data structures and their relationships—to say nothing of the complex syntax—is high. Beyond two or three levels of nesting, consider whether modeling various components of your system with classes and objects (Moose, pp. 165) will allow for clearer code.

# CHAPTER 4

# Operators

Some people call Perl an "operator-oriented language". To understand a Perl program, you must understand how its operators interact with their operands.

A Perl *operator* is a series of one or more symbols used as part of the syntax of a language. Each operator operates on zero or more *operands*. Think of an operator as a special sort of function the parser understands and its operands as arguments.

## Operator Characteristics

Every operator possesses several important characteristics which govern its behavior: the number of operands on which it operates, its relationship to other operators, the contexts it enforces, and the syntax it provides.

`perldoc perlop` and `perldoc perlsyn` provide voluminous information about Perl's operators, but the documentation assumes you're already familiar with a few essential computer science concepts. These ideas sound complicated, but they use complex names for ideas you already understand, even if you've never thought about them. If you can do elementary math in your head, you'll do fine.

### Precedence

The *precedence* of an operator governs when Perl should evaluate it in an expression. Evaluation order proceeds from highest to lowest precedence. Remember basic math? Multiply and divide before you add and subtract. That's precedence. Because the precedence of multiplication is higher than the precedence of addition, in Perl 7 + 7 * 10 evaluates to 77, not 140.

To force the evaluation of some operators before others, group their subexpressions in parentheses. In (7 + 7) * 10, grouping the addition into a single unit forces its evaluation before the multiplication. The result is 140.

`perldoc perlop` contains a table of precedence. Skim it a few times, but don't bother memorizing it (almost no one does). Spend your time simplifying your code where you can and then adding clarifying parentheses where you need them.

In cases where two operators have the same precedence, other factors such as associativity (Associativity, pp. 100) and fixity (Fixity, pp. 101) break the tie.

## Associativity

The *associativity* of an operator governs whether it evaluates from left to right or right to left. Addition is left associative, such that 2 + 3 + 4 evaluates 2 + 3 first, then adds 4 to the result. Exponentiation is right associative, such that 2 ** 3 ** 4 evaluates 3 ** 4 first, then raises 2 to the 81st power. As usual, grouping with parentheses will let you change the order of evaluation.

If you memorize only the precedence and associativity of the common mathematical operators, you'll be fine. Simplify your code and you won't have to memorize other associativities.

> The core B::Deparse module is an invaluable debugging tool. Run perl
> -MO=Deparse,-p on a snippet of code to see exactly how Perl handles operator
> precedence and associativity. The -p flag adds extra grouping parentheses which
> often clarify evaluation order.
> Beware that Perl's optimizer will simplify mathematical operations using constant
> values. To work around this, use named variables instead, as in $x ** $y ** $z.

## Arity

The *arity* of an operator is the number of operands on which it operates. A *nullary* operator operates on zero operands. A *unary* operator operates on one operand. A *binary* operator operates on two operands. A *trinary* operator operates on three operands. A *listary* operator operates on a list of operands.

The arithmetic operators are binary operators and are usually left associative. 2 + 3 - 4 evaluates 2 + 3 first; addition and subtraction have the same precedence, but they're left associative and binary, so the proper evaluation order applies the leftmost operator (+) to the leftmost two operands (2 and 3) with the leftmost operator (+), then applies the rightmost operator (-) to the result of the first operation and the rightmost operand (4).

Perl novices often find confusion between the interaction of listary operators–especially function calls–and nested expressions. Where parentheses usually help, beware of the parsing complexity of:

```
# probably buggy code
say ( 1 + 2 + 3 ) * 4;
```

...which prints the value 6 and (probably) evaluates as a whole to 4 (the return value of say multiplied by 4). Perl's parser happily interprets the parentheses as postcircumfix (Fixity, pp. 101) operators denoting the arguments to say, not circumfix parentheses grouping an expression to change precedence.

## Fixity

An operator's *fixity*[1] is its position relative to its operands:

- *Infix* operators appear between their operands. Most mathematical operators are infix operators, such as the multiplication operator in $length * $width.

- *Prefix* operators precede their operands. *Postfix* operators follow their operands. These operators tend to be unary, such as mathematic negation (-$x), boolean negation (!$y), and postfix increment ($z++).

- *Circumfix* operators surround their operands, as with the anonymous hash constructor ({ ... }) and quoting operators (qq[ ... ]).

- *Postcircumfix* operators follow certain operands and surround others, as seen in hash and array element access ($hash{$x} and $array[$y]).

# Operator Types

Perl operators provide value contexts (Numeric, String, and Boolean Context, pp. 8) to their operands. To choose the appropriate operator, you must know the values of the operands you provide as well as the value you expect to receive.

## Numeric Operators

Numeric operators impose numeric contexts on their operands. These operators are the standard arithmetic operators such as addition (+), subtraction (-), multiplication (*), division (/), exponentiation (**), and modulo (%), their in-place variants (+=, -=, *=, /=, **=, and %=), and both postfix and prefix auto-decrement (--).

The auto-increment operator has special string behavior (Special Operators, pp. 103).

Several comparison operators impose numeric contexts upon their operands. These are numeric equality (==), numeric inequality (!=), greater than (>), less than (<),

---

[1] Don't memorize all of these words. Just remember what they mean.

greater than or equal to (>=), less than or equal to (<=), and the sort comparison operator (<=>).

## String Operators

String operators impose string contexts on their operands. These operators are positive and negative regular expression binding (=~ and !~, respectively), and concatenation (.).

Several comparison operators impose string contexts upon their operands. These are string equality (eq), string inequality (ne), greater than (gt), less than (lt), greater than or equal to (ge), less than or equal to (le), and the string sort comparison operator (cmp).

## Logical Operators

Logical operators impose a boolean context on their operands. These operators are &&, and, ||, and or. All are infix and all exhibit *short-circuiting* behavior (Short Circuiting, pp. 44). The word forms have lower precedence than their punctuation forms.

The defined-or operator, //, tests the *definedness* of its operand. Unlike || which tests the *truth* of its operand, // evaluates to a true value even if its operand evaluates to a numeric zero or the empty string. This is especially useful for setting default parameter values:

```perl
sub name_pet
{
    my $name = shift // 'Fluffy';
    ...
}
```

The ternary conditional operator (?:) takes three operands. It evaluates the first in boolean context and evaluates to the second if the first is true and the third otherwise:

```perl
my $truthiness = $value ? 'true' : 'false';
```

The prefix ! and not operators return the logical opposites of the boolean values of their operands. not is a lower precedence version of !.

The xor operator is an infix operator which evaluates to the exclusive-or of its operands.

# Bitwise Operators

Bitwise operators treat their operands numerically at the bit level. These operations are uncommon. They consist of left shift (<<), right shift (>>), bitwise and (&), bitwise or ( | ), and bitwise xor (^), as well as their in-place variants (<<=, >>=, &=, | =, and ^=).

# Special Operators

The auto-increment operator has special behavior. When used on a value with a numeric component (Cached Coercions, pp. 79), the operator increments that numeric component. If the value is obviously a string (and has no numeric component), the operator increments the value's string component such that a becomes b, zz becomes aaa, and a9 becomes b0.

```
my $num = 1;
my $str = 'a';

$num++;
$str++;
is( $num,    2, 'numeric autoincrement' );
is( $str, 'b', 'string autoincrement'  );

no warnings 'numeric';
$num += $str;
$str++;

is( $num, 2, 'numeric addition with $str'    );
is( $str, 1, '... gives $str a numeric part' );
```

The repetition operator (x) is an infix operator with complex behavior. When evaluated in list context with a list as its first operand, it evaluates to that list repeated the number of times specified by its second operand. When evaluated in list context with a scalar as its first operand, it produces a string consisting of the string value of its first operand concatenated to itself the number of times specified by its second operand.

In scalar context, the operator repeats and concatenates a string:

```
my @scheherazade = ('nights') x 1001;
my $calendar     = 'nights'   x 1001;
my $cal_length   = length $calendar;
```

```
is( @scheherazade, 1001, 'list repeated' );
is( $cal_length,   1001 * length 'nights',
                   'word repeated' );

my @schenolist   = 'nights' x 1001;
my $calscalar    = ('nights') x 1001;

is( @schenolist, 1, 'no lvalue list' );
is( length $calscalar,
    1001 * length 'nights', 'word still repeated' );
```

The infix *range* operator (..) produces a list of items in list context:

```
my @cards = ( 2 .. 10, 'J', 'Q', 'K', 'A' );
```

It can *only* produce simple, incrementing ranges of integers or strings.

In boolean context, the range operator becomes the *flip-flop* operator. This operator produces a false value until its left operand is true. That value stays true until the right operand is true, after which the value is false again until the left operand is true again. Imagine parsing the text of a formal letter with:

```
while (/Hello, $user/ .. /Sincerely,/)
{
    say "> $_";
}
```

The *comma* operator (,) is an infix operator. In scalar context it evaluates its left operand then returns the value produced by evaluating its right operand. In list context, it evaluates both operands in left-to-right order.

The fat comma operator (=>) also automatically quotes any bareword used as its left operand (Hashes, pp. 68).

The *triple-dot* or *whatever* operator stands in for a single statement. It is nullary and has neither precedence nor associativity. It parses, but when executed it throws an exception with the string Unimplemented. This makes a great placeholder in example code you don't expect anyone to execute:

```
sub some_example {
    # implement this yourself
    ...
}
```

# CHAPTER 5

# Functions

A *function* (or *subroutine*) in Perl is a discrete, encapsulated unit of behavior. A program is a collection of little black boxes where the interaction of these functions governs the control flow of the program. A function may have a name. It may consume incoming information. It may produce outgoing information.

Functions are a prime mechanism for abstraction, encapsulation, and re-use in Perl.

## Declaring Functions

Use the sub builtin to declare a function:

```
sub greet_me  { ... }
```

Now greet_me() is available for invocation anywhere else within the program.

Just as you may *declare* a lexical variable but leave its value undefined, you may declare a function without defining it. A *forward declaration* tells Perl to record that a named function exists. You may define it later:

```
sub greet_sun;
```

## Invoking Functions

Use postfix (Fixity, pp. 101) parentheses to invoke a named function. Any arguments to the function may go within the parentheses:

```
greet_me( 'Jack', 'Tuxie' );
greet_me( 'Snowy' );
greet_me();
```

While these parentheses are not strictly necessary for these examples–even with strict enabled–they provide clarity to human readers as well as Perl's parser. When in doubt, leave them in.

Function arguments can be arbitrary expressions–including variables and function calls:

```
greet_me( $name );
greet_me( @authors );
greet_me( %editors );
greet_me( get_readers() );
```

...though Perl's default parameter handling sometimes surprises novices.

# Function Parameters

A function receives its parameters in a single array, @_ (The Default Array Variables, pp. 12). When you invoke a function, Perl *flattens* all provided arguments into a single list. The function must either unpack its parameters into variables or operate on @_ directly:

```
sub greet_one
{
    my ($name) = @_;
    say "Hello, $name!";
}

sub greet_all
{
    say "Hello, $_!" for @_;
}
```

@_ behaves as a normal array. Most Perl functions shift off parameters or use list assignment, but some code will access individual elements by index:

```
sub greet_one_shift
{
    my $name = shift;
    say "Hello, $name!";
}
```

```
sub greet_two_list_assignment
{
    my ($hero, $sidekick) = @_;
    say "Well if it isn't $hero and $sidekick. Welcome!";
}

sub greet_one_indexed
{
    my $name = $_[0];
    say "Hello, $name!";

    # or, less clear
    say "Hello, $_[0]!";
}
```

You may also unshift, push, pop, splice, and slice @_. Remember that the
array builtins use @_ as the default operand *within functions*, so that my $name =
shift; works. Take advantage of this idiom.

Assigning a scalar parameter from @_ requires shift, indexed access to @_, or
lvalue list context parentheses. Otherwise, Perl will happily evaluate @_ in scalar
context for you and assign the number of parameters passed:

```
sub bad_greet_one
{
    my $name = @_;   # buggy
    say "Hello, $name; you look numeric today!"
}
```

List assignment of multiple parameters is often clearer than multiple lines of
shift. Compare:

```
my $left_value  = shift;
my $operation   = shift;
my $right_value = shift;
```

... to:

```
my ($left_value, $operation, $right_value) = @_;
```

The latter is simpler to read and is even slightly more efficient (though its improved readability is much more important).

107

Occasionally it's necessary to extract parameters from @_ and pass the rest to another function:

```
sub delegated_method
{
    my $self = shift;
    say 'Calling delegated_method()'

    $self->delegate->delegated_method( @_ );
}
```

Use shift when your function needs only a single parameter. Use list assignment when accessing multiple parameters.

---

**Real Function Signatures**

Several CPAN distributions extend Perl's parameter handling with additional syntax and options. signatures and Method::Signatures are powerful. Method::Signatures::Simple is basic, but useful. MooseX::Method::Signatures works very well with Moose (Moose, pp. 165). Function::Parameters is worth exploring. Moops goes much further to add OO syntax, but bundles good function signatures as well.

---

## Flattening

List flattening into @_ happens on the caller side of a function call. Passing a hash as an argument produces a list of key/value pairs:

```
my %pet_names_and_types = (
    Lucky   => 'dog',
    Rodney  => 'dog',
    Tuxedo  => 'cat',
    Petunia => 'cat',
    Rosie   => 'dog',
);

show_pets( %pet_names_and_types );

sub show_pets
```

```
{
    my %pets = @_;
    while (my ($name, $type) = each %pets)
    {
        say "$name is a $type";
    }
}
```

When Perl flattens %pet_names_and_types into a list, the order of the key/value pairs from the hash will vary, but the list will always contain a key immediately followed by its value. Hash assignment inside show_pets() works the same way as the explicit assignment to %pet_names_and_types.

This flattening is often useful, but beware of mixing scalars with flattened aggregates in parameter lists. To write a show_pets_of_type() function, where one parameter is the type of pet to display, pass that type as the *first* parameter (or use pop to remove it from the end of @_, if you like to confuse people):

```
sub show_pets_by_type
{
    my ($type, %pets) = @_;

    while (my ($name, $species) = each %pets)
    {
        next unless $species eq $type;
        say "$name is a $species";
    }
}

my %pet_names_and_types = (
    Lucky   => 'dog',
    Rodney  => 'dog',
    Tuxedo  => 'cat',
    Petunia => 'cat',
    Rosie   => 'dog',
);

show_pets_by_type( 'dog',   %pet_names_and_types );
show_pets_by_type( 'cat',   %pet_names_and_types );
show_pets_by_type( 'moose', %pet_names_and_types );
```

## Slurping

List assignment with an aggregate is always greedy, so assigning to %pets *slurps* all of the remaining values from @_. If the $type parameter came at the end of @_, Perl would warn about assigning an odd number of elements to the hash. You *could* work around that:

```
sub show_pets_by_type
{
    my $type = pop;
    my %pets = @_;

    ...
}
```

...at the expense of clarity. The same principle applies when assigning to an array as a parameter. Use references (References, pp. 83) to avoid unwanted aggregate flattening.

## Aliasing

@_ contains a subtlety; it *aliases* function arguments. In other words, if you access @_ directly, you can modify the arguments passed to the function:

```
sub modify_name
{
    $_[0] = reverse $_[0];
}

my $name = 'Orange';
modify_name( $name );
say $name;

# prints egnarO
```

Modify an element of @_ directly and you will modify the original argument. Be cautious and unpack @_ rigorously–or document the modification carefully.

# Functions and Namespaces

Every function has a containing namespace (Packages, pp. 80). Functions in an un-declared namespace–functions not declared within the reach of an explicit package statement–exist in the `main` namespace. You may also declare a function within another namespace by prefixing its name:

```
sub Extensions::Math::add { ... }
```

This will declare the function and create the namespace as necessary. Remember that Perl packages are open for modification at any point–even while your program is running. If you declare multiple functions with the same name in a single namespace, Perl will issue a warning.

You can refer to other functions within a namespace with their short names. Use a fully-qualified name to invoke a function in another namespace:

```
package main;

Extensions::Math::add( $scalar, $vector );
```

Remember, functions are *visible* outside of their own namespaces through their fully-qualified names. Alternately, you may import names from other namespaces.

---

**Lexical Functions**

Perl 5.18 added an experimental feature to declare functions lexically. They're visible only within lexical scopes after declaration. See the "Lexical Subroutines" section of `perldoc perlsub` for more details.

---

## Importing

When loading a module with the `use` builtin (Modules, pp. 223), Perl automatically calls a method named `import()`. Modules can provide their own `import()` method which makes some or all defined symbols available to the calling package. Any arguments after the name of the module in the `use` statement get passed to the module's `import()` method. Thus:

```
use strict;
```

...loads the *strict.pm* module and calls `strict->import()` with no arguments, while:

```
use strict 'refs';
use strict qw( subs vars );
```

111

...loads the *strict.pm* module, calls `strict->import( 'refs' )`, then calls `strict->import( 'subs', vars' )`.

use has special behavior with regard to `import()`, but you may call `import()` directly. The use example is equivalent to:

```
BEGIN
{
    require strict;
    strict->import( 'refs' );
    strict->import( qw( subs vars ) );
}
```

The use builtin adds an implicit `BEGIN` block around these statements so that the `import()` call happens *immediately* after the parser has compiled the entire use statement. This ensures that the parser knows about any symbols imported by `strict` before it compiles the rest of the program. Otherwise, any functions *imported* from other modules but not *declared* in the current file would look like barewords, and would violate `strict`, for example.

Of course, `strict` is a pragma (Pragmas, pp. 200), so it has other effects.

# Reporting Errors

Almost every function has a caller. Use the `caller` builtin to inspect a function's calling context. When passed no arguments, `caller` returns a list containing the name of the calling package, the name of the file containing the call, and the line number of the file on which the call occurred:

```
package main;

main();

sub main
{
    show_call_information();
}

sub show_call_information
{
    my ($package, $file, $line) = caller();
    say "Called from $package in $file:$line";
}
```

112

The full call chain is available for inspection. Pass a single integer argument *n* to caller() to inspect the caller of the caller of the caller *n* times back. In other words, if show_call_information() used caller(0), it would receive information about the call from main(). If it used caller(1), it would receive information about the call from the start of the program.

This optional argument also tells caller to provide additional return values, including the name of the function and the context of the call:

```
sub show_call_information
{
    my ($package, $file, $line, $func) = caller(0);
    say "Called $func from $package in $file:$line";
}
```

The standard Carp module uses caller to report errors and throwing warnings in functions. When used in place of die in library code, croak() throws an exception from the point of view of its caller. carp() reports a warning from the file and line number of its caller (Producing Warnings, pp. 210).

Use caller (or Carp) when validating parameters or preconditions of a function to indicate that whatever called the function did so erroneously.

## Validating Arguments

While Perl does its best to do what you mean, it offers few native ways to test the validity of arguments provided to a function. Evaluate @_ in scalar context to check that the *number* of parameters passed to a function is correct:

```
sub add_numbers
{
    croak 'Expected two numbers, received: ' . @_
        unless @_ == 2;

    . . .
}
```

This validation reports any parameter count error from the point of view of its caller, thanks to the use of croak.

Type checking is more difficult, because of Perl's operator-oriented type conversions (Context, pp. 5). If you want additional safety of function parameters, see CPAN modules such as Params::Validate or MooseX::Method::Signatures.

113

# Advanced Functions

Functions are the foundation of many advanced Perl features.

## Context Awareness

Perl's builtins know whether you've invoked them in void, scalar, or list context. So too can your functions. The misnamed[1] `wantarray` builtin returns `undef` to signify void context, a false value to signify scalar context, and a true value to signify list context.

```
sub context_sensitive
{
    my $context = wantarray();

    return qw( List context )    if        $context;
    say     'Void context'    unless defined $context;
    return 'Scalar context' unless        $context;
}

context_sensitive();
say my $scalar = context_sensitive();
say context_sensitive();
```

This can be useful for functions which might produce expensive return values to avoid doing so in void context. Some idiomatic functions return a list in list context and the first element of the list or an array reference in scalar context. Remember, however, that there exists no single best recommendation for the use `wantarray`. Sometimes it's clearer to write separate and unambiguous functions, such as `get_all_toppings()` and `get_next_topping()`.

> **Putting it in Context**
>
> Robin Houston's `Want` and Damian Conway's `Contextual::Return` distributions from the CPAN offer many possibilities for writing powerful context-aware interfaces.

---

[1]See `perldoc -f wantarray`.

# Recursion

Suppose you want to find an element in a sorted array. You *could* iterate through every element of the array individually, looking for the target, but on average, you'll have to examine half of the elements of the array. Another approach is to halve the array, pick the element at the midpoint, compare, then repeat with either the lower or upper half. Divide and conquer. When you run out of elements to inspect or find the element, stop.

An automated test for this technique could be:

```
use Test::More;

my @elements =
(
    1, 5, 6, 19, 48, 77, 997, 1025, 7777, 8192, 9999
);

ok   elem_exists(    1, @elements ),
        'found first element in array';
ok   elem_exists( 9999, @elements ),
         'found last element in array';
ok ! elem_exists(  998, @elements ),
        'did not find element not in array';
ok ! elem_exists(   -1, @elements ),
        'did not find element not in array';
ok ! elem_exists( 10000, @elements ),
        'did not find element not in array';

ok   elem_exists(   77, @elements ),
        'found midpoint element';
ok   elem_exists(   48, @elements ),
        'found end of lower half element';
ok   elem_exists(  997, @elements ),
        'found start of upper half element';

done_testing();
```

Recursion is a deceptively simple concept. Every call to a function in Perl creates a new *call frame*, an data structure internal to Perl itself which represents the fact that you've called a function. This call frame includes the lexical environment of the function's current invocation–the values of all lexical variables within the

115

function as invoked. Because the storage of the values of the lexical variables is separate from the function itself, you can have multiple calls to a function active at the same time. A function can even call itself, or *recur*.

To make the previous test pass, write the recursive function `elem_exists()`:

```
sub elem_exists
{
    my ($item, @array) = @_;

    # break recursion with no elements to search
    return unless @array;

    # bias down with odd number of elements
    my $midpoint = int( (@array / 2) - 0.5 );
    my $miditem  = $array[ $midpoint ];

    # return true if found
    return 1 if $item  == $miditem;

    # return false with only one element
    return   if @array == 1;

    # split the array down and recurse
    return elem_exists(
        $item, @array[0 .. $midpoint]
    ) if $item < $miditem;

    # split the array and recurse
    return elem_exists(
        $item, @array[ $midpoint + 1 .. $#array ]
    );
}
```

Keep in mind that the arguments to the function will be *different* for every call, otherwise the function would always behave the same way (it would continue recursing until the program crashes).That's why the termination condition is so important.

Every recursive program can be written without recursion[2], but this divide-and-

---

[2]See the free book *Higher Order Perl* at http://hop.perl.plover.com/.

conquer approach is an effective way to manage many similar types of problems.

## Lexicals

As implied by recursion, every invocation of a function creates its own *instance* of a lexical scope represented internally by a call frame. Even though the declaration of elem_exists() creates a single scope for the lexicals $item, @array, $midpoint, and $miditem, every *call* to elem_exists()–even recursively–stores the values of those lexicals separately.

Not only can elem_exists() call itself, but the lexical variables of each invocation are safe and separate:

```
use Carp 'cluck';

sub elem_exists
{
    my ($item, @array) = @_;

    cluck "[$item] (@array)";
    ...
}
```

## Tail Calls

One *drawback* of recursion is that you must get your return conditions correct, lest your function call itself an infinite number of times. elem_exists() function has several return statements for this reason. Perl offers a helpful Deep recursion on subroutine warning when it suspects runaway recursion. The limit of 100 recursive calls is arbitrary, but often useful. Disable this warning with no warnings 'recursion'.

Because each call to a function requires a new call frame and lexical storage space, highly-recursive code can use more memory than iterative code. *Tail call elimination* can help.

A *tail call* is a call to a function which directly returns that function's results. These recursive calls to elem_exists():

```
# split the array down and recurse
return elem_exists(
    $item, @array[0 .. $midpoint]
) if $item < $miditem;
```

117

```
# split the array and recurse
return elem_exists(
    $item, @array[ $midpoint + 1 .. $#array ]
);
```

. . . are candidates for tail call elimination. This optimization would avoid returning to the current call and then returning to the parent call. Instead, it returns to the parent call directly.

Perl does not eliminate tail calls automatically, but you can get the same effect by using a special form of the goto builtin. Unlike the form which often produces spaghetti code[3], the goto function form replaces the current function call with a call to another function. You may use a function by name or by reference. You can even modify the arguments passed to the replacement function by modifying @_:

```
# split the array down and recurse
if ($item < $miditem)
{
    @_ = ($item, @array[0 .. $midpoint]);
    goto &elem_exists;
}

# split the array up and recurse
else
{
    @_ = ($item, @array[$midpoint + 1 .. $#array] );
    goto &elem_exists;
}
```

Sometimes optimizations are ugly, but if the alternative is highly recursive code which runs out of memory, embrace the ugly and rejoice in the practical.

## Pitfalls and Misfeatures

Perl still supports old-style invocations of functions, carried over from ancient versions of Perl. Previous versions of Perl required you to invoke functions with a leading ampersand (&) character. Perl 1 even required you to use the do builtin:

```
# outdated style; avoid
my $result = &calculate_result( 52 );
```

---

[3]Named because control flow is as simple and straightforward as a plate of spaghetti.

```
# Perl 1 style; avoid
my $result = do calculate_result( 42 );

# crazy mishmash; really truly avoid
my $result = do &calculate_result( 42 );
```

While the vestigial syntax is visual clutter, the leading ampersand form has other surprising behaviors. First, it disables any prototype checking. Second, it *implicitly* passes the contents of @_ unmodified, unless you've explicitly passed arguments yourself. Yes, that's invisible action at a distance.

A final pitfall comes from leaving the parentheses off of function calls. The Perl parser uses several heuristics to resolve ambiguous barewords and the number of parameters passed to a function. Heuristics can be wrong:

```
# warning; contains a subtle bug
ok elem_exists 1, @elements, 'found first element';
```

The call to elem_exists() will gobble up the test description intended as the second argument to ok(). Because elem_exists() uses a slurpy second parameter, this may go unnoticed until Perl produces warnings about comparing a non-number (the test description, which it cannot convert into a number) with the element in the array.

While extraneous parentheses can hamper readability, thoughtful use of parentheses can clarify code and make subtle bugs unlikely.

# Scope

*Scope* in Perl refers to the lifespan and visibility of named entities. Everything with a name in Perl (a variable, a function, a filehandle, a class) has a scope. Scoping helps to enforce *encapsulation*–keeping related concepts together and preventing their details from leaking.

## Lexical Scope

*Lexical scope* is the scope visible to you as you *read* a program. A block delimited by curly braces creates a new scope, whether a bare block, the block of a loop construct, the block of a sub declaration, an eval block, a package block, or any other non-quoting block. The Perl compiler resolves this scope during compilation.

119

Lexical scope describes the visibility of variables declared with my–*lexical* variables. A lexical variable declared in one scope is visible in that scope and any scopes nested within it, but is invisible to sibling or outer scopes:

```
# outer lexical scope
{
    package Robot::Butler

    # inner lexical scope
    my $battery_level;

    sub tidy_room
    {
        # further inner lexical scope
        my $timer;

        do {
            # innermost lexical scope
            my $dustpan;
            ...
        } while (@_);

        # sibling inner lexical scope
        for (@_)
        {
            # separate innermost scope
            my $polish_cloth;
            ...
        }
    }
}
```

...$battery_level is visible in all four scopes. $timer is visible in the method, the do block, and the for loop. $dustpan is visible only in the do block and $polish_cloth within the for loop.

Declaring a lexical in an inner scope with the same name as a lexical in an outer scope hides, or *shadows*, the outer lexical within the inner scope. For example:

```
my $name = 'Jacob';
```

```
{
    my $name = 'Edward';
    say $name;
}

say $name;
```

In longer code with larger scopes, this shadowing behavior is often desirable–it's easier to understand code when the scope of a lexical variable is no more than a couple of dozen lines.

> **Name Collisions**
>
> Lexical shadowing can happen by accident. Limit the scope of variables and the nesting of scopes to lessen your risk.

The silly lexical shadowing example program prints Edward and then Jacob[4] because the lexical in the nested scope hides the lexical in the outer scope. Shadowing a lexical is a feature of encapsulation. Declaring multiple variables with the same name and type *in the same lexical scope* produces a warning message.

Some lexical declarations have subtleties, such as a lexical variable used as the iterator variable of a for loop. Its declaration comes outside of the block, but its scope is that *within* the loop block:

```
my $cat = 'Brad';

for my $cat (qw( Jack Daisy Petunia Tuxedo Choco ))
{
    say "Iterator cat is $cat";
}

say "Static cat is $cat";
```

Functions–named and anonymous–provide lexical scoping to their bodies. This enables closures (Closures, pp. 130).

---

[4]Family members, not vampires.

## Our Scope

Within given scope, declare an alias to a package variable with the our builtin. Like my, our enforces lexical scoping of the alias. The fully-qualified name is available everywhere, but the lexical alias is visible only within its scope.

our is most useful with package global variables like $VERSION and $AUTOLOAD. You get a little bit of typo detection (declaring a package global with our satisfies the strict pragma's vars rule), but you still have to deal with a global variable.

## Dynamic Scope

Dynamic scope resembles lexical scope in its visibility rules, but instead of looking outward in compile-time scopes, lookup traverses backwards through all of the function calls you've made to reach the current code. Dynamic scope applies only to global and package global variables (because lexicals aren't visible outside their scopes), and is easiest to understand with an example. While a package global variable may be *visible* within all scopes, its *value* may change depending on localization and assignment:

```
our $scope;

sub inner
{
    say $scope;
}

sub main
{
    say $scope;
    local $scope = 'main() scope';
    middle();
}

sub middle
{
    say $scope;
    inner();
}

$scope = 'outer scope';
main();
say $scope;
```

The program begins by declaring an our variable, $scope, as well as three functions. It ends by assigning to $scope and calling main().

Within main(), the program prints $scope's current value, outer scope, then localizes the variable. This changes the visibility of the symbol within the current lexical scope *as well as* in any functions called from the *current* lexical scope; that *as well as* condition is what dynamic scoping does. Thus, $scope contains main() scope within the body of both middle() and inner(). After main() returns, when control flow reaches the end of its block, Perl restores the original value of the localized $scope. The final say prints outer scope once again.

Perl uses different visibility rules and storage mechanisms for package variables and lexical variables. Every scope which contains lexical variables uses a data structure called a *lexical pad* or *lexpad* to store the values for its enclosed lexical variables. Every time control flow enters one of these scopes, Perl creates another lexpad to contain the values of the lexical variables for that particular call. This makes functions work correctly, especially in recursive calls (Recursion, pp. 115).

Each package has a single *symbol table* which holds package variables and well as named functions. Importing (Importing, pp. 111) works by inspecting and manipulating this symbol table. So does local. You may only localize global and package global variables–never lexical variables.

local is most often useful with magic variables. For example, $/, the input record separator, governs how much data a readline operation will read from a filehandle. $!, the system error variable, contains error details for the most recent system call. $@, the Perl eval error variable, contains any error from the most recent eval operation. $|, the autoflush variable, governs whether Perl will flush the currently selected filehandle after every write operation.

localizing these in the narrowest possible scope limits the effect of your changes. This can prevent strange behavior in other parts of your code.

## State Scope

Perl 5.10 added a new scope to support the state builtin. State scope resembles lexical scope in terms of visibility, but adds a one-time initialization as well as value persistence:

```
sub counter
{
    state $count = 1;
    return $count++;
}
```

123

```
say counter();
say counter();
say counter();
```

On the first call to `counter`, Perl performs its single initialization of $count. On subsequent calls, $count retains its previous value. This program prints 1, 2, and 3. Change `state` to `my` and the program will print 1, 1, and 1.

You may use an expression to set a `state` variable's initial value:

```
sub counter
{
    state $count = shift;
    return $count++;
}

say counter(2);
say counter(4);
say counter(6);
```

Even though a simple reading of the code may suggest that the output should be 2, 4, and 6, the output is actually 2, 3, and 4. The first call to the sub `counter` sets the $count variable. Subsequent calls will not change its value.

`state` can be useful for establishing a default value or preparing a cache, but be sure to understand its initialization behavior if you use it:

```
sub counter
{
    state $count = shift;
    say 'Second arg is: ', shift;
    return $count++;
}

say counter(2, 'two');
say counter(4, 'four');
say counter(6, 'six');
```

The counter for this program prints 2, 3, and 4 as expected, but the values of the intended second arguments to the `counter()` calls are two, 4, and 6–because the `shift` of the first argument only happens in the first call to `counter()`. Either change the API to prevent this mistake, or guard against it with:

```
sub counter
{
    my ($initial_value, $text) = @_;

    state $count = $initial_value;
    say "Second arg is: $text";
    return $count++;
}

say counter(2, 'two');
say counter(4, 'four');
say counter(6, 'six');
```

# Anonymous Functions

An *anonymous function* is a function without a name. It behaves exactly like a named function–you can invoke it, pass arguments to it, return values from it, and copy references to it. Yet the only way to deal with it is by reference (Function References, pp. 89), not by name.

A common Perl idiom known as a *dispatch table* uses hashes to associate input with behavior:

```
my %dispatch =
(
    plus    => \&add_two_numbers,
    minus   => \&subtract_two_numbers,
    times   => \&multiply_two_numbers,
);

sub add_two_numbers      { $_[0] + $_[1] }
sub subtract_two_numbers { $_[0] - $_[1] }
sub multiply_two_numbers { $_[0] * $_[1] }

sub dispatch
{
    my ($left, $op, $right) = @_;

    return unless exists $dispatch{ $op };

    return $dispatch{ $op }->( $left, $right );
}
```

The dispatch() function takes arguments of the form (2, 'times', 2) and returns the result of evaluating the operation. If you were writing a trivial calculator application, you could use dispatch to figure out which calculation to perform based on a name provided by a user.

## Declaring Anonymous Functions

The sub builtin used without a name creates and returns an anonymous function. Use this function reference any place you'd use a reference to a named function, such as to declare the dispatch table's functions in place:

```
my %dispatch =
(
    plus      => sub { $_[0]  + $_[1] },
    minus     => sub { $_[0]  - $_[1] },
    times     => sub { $_[0]  * $_[1] },
    dividedby => sub { $_[0]  / $_[1] },
    raisedto  => sub { $_[0] ** $_[1] },
);
```

**Defensive Dispatch**

Only those functions within this dispatch table are available for users to call. If your dispatch function used a user-provided string as the literal name of functions, a malicious user could call any function anywhere by passing 'Internal::Functions::malicious_function'.

You may also see anonymous functions passed as function arguments:

```
sub invoke_anon_function
{
    my $func = shift;
    return $func->( @_ );
}

sub named_func
{
    say 'I am a named function!';
}
```

```
invoke_anon_function( \&named_func );
invoke_anon_function( sub { say 'Who am I?' } );
```

## Anonymous Function Names

Use introspection[5]: to determine whether a function is named or anonymous:

```
package ShowCaller;

sub show_caller
{
    my ($package, $file, $line, $sub) = caller(1);
    say "Called from $sub in $package:$file:$line";
}

sub main
{
    my $anon_sub = sub { show_caller() };
    show_caller();
    $anon_sub->();
}

main();
```

The result may be surprising:

```
Called from ShowCaller::main
        in ShowCaller:anoncaller.pl:20
Called from ShowCaller::__ANON__
        in ShowCaller:anoncaller.pl:17
```

The __ANON__ in the second line of output demonstrates that the anonymous function has no name that Perl can identify. This can complicate debugging. The CPAN module Sub::Name's subname() function allows you to attach names to anonymous functions:

```
use Sub::Name;
use Sub::Identify 'sub_name';
```

---

[5]See also sub_name from the CPAN module Sub::Identify.

127

```
my $anon   = sub {};
say sub_name( $anon );

my $named = subname( 'pseudo-anonymous', $anon );
say sub_name( $named );
say sub_name( $anon );

say sub_name( sub {} );
```

This program produces:

```
__ANON__
pseudo-anonymous
pseudo-anonymous
__ANON__
```

Be aware that both references refer to the same underlying anonymous function. Using subname() on one reference to a function will modify that anonymous function's name such that all other references to it will see the new name.

## Implicit Anonymous Functions

Perl allows you to declare anonymous functions as function arguments without using the sub keyword. Though this feature exists nominally to enable programmers to write their own syntax such as that for map and eval (Prototypes, pp. 265), an interesting example is the use of *delayed* functions that don't look like functions. It's not perfect, but it can make code easier to read.

Consider the CPAN module Test::Fatal, which takes an anonymous function as the first argument to its exception() function:

```
use Test::More;
use Test::Fatal;

my $croaker = exception { die 'I croak!' };
my $liver   = exception { 1 + 1 };

like( $croaker, qr/I croak/, 'die() should croak'   );
is(   $liver,   undef,       'addition should live' );

done_testing();
```

You might rewrite this more verbosely as:

```
my $croaker = exception( sub { die 'I croak!' } );
my $liver   = exception( sub { 1 + 1 } );
```

... or to pass named functions by reference:

```
sub croaker { die 'I croak!' }
sub liver   { 1 + 1 }

my $croaker = exception \&croaker;
my $liver   = exception \&liver;

like( $croaker, qr/I croak/, 'die() should die'     );
is(   $liver,   undef,        'addition should live' );
```

... but you may *not* pass them as scalar references:

```
my $croak_ref = \&croaker;
my $live_ref  = \&liver;

# BUGGY: does not work
my $croaker = exception $croak_ref;
my $liver   = exception $live_ref;
```

... because the prototype changes the way the Perl parser interprets this code. It cannot determine with 100% clarity *what* `$croaker` and `$liver` will contain, and so will throw an exception.

```
Type of arg 1 to Test::Fatal::exception
    must be block or sub {} (not private variable)
```

Also be aware that a function which takes an anonymous function as the first of multiple arguments cannot have a trailing comma after the function block:

```
use Test::More;
use Test::Fatal 'dies_ok';

dies_ok { die 'This is my boomstick!' }
        'No movie references here';
```

This is an occasionally confusing wart on otherwise helpful syntax, courtesy of a quirk of the Perl parser. The syntactic clarity available by promoting bare blocks to anonymous functions can be helpful, but use it sparingly and document the API with care.

# Closures

Every time control flow enters a function, that function gets a new environment representing that invocation's lexical scope (Scope, pp. 119). That applies equally well to anonymous functions (Anonymous Functions, pp. 125). The implication is powerful. The computer science term *higher order functions* refers to functions which manipulate other functions. Closures show off this power.

## Creating Closures

A *closure* is a function that uses lexical variables from an outer scope. You've probably already created and used closures without realizing it:

```
use Modern::Perl '2014';

my $filename = shift @ARGV;

sub get_filename { return $filename }
```

If this code seems straightforward to you, good! *Of course* the get_filename() function can see the $filename lexical. That's how scope works!

Suppose you want to iterate over a list of items without managing the iterator yourself. You can create a function which returns a function that, when invoked, will return the next item in the iteration:

```
sub make_iterator
{
    my @items = @_;
    my $count = 0;

    return sub
    {
        return if $count == @items;
        return $items[ $count++ ];
    }
}
```

```
my $cousins = make_iterator(qw(
    Rick Alex Kaycee Eric Corey Mandy Christine Alex
));

say $cousins->() for 1 .. 6;
```

Even though make_iterator() has returned, the anonymous function stored in $cousins has closed over the values of these variables *as they existed within* the invocation of make_iterator(). Their values persist (Reference Counts, pp. 91).

Because invoking make_iterator() creates a separate lexical environment, the anonymous sub it creates and returns closes over a unique lexical environment for each invocation:

```
my $aunts = make_iterator(qw(
    Carole Phyllis Wendy Sylvia Monica Lupe
));

say $cousins->();
say $aunts->();
```

Because make_iterator() does not return these lexicals by value or by reference, no other Perl code besides the closure can access them. They're encapsulated as effectively as any other lexical is, although any code which shares a lexical environment can access these values. This idiom provides better encapsulation of what would otherwise be a file or package global variable:

```
{
    my $private_variable;

    sub set_private { $private_variable = shift }
    sub get_private { $private_variable }
}
```

Be aware that you cannot *nest* named functions. Named functions have package global scope. Any lexical variables shared between nested functions will go unshared when the outer function destroys its first lexical environment[6].

---

[6] If that's confusing to you, imagine the implementation.

> ### Invasion of Privacy
>
> The CPAN module `PadWalker` lets you violate lexical encapsulation, but anyone who uses it gets to fix any bugs that result.

## Uses of Closures

Iterating over a fixed-sized list with a closure is interesting, but closures can do much more, such as iterating over a list which is too expensive to calculate or too large to maintain in memory all at once. Consider a function to create the Fibonacci series as you need its elements[7]. Instead of recalculating the series recursively, use a cache and lazily create the elements you need:

```
sub gen_fib
{
    my @fibs = (0, 1);

    return sub
    {
        my $item = shift;

        if ($item >= @fibs)
        {
            for my $calc (@fibs .. $item)
            {
                $fibs[$calc] = $fibs[$calc - 2]
                             + $fibs[$calc - 1];
            }
        }
        return $fibs[$item];
    }
}

# calculate 42nd Fibonacci number
my $fib = gen_fib();
say $fib->( 42 );
```

---

[7]Why? To check your Haskell homework.

Every call to the function returned by gen_fib() takes one argument, the *n*th element of the Fibonacci series. The function generates and caches all preceding values in the series as necessary, and returns the requested element.

Here's where closures and first class functions get interesting. This code does two things; there's a pattern specific to caching intertwined with the numeric series. What happens if you extract the cache-specific code (initialize a cache, execute custom code to populate cache elements, and return the calculated or cached value) to a function gen_caching_closure()?

```perl
sub gen_caching_closure
{
    my ($calc_element, @cache) = @_;

    return sub
    {
        my $item = shift;

        $calc_element->($item, \@cache)
            unless $item < @cache;

        return $cache[$item];
    };
}

sub gen_fib
{
    my @fibs = (0, 1, 1);

    return gen_caching_closure( sub
        {
            my ($item, $fibs) = @_;

            for my $calc ((@$fibs - 1) .. $item)
            {
                $fibs->[$calc] = $fibs->[$calc - 2]
                                 + $fibs->[$calc - 1];
            }
        }, @fibs
    );
}
```

The program behaves as it did before, but now function references and closures separate the cache initialization behavior from the calculation of the next number in the Fibonacci series. Customizing the behavior of code–in this case, gen_-caching_closure()–by passing in a function allows tremendous flexibility and can clean up your code.

> **Fold, Apply, and Filter**
>
> The builtins map, grep, and sort are themselves higher-order functions.

## Closures and Partial Application

Closures can also *remove* unwanted genericity. Consider the case of a function which takes several parameters:

```perl
sub make_sundae
{
    my %args        = @_;

    my $ice_cream = get_ice_cream( $args{ice_cream} );
    my $banana    = get_banana(    $args{banana}    );
    my $syrup     = get_syrup(     $args{syrup}     );
    ...
}
```

Myriad customization possibilities might work very well in a full-sized ice cream store, but for a drive-through ice cream cart where you only serve French vanilla ice cream on Cavendish bananas, every call to make_sundae() passes arguments that never change.

*Partial application* allows you to bind *some* of the arguments to a function now so that you can provide the others later. Wrap the function you intend to call in a closure and pass the bound arguments. For your ice cream cart:

```perl
my $make_cart_sundae = sub
{
    return make_sundae( @_,
        ice_cream => 'French Vanilla',
        banana    => 'Cavendish',
    );
};
```

Now whenever you process an order, invoke the function reference in $make_-cart_sundae and pass only the interesting arguments. You'll never forget the invariants or pass them incorrectly. You can even use Sub::Install from the CPAN to import $make_cart_sundae function into another namespace.

This is only the start of what you can do with higher order functions. Mark Jason Dominus's *Higher Order Perl* is the canonical reference on first-class functions and closures in Perl. Read it online at http://hop.perl.plover.com/.

## State versus Closures

Closures (Closures, pp. 130) use lexical scope (Scope, pp. 119) to control access to lexical variables–even with named functions:

```
{
    my $safety = 0;

    sub enable_safety  { $safety = 1 }
    sub disable_safety { $safety = 0 }

    sub do_something_awesome
    {
        return if $safety;
        ...
    }
}
```

All three functions encapsulate that shared state without exposing the lexical variable directly to external code. This idiom works well for cases where multiple functions access that lexical, but it's clunky when only one function does. Suppose every hundredth ice cream parlor customer gets free sprinkles:

```
my $cust_count = 0;

sub serve_customer
{
    $cust_count++;
    my $order = shift;

    add_sprinkles($order) if $cust_count % 100 == 0;
    ...
}
```

This approach *works*, but creating a new outer lexical scope for a single function is a little bit noisy. The `state` builtin allows you to declare a lexically scoped variable with a value that persists between invocations:

```
sub serve_customer
{
    state $cust_count = 0;
    $cust_count++;

    my $order = shift;
    add_sprinkles($order)
        if ($cust_count % 100 == 0);

    ...
}
```

You must enable this feature explicitly by using a module such as `Modern::Perl`, the `feature` pragma (Pragmas, pp. 200), or requiring the features of at least Perl 5.10 (use `5.010;`, use `5.012;`, and so on).

`state` also works within anonymous functions:

```
sub make_counter
{
    return sub
    {
        state $count = 0;
        return $count++;
    }
}
```

... though there are few obvious benefits to this approach.

## State versus Pseudo-State

In old versions of Perl, a named function could close over its previous lexical scope by abusing a quirk of implementation. Using a postfix conditional which evaluates to false with a `my` declaration avoided *reinitializing* a lexical variable to undef or its initialized value.

In modern versions of Perl, any use of a postfix conditional expression modifying a lexical variable declaration produces a deprecation warning. It's too easy to write inadvertently buggy code with this technique; use `state` instead where available, or a true closure otherwise. Rewrite this idiom when you encounter it:

```
sub inadvertent_state
{
    # my $counter  = 1 if 0;  # DEPRECATED; don't use
    state $counter = 1;       # prefer

    ...
}
```

You may only initialize a state variable with a scalar value. If you need to keep track of an aggregate, use a hash or array reference (References, pp. 83).

# Attributes

Named entities in Perl–variables and functions–can have additional metadata attached. This metadata takes the form of *attributes*, arbitrary names and values used with certain types of metaprogramming (Code Generation, pp. 234).

Attribute declaration syntax is awkward, and using attributes effectively is more art than science. Most programs never use them, but when used well they offer clarity and maintenance benefits.

A simple attribute is a colon-preceded identifier attached to a declaration:

```
my $fortress       :hidden;

sub erupt_volcano :ScienceProject { ... }
```

When Perl parses these declarations, it invokes attribute handlers named `hidden` and `ScienceProject`, if they exist for the appropriate types (scalars and functions, respectively). These handlers can do *anything*. If the appropriate handlers do not exist, Perl will throw a compile-time exception.

Attributes may include a list of parameters. Perl treats these parameters as lists of constant strings. The `Test::Class` module from the CPAN uses such parametric arguments to good effect[8]:

```
sub setup_tests         :Test(setup)    { ... }
sub test_monkey_creation :Test(10)      { ... }
sub shutdown_tests      :Test(teardown) { ... }
```

---

[8] See the Catalyst web framework for another, different, example.

The Test attribute identifies methods which include test assertions and optionally identifies the number of assertions the method intends to run. While introspection (Reflection, pp. 187) of these classes could discover the appropriate test methods, given well-designed solid heuristics, the :Test attribute is unambiguous. Test::Class provides attribute handlers which keep track of these methods. When the class has finished parsing, Test::Class can loop through the list of test methods and run them.

The setup and teardown parameters allow test classes to define their own support methods without worrying about conflicts with other such methods in other classes. This separates the idea of what this class must do from how other classes do their work. Otherwise a test class might have only one method named setup and one named teardown and would have to do everything there, then call the parent methods, and so on.

## Drawbacks of Attributes

Attributes have their drawbacks. The canonical pragma for working with attributes (the attributes pragma) has listed its interface as experimental for many years, and for good reason. Damian Conway's core module Attribute::Handlers is much easier to use, and Andrew Main's Attribute::Lexical is a newer approach. Prefer either to attributes whenever possible.

The worst feature of attributes is that they make it easy to warp the syntax of Perl in unpredictable ways. It's not always easy to predict what code with attributes will do. Good documentation helps, but if an innocent-looking declaration on a lexical variable stores a reference to that variable somewhere, your expectations of its lifespan may be wrong. Likewise, a handler may wrap a function in another function and replace it in the symbol table without your knowledge–consider a :memoize attribute which automatically invokes the core Memoize module.

Attributes *can* help you to solve difficult problems or to make an API much easier to use. When used properly, they're powerful–but most programs never need them.

# AUTOLOAD

Perl does not require you to declare every function before you call it. Perl will happily attempt to call a function even if it doesn't exist. Consider the program:

```
use Modern::Perl;

bake_pie( filling => 'apple' );
```

When you run it, Perl will throw an exception due to the call to the undefined function `bake_pie()`.

Now add a function called `AUTOLOAD()`:

```
sub AUTOLOAD {}
```

When you run the program now, nothing obvious will happen. Perl will call a function named `AUTOLOAD()` in a package–if it exists–whenever normal dispatch fails. Change the `AUTOLOAD()` to emit a message to demonstrate that it gets called:

```
sub AUTOLOAD { say 'In AUTOLOAD()!' }
```

The `AUTOLOAD()` function receives the arguments passed to the undefined function in `@_` and the fully-qualified *name* of the undefined function in the package global `$AUTOLOAD` (here, `main::bake_pie`):

```
sub AUTOLOAD
{
    our $AUTOLOAD;

    # pretty-print the arguments
    local $" = ', ';
    say "In AUTOLOAD(@_) for $AUTOLOAD!"
}
```

Extract the method name with a regular expression (Regular Expressions and Matching, pp. 145):

```
sub AUTOLOAD
{
    my ($name) = our $AUTOLOAD =~ /::(\w+)$/;

    # pretty-print the arguments
    local $" = ', ';
    say "In AUTOLOAD(@_) for $name!"
}
```

Whatever `AUTOLOAD()` returns, the original call receives:

```
say secret_tangent( -1 );

sub AUTOLOAD { return 'mu' }
```

So far, these examples have merely intercepted calls to undefined functions. You have other options.

## Redispatching Methods in AUTOLOAD()

A common pattern in OO programming (Moose, pp. 165) is to *delegate* or *proxy* certain methods in one object to another object somehow available to the former. A logging proxy can help with debugging:

```
package Proxy::Log;

# constructor blesses reference to a scalar

sub AUTOLOAD
{
    my ($name) = our $AUTOLOAD =~ /::(\w+)$/;
    Log::method_call( $name, @_ );

    my $self = shift;
    return $$self->$name( @_ );
}
```

This AUTOLOAD() extracts the name of the undefined method. Then it dereferences the proxied object from a blessed scalar reference, logs the method call, then invokes that method on the proxied object with the provided parameters.

## Generating Code in AUTOLOAD()

This double dispatch is easy to write but inefficient. Every method call on the proxy must fail normal dispatch to end up in AUTOLOAD(). Pay that penalty only once by installing new methods into the proxy class as the program needs them:

```
sub AUTOLOAD
{
    my ($name) = our $AUTOLOAD =~ /::(\w+)$/;
    my $method = sub { ... };

    no strict 'refs';
    *{ $AUTOLOAD } = $method;
    return $method->( @_ );
}
```

The body of the previous AUTOLOAD() has become a closure (Closures, pp. 130) bound over the *name* of the undefined method. Installing that closure in the appropriate symbol table allows all subsequent dispatch to that method to find the created closure (and avoid AUTOLOAD()). This code finally invokes the method directly and returns the result.

Though this approach is cleaner and almost always more transparent than handling the behavior directly in AUTOLOAD(), the code *called* by AUTOLOAD() may see AUTOLOAD() in its caller() list. While it may violate encapsulation to care that this occurs, leaking the details of *how* an object provides a method may also violate encapsulation.

Some code uses a tailcall (Tailcalls, pp. 58) to *replace* the current invocation of AUTOLOAD() with a call to the destination method:

```
sub AUTOLOAD
{
    my ($name) = our $AUTOLOAD =~ /::(\w+)$/;
    my $method = sub { ... }

    no strict 'refs';
    *{ $AUTOLOAD } = $method;
    goto &$method;
}
```

This has the same effect as invoking $method directly, except that AUTOLOAD() will no longer appear in the list of calls available from caller(), so it looks like the generated method was simply called directly.

## Drawbacks of AUTOLOAD

AUTOLOAD() can be useful, though it is difficult to use properly. The naïve approach to generating methods at runtime means that the can() method will not report the right information about the capabilities of objects and classes. The easiest solution is to predeclare all functions you plan to AUTOLOAD() with the subs pragma:

```
use subs qw( red green blue ochre teal );
```

---

> **Now You See Them**
>
> Forward declarations are useful only in the two rare cases of attributes and autoloading (AUTOLOAD, pp. 138).

That technique documents your intent well, but requires you to maintain a static list of functions or methods. Overriding can() (The UNIVERSAL Package, pp. 230) sometimes works better:

```
sub can
{
    my ($self, $method) = @_;

    # use results of parent can()
    my $meth_ref = $self->SUPER::can( $method );
    return $meth_ref if $meth_ref;

    # add some filter here
    return unless $self->should_generate( $method );

    $meth_ref = sub { ... };
    no strict 'refs';
    return *{ $method } = $meth_ref;
}

sub AUTOLOAD
{
    my ($self) = @_;
    my ($name) = our $AUTOLOAD =~ /::(\w+)$/;>

    return unless my $meth_ref = $self->can( $name );
    goto &$meth_ref;
}
```

AUTOLOAD() is a big hammer; it can catch functions and methods you had no intention of autoloading, such as DESTROY(), the destructor of objects. If you write a DESTROY() method with no implementation, Perl will happily dispatch to it instead of AUTOLOAD():

```
# skip AUTOLOAD()
sub DESTROY {}
```

---

**A Very Special Method**

The special methods `import()`, `unimport()`, and `VERSION()` never go through `AUTOLOAD()`.

---

If you mix functions and methods in a single namespace which inherits from another package which provides its own `AUTOLOAD()`, you may see the strange error:

```
Use of inherited AUTOLOAD for non-method
    slam_door() is deprecated
```

If this happens to you, simplify your code; you've called a function which does not exist in a package which inherits from a class which contains its own `AUTOLOAD()`. The problem compounds in several ways: mixing functions and methods in a single namespace is often a design flaw, inheritance and `AUTOLOAD()` get complex very quickly, and reasoning about code when you don't know what methods objects provide is difficult.

`AUTOLOAD()` is useful for quick and dirty programming, but robust code avoids it.

# CHAPTER 6

# Regular Expressions and Matching

Much of Perl's text processing power comes from its use of *regular expressions*. A regular expression (also *regex* or *regexp*) is a *pattern* which describes characteristics of a piece of text. A *regular expression engine* applies these patterns to match or to replace portions of text.

While mastering regular expressions is a daunting pursuit, a little knowledge will give you great power. Perl's core regex documentation includes a tutorial (perldoc perlretut), a reference guide (perldoc perlreref), and full documentation (perldoc perlre). Jeffrey Friedl's book *Mastering Regular Expressions* explains the theory and the mechanics of how regular expressions work.

## Literals

A regex can be as simple as a substring pattern:

```
my $name = 'Chatfield';
say 'Found a hat!' if $name =~ /hat/;
```

The match operator (m//, abbreviated //) identifies a regular expression–in this example, hat. This pattern is *not* a word. Instead it means "the h character, followed by the a character, followed by the t character." Each character in the pattern is an indivisible element (an *atom*). An atom matches or it doesn't.

The regex binding operator (=~) is an infix operator (Fixity, pp. 101) which applies the regex of its second operand to a string as its first operand. When evaluated in scalar context, a match evaluates to a true value if it succeeds. The negated form of the binding operator (!~) evaluates to a true value *unless* the match succeeds.

> **Remember index!**
>
> The `index` builtin can also search for a literal substring within a string.
> Using a regex engine for that is like flying an autonomous combat drone
> to the corner store to buy cheese–but Perl lets you write code as it seems
> most clear to you.

The substitution operator, `s///`, is in one sense a circumfix operator (Fixity, pp.
101) with two operands. Its first operand (the part between the first and second
delimiters) is a regular expression to match when used with the regex binding
operator. The second operand (the part between the second and third delimiters)
is a substring used to replace the matched portion of the string operand used with
the regex binding operator. For example, to cure pesky summer allergies:

```
my $status = 'I feel ill.';
$status    =~ s/ill/well/;
say $status;
```

# The qr// Operator and Regex Combinations

The `qr//` operator creates first-class regexes. Use them as the operand of the
match operator or the first operand of the substitution operator:

```
my $hat = qr/hat/;
say 'Found a hat!' if $name =~ /$hat/;
```

. . . or combine multiple regex objects into complex patterns:

```
my $hat   = qr/hat/;
my $field = qr/field/;

say 'Found a hat in a field!'
    if $name =~ /$hat$field/;

like( $name, qr/$hat$field/,
              'Found a hat in a field!' );
```

> **Like is, with More `like`**
>
> `Test::More`'s `like` function tests that the first argument matches the regex provided as the second argument.

# Quantifiers

Regular expressions get more powerful through the use of *regex quantifiers*. These metacharacters govern how often a regex component may appear in a matching string. The simplest quantifier is the *zero or one quantifier*, or ?:

```
my $cat_or_ct = qr/ca?t/;

like( 'cat', $cat_or_ct, "'cat' matches /ca?t/" );
like( 'ct',  $cat_or_ct, "'ct' matches /ca?t/"  );
```

Any atom in a regular expression followed by the ? character means "match zero or one of this atom." This regular expression matches if zero or one a characters immediately follow a c character *and* immediately precede a t character. This regex matches both the literal substrings cat and ct.

The *one or more quantifier*, or +, matches at least one of the quantified atom:

```
my $some_a = qr/ca+t/;

like( 'cat',    $some_a, "'cat' matches /ca+t/" );
like( 'caat',   $some_a, "'caat' matches/"      );
like( 'caaat',  $some_a, "'caaat' matches"      );
like( 'caaaat', $some_a, "'caaaat' matches"     );

unlike( 'ct',   $some_a, "'ct' does not match"  );
```

There is no theoretical limit to the maximum number of quantified atoms which can match.

The *zero or more quantifier*, *, matches zero or more instances of the quantified atom:

```
my $any_a = qr/ca*t/;
```

147

```
like( 'cat',    $any_a, "'cat' matches /ca*t/" );
like( 'caat',   $any_a, "'caat' matches"       );
like( 'caaat',  $any_a, "'caaat' matches"      );
like( 'caaaat', $any_a, "'caaaat' matches"     );
like( 'ct',     $any_a, "'ct' matches"         );
```

As silly as this seems, it allows you to specify optional components of a regex. Use it sparingly, though: it's a blunt and expensive tool. *Most* regular expressions benefit from using the ? and + quantifiers far more than *. Precision of intent often improves clarity.

*Numeric quantifiers* express the number of times an atom may match. {n} means that a match must occur exactly *n* times.

```
# equivalent to qr/cat/;
my $only_one_a = qr/ca{1}t/;

like( 'cat', $only_one_a, "'cat' matches /ca{1}t/" );
```

{n,} matches an atom *at least n* times:

```
# equivalent to qr/ca+t/;
my $some_a = qr/ca{1,}t/;

like( 'cat',    $some_a, "'cat' matches /ca{1,}t/" );
like( 'caat',   $some_a, "'caat' matches"          );
like( 'caaat',  $some_a, "'caaat' matches"         );
like( 'caaaat', $some_a, "'caaaat' matches"        );
```

{n,m} means that a match must occur at least *n* times and cannot occur more than *m* times:

```
my $few_a = qr/ca{1,3}t/;

like( 'cat',    $few_a, "'cat' matches /ca{1,3}t/" );
like( 'caat',   $few_a, "'caat' matches"           );
like( 'caaat',  $few_a, "'caaat' matches"          );

unlike( 'caaaat', $few_a, "'caaaat' doesn't match" );
```

You may express the symbolic quantifiers in terms of the numeric quantifiers, but the symbolic quantifiers are shorter and get used more often.

# Greediness

The + and * quantifiers are *greedy*: they try to match as much of the input string as possible. This is particularly pernicious. Consider a naïve use of the "zero or more non-newline characters" pattern of .*:

```
# a poor regex
my $hot_meal = qr/hot.*meal/;

say 'Found a hot meal!'
    if 'I have a hot meal' =~ $hot_meal;

say 'Found a hot meal!'
     if 'one-shot, piecemeal work!' =~ $hot_meal;
```

Greedy quantifiers start by matching *everything* at first. If that match does not succeed, the regex engine will back off one character at a time until it finds a match.

The ? quantifier modifier turns a greedy-quantifier non-greedy:

```
my $minimal_greedy = qr/hot.*?meal/;
```

When given a non-greedy quantifier, the regular expression engine will prefer the *shortest* possible potential match. If that match fails, the engine will increase the number of characters identified by the .*? token combination one character at a time. Because * matches zero or more times, the minimal potential match for this token combination is zero characters:

```
say 'Found a hot meal'
if 'ilikeahotmeal' =~ /$minimal_greedy/;
```

Use +? to match one or more items non-greedily:

```
my $minimal_greedy_plus = qr/hot.+?meal/;

unlike( 'ilikeahotmeal',   $minimal_greedy_plus );

like( 'i like a hot meal', $minimal_greedy_plus );
```

The ? quantifier modifier applies to the ? (zero or one matches) quantifier as well as the range quantifiers. It always causes the regex to match as little of the input as possible.

Regexes are powerful, but they're not always the best way to solve a problem. This is doubly true for the greedy patterns .+ and .*. A crossword puzzle fan who needs to fill in four boxes of 7 Down ("Rich soil") will find too many invalid candidates with the pattern:

```
my $seven_down = qr/l$letters_only*m/;
```

If she runs this against all of the words in a dictionary, it'll match Alabama, Belgium, and Bethlehem long before it reaches the answer of loam. Not only are those words too long, but the matches start in the middle of the words.

# Regex Anchors

It's important to know how the regex engine handles greedy matches—but it's equally as important to know what kind of matches you do and don't want. *Regex anchors* force the regex engine to start or end a match at a fixed position. The *start of string anchor* (\A) dictates that any match must start at the very beginning of the string:

```
# also matches "lammed", "lawmaker", and "layman"
my $seven_down = qr/\Al$ {letters_only}{2}m/;
```

The *end of line string anchor* (\z) requires that a match end at the very end of the string.

```
# also matches "loom", but an obvious improvement
my $seven_down = qr/\Al$ {letters_only}{2}m\z/;
```

You will often see the ^ and $ assertions used to match the start and end of strings. ^ *does* match the start of the string, but in certain circumstances it can match just after a newline within the string. Similarly, $ *does* match the end of the string (just before a newline, if it exists), but it can match just before a newline in the middle of the string. \A and \z are more specific and, thus, more useful.

The *word boundary anchor* (\b) matches only at the boundary between a word character (\w) and a non-word character (\W). That boundary isn't a character in and of itself; it has no width. It's invisible. Use an anchored regex to find loam while prohibiting Belgium:

```
my $seven_down = qr/\bl$ {letters_only}{2}m\b/;
```

# Metacharacters

Perl interprets several characters in regular expressions as *metacharacters*, characters represent something other than their literal interpretation. You've seen a few metacharacters already (\b, ., and ?, for example). Metacharacters give regex wielders power far beyond mere substring matches. The regex engine treats all metacharacters as atoms.

The . metacharacter means "match any character except a newline". Many novices forget that nuance. A simple regex search–ignoring the obvious improvement of using anchors–for 7 Down might be /1..m/. Of course, there's always more than one way to get the right answer:

```
for my $word (@words)
{
    next unless length( $word ) == 4;
    next unless $word =~ /1..m/;
    say "Possibility: $word";
}
```

If the potential matches in @words are more than the simplest English words, you will get false positives. . also matches punctuation characters, whitespace, and numbers. Be specific! The \w metacharacter represents all alphanumeric characters (Unicode and Strings, pp. 30) and the underscore:

```
next unless $word =~ /1\w\wm/;
```

The \d metacharacter matches digits (also in the Unicode sense):

```
# not a robust phone number matcher
next unless $number =~ /\d{3}-\d{3}-\d{4}/;
say "I have your number: $number";
```

Use the \s metacharacter to match whitespace. *Whitespace* means a literal space, a tab character, a carriage return, a form-feed, or a newline:

```
my $two_three_letter_words = qr/\w{3}\s\w{3}/;
```

151

> ### Negated Metacharacters
>
> These metacharacters have negated forms. Use \W to match any character *except* a word character. Use \D to match a non-digit character. Use \S to match anything but whitespace. Use \B to match anywhere except a word boundary.

## Character Classes

When none of those metacharacters is specific enough, you can make your own group of characters into *character class* by enclosing them in square brackets. A character class allows you to treat a group of alternatives as a single atom.

```
my $ascii_vowels = qr/[aeiou]/;
my $maybe_cat    = qr/c${ascii_vowels}t/;
```

> ### Interpolation Happens
>
> Without those curly braces, Perl's parser would interpret the variable name as $ascii_vowelst, which either causes a compile-time error about an unknown variable or interpolates the contents of an existing $ascii_-vowelst into the regex.

The hyphen character (-) allows you to include a contiguous range of characters in a class, such as this $ascii_letters_only regex:

```
my $ascii_letters_only = qr/[a-zA-Z]/;
```

To include the hyphen as a member of the class, use it at the start or end of the class:

```
my $interesting_punctuation = qr/[-!?]/;
```

...or escape it:

```
my $line_characters = qr/[|=\-_]/;
```

Use the caret (^) as the first element of the character class to mean "anything *except* these characters":

```
my $not_an_ascii_vowel = qr/[^aeiou]/;
```

Use a caret anywhere but the first position to make it a member of the character class. To include a hyphen in a negated character class, place it after the caret or at the end of the class, or escape it.

# Capturing

Regular expressions allow you to group and capture portions of the match for later use. To extract an American telephone number of the form (202) 456-1111 from a string:

```
my $area_code    = qr/\(\d{3}\)/;
my $local_number = qr/\d{3}-?\d{4}/;
my $phone_number = qr/$area_code\s?$local_number/;
```

Note especially the escaping of the parentheses within $area_code. Parentheses are special in Perl regular expressions. They group atoms into larger units and also capture portions of matching strings. To match literal parentheses, escape them with backslashes as seen in $area_code.

## Named Captures

Perl 5.10 added *named captures*, which allow you to capture portions of matches from applying a regular expression and access them later. For example, when extracting a phone number from contact information:

```
if ($contact_info =~ /(?<phone>$phone_number)/)
{
    say "Found a number $+{phone}";
}
```

Regexes tend to look like punctuation soup until you can group various portions together as chunks. Named capture syntax has the form:

```
(?<capture name> ... )
```

Parentheses enclose the capture. The `?< name >` construct immediately follows the opening parenthesis and provides a name for this particular capture. The remainder of the capture is a regular expression.

When a match against the enclosing pattern succeeds, Perl updates the magic variable %+. In this hash, the key is the name of the capture and the value is the portion of the string which matched the capture.

## Numbered Captures

Perl has supported *numbered captures* for ages:

```perl
if ($contact_info =~ /($phone_number)/)
{
    say "Found a number $1";
}
```

This form of capture provides no identifying name and does nothing to %+. Instead, Perl stores the captured substring in a series of magic variables. The *first* matching capture that Perl finds goes into $1, the second into $2, and so on. Capture counts start at the *opening* parenthesis of the capture. Thus the first left parenthesis begins the capture into $1, the second into $2, and so on.

While the syntax for named captures is longer than for numbered captures, it provides additional clarity. Counting left parentheses is tedious work, and combining regexes which each contain numbered captures is difficult. Named captures improve regex maintainability–though name collisions are possible, they're relatively infrequent. Minimize the risk by using named captures only in top-level regexes.

In list context, a regex match returns a list of captured substrings:

```perl
if (my ($number) = $contact_info =~ /($phone_number)/)
{
    say "Found a number $number";
}
```

Numbered captures are also useful in simple substitutions, where named captures may be more verbose:

```perl
my $order = 'Vegan brownies!';

$order =~ s/Vegan (\w+)/Vegetarian $1/;
# or
$order =~ s/Vegan (?<food>\w+)/Vegetarian $+{food}/;
```

# Grouping and Alternation

Previous examples have all applied quantifiers to simple atoms. You may apply them to any regex element:

```
my $pork  = qr/pork/;
my $beans = qr/beans/;

like( 'pork and beans', qr/\A$pork?.*?$beans/,
    'maybe pork, definitely beans' );
```

If you expand the regex manually, the results may surprise you:

```
my $pork_and_beans = qr/\Apork?.*beans/;

like( 'pork and beans', qr/$pork_and_beans/,
    'maybe pork, definitely beans' );
like( 'por and beans', qr/$pork_and_beans/,
    'wait... no phylloquinone here!' );
```

Sometimes specificity helps pattern accuracy:

```
my $pork  = qr/pork/;
my $and   = qr/and/;
my $beans = qr/beans/;

like( 'pork and beans', qr/\A$pork? $and? $beans/,
    'maybe pork, maybe and, definitely beans' );
```

Some regexes need to match either one thing or another. The *alternation* metacharacter ( | ) indicates that either possibility may match.

```
my $rice  = qr/rice/;
my $beans = qr/beans/;

like( 'rice',  qr/$rice|$beans/, 'Found rice'  );
like( 'beans', qr/$rice|$beans/, 'Found beans' );
```

While it's easy to interpret rice|beans as meaning ric, followed by either e or b, followed by eans, alternations always include the *entire* fragment to the nearest

155

regex delimiter, whether the start or end of the pattern, an enclosing parenthesis, another alternation character, or a square bracket.

Alternation has a lower precedence (Precedence, pp. 99) than even atoms:

```
like(   'rice',   qr/rice|beans/, 'Found rice'   );
like(   'beans',  qr/rice|beans/, 'Found beans'  );
unlike( 'ricb',   qr/rice|beans/, 'Found hybrid' );
```

To reduce confusion, use named fragments in variables ($rice|$beans) or group alternation candidates in *non-capturing groups*:

```
my $starches = qr/(?:pasta|potatoes|rice)/;
```

The (?:) sequence groups a series of atoms without making a capture.

> ### Non-Captured For Your Protection
>
> A stringified regular expression includes an enclosing non-capturing group; qr/rice|beans/ stringifies as (?^u:rice|beans).

# Other Escape Sequences

To match a *literal* instance of a metacharacter, *escape* it with a backslash (\). You've seen this before, where \( refers to a single left parenthesis and \] refers to a single right square bracket. \. refers to a literal period character instead of the "match anything but an explicit newline character" atom.

You will likely need to escape the alternation metacharacter (|) as well as the end of line metacharacter ($) and the quantifiers (+, ?, *).

The *metacharacter disabling characters* (\Q and \E) disable metacharacter interpretation within their boundaries. This is especially useful when taking match text from a source you don't control:

```
my ($text, $literal_text) = @_;

return $text =~ /\Q$literal_text\E/;
```

The $literal_text argument can contain anything–the string ** ALERT **, for example. Within the fragment bounded by \Q and \E, Perl will interpret the regex as \*\* ALERT \*\* and attempt to match literal asterisk characters instead of treating the asterisks as greedy quantifiers.

> **Regex Security**
>
> Be cautious when processing regular expressions from untrusted user input. A malicious regex master can craft a regular expression which may take *years* to match input strings, creating a denial-of-service attack against your program.

# Assertions

Regex anchors such as \A, \b, \B, and \Z are a form of *regex assertion*, which requires that the string meet some condition. These assertions do not match individual characters within the string. No matter what the string contains, the regex qr/\A/ will *always* match..

*Zero-width assertions* match a *pattern*. Most importantly, they do not *consume* the portion of the pattern that they match. For example, to find a cat on its own, you might use a word boundary assertion:

```
my $just_a_cat = qr/cat\b/;
```

...but if you want to find a non-disastrous feline, you might use a *zero-width negative look-ahead assertion*:

```
my $safe_feline = qr/cat(?!astrophe)/;
```

The construct (?!...) matches the phrase cat only if the phrase astrophe does not immediately follow. The *zero-width positive look-ahead assertion*:

```
my $disastrous_feline = qr/cat(?=astrophe)/;
```

...matches the phrase cat only if the phrase astrophe immediately follows. While a normal regular expression can accomplish the same thing, consider a regex to find all non-catastrophic words in the dictionary which start with cat:

```
my $disastrous_feline = qr/cat(?!astrophe)/;

while (<$words>)
{
    chomp;
```

157

```
    next unless /\A(?<cat>$disastrous_feline.*)\Z/;
    say "Found a non-catastrophe '$+{cat}'";
}
```

The zero-width assertion consumes none of the source string, leaving the anchored fragment <.*\Z> to match. Otherwise, the capture would only capture the cat portion of the source string.

To assert that your feline never occurs at the start of a line, you might use a *zero-width negative look-behind assertion*. These assertions must have fixed sizes. You may not use quantifiers:

```
my $middle_cat = qr/(?<!\A)cat/;
```

The construct (?<!...) contains the fixed-width pattern. You could also express that the cat must always occur immediately after a space character with a *zero-width positive look-behind assertion*:

```
my $space_cat = qr/(?<=\s)cat/;
```

The construct (?<=...) contains the fixed-width pattern. This approach can be useful when combining a global regex match with the \G modifier.

A newer feature of Perl regexes is the *keep* assertion \K. This zero-width positive look-behind assertion *can* have a variable length:

```
my $spacey_cat = qr/\s+\Kcat/;

like( 'my cat has been to space', $spacey_cat );
like( 'my  cat  has  been  to  doublespace',
        $spacey_cat );
```

\K is surprisingly useful for certain substitutions which remove the end of a pattern. It lets you match a pattern but remove only a portion of it:

```
my $exclamation = 'This is a catastrophe!';
$exclamation    =~ s/cat\K\w+!/./;

like( $exclamation, qr/\bcat\./,
                    "That wasn't so bad!" );
```

Everything up until the \K assertion matches, but only the portion of the match after the assertion gets substituted away.

# Regex Modifiers

Several modifiers change the behavior of the regular expression operators. These modifiers appear at the end of the match, substitution, and qr// operators. For example, to enable case-insensitive matching:

```
my $pet = 'CaMeLiA';

like( $pet, qr/Camelia/,  'Nice butterfly!'  );
like( $pet, qr/Camelia/i, 'shift key br0ken' );
```

The first like() will fail, because the strings contain different letters. The second like() will pass, because the /i modifier causes the regex to ignore case distinctions. M and m are equivalent in the second regex due to the modifier.

You may also embed regex modifiers within a pattern:

```
my $find_a_cat = qr/(?<feline>(?i)cat)/;
```

The (?i) syntax enables case-insensitive matching only for its enclosing group. In this case, that's the named capture. You may use multiple modifiers with this form. Disable specific modifiers by preceding them with the minus character (-):

```
my $find_a_rational = qr/(?<number>(?-i)Rat)/;
```

The multiline operator, /m, allows the ^ and $ anchors to match at any newline embedded within the string.

The /s modifier treats the source string as a single line such that the . metacharacter matches the newline character. Damian Conway suggests the mnemonic that /m modifies the behavior of *multiple* regex metacharacters, while /s modifies the behavior of a *single* regex metacharacter.

The /r modifier causes a substitution operation to return the result of the substitution, leaving the original string unchanged. If the substitution succeeds, the result is a modified copy of the original. If the substitution fails (because the pattern does not match), the result is an unmodified copy of the original:

```
my $status    = 'I am hungry for pie.';
my $newstatus = $status =~ s/pie/cake/r;
my $statuscopy = $status
                =~ s/liver and onions/bratwurst/r;
```

```
is( $status, 'I am hungry for pie.',
    'original string should be unmodified' );

like( $newstatus,    qr/cake/,      'cake wanted' );
unlike( $statuscopy, qr/bratwurst/, 'wurst not'  );
```

The /x modifier allows you to embed additional whitespace and comments within patterns. With this modifier in effect, the regex engine ignores whitespace and comments, so your code can be more readable:

```
my $attr_re = qr{
    \A                      # start of line

    (?:
      [;\n\s]*               # spaces and semicolons
      (?:/\*.*?\*/)?          # C comments
    )*

    ATTR

    \s+
    (    U?INTVAL
     |   FLOATVAL
     |   STRING\s+\*
    )
}x;
```

This regex isn't *simple*, but comments and whitespace improve its readability. Even if you compose regexes together from compiled fragments, the /x modifier can still improve your code.

The /g modifier matches a regex globally throughout a string. This makes sense when used with a substitution:

```
# appease the Mitchell estate
my $contents = slurp( $file );
$contents    =~ s/Scarlett O'Hara/Mauve Midway/g;
```

When used with a match–not a substitution–the \G metacharacter allows you to process a string within a loop one chunk at a time. \G matches at the position where the most recent match ended. To process a poorly-encoded file full of American telephone numbers in logical chunks, you might write:

```
while ($contents =~ /\G(\w{3})(\w{3})(\w{4})/g)
{
    push @numbers, "($1) $2-$3";
}
```

Be aware that the \G anchor will begin at the last point in the string where the previous iteration of the match occurred. If the previous match ended with a greedy match such as .*, the next match will have less available string to match. Lookahead assertions can also help.

The /e modifier allows you to write arbitrary code on the right side of a substitution operation. If the match succeeds, the regex engine will run the code, using its return value as the substitution value. The earlier global substitution example could be simpler with code like:

```
# appease the Mitchell estate
$sequel  =~ s{Scarlett( O'Hara)?}
             {
                 'Mauve' . defined $1
                         ? ' Midway'
                         : ''
             }ge;
```

Each additional occurrence of the /e modifier will cause another evaluation of the result of the expression, though only Perl golfers use anything beyond /ee.

# Smart Matching

The smart match operator, ~~, compares two operands and returns a true value if they match. The type of comparison depends on the type of both operands. given (Switch Statements, pp. 56) performs an implicit smart match.

As of Perl 5.18, this feature is experimental. The details of the current design are complex and unwieldy, and no proposal for simplifying things has gained enough popular support to warrant a complete overhaul. The more complex your operands, the more likely you are to receive confusing results. Avoid comparing objects and stick to simple operations between two scalars or one scalar and one aggregate for the best results.

The smart match operator is an infix operator:

```
say 'They match (somehow)' if $loperand ~~ $roperand;
```

The type of comparison *generally* depends first on the type of the right operand and then on the left operand. For example, if the right operand is a scalar with a numeric component, the comparison will use numeric equality. If the right operand is a regex, the comparison will use a grep or a pattern match. If the right operand is an array, the comparison will perform a grep or a recursive smart match. If the right operand is a hash, the comparison will check the existence of one or more keys. A large and intimidating chart in `perldoc perlsyn` gives far more details about all the comparisons smart match can perform.

These examples are deliberately simple, because smart match can be confusing:

```
my ($x, $y) = (10, 20);
say 'Not equal numerically' unless $x ~~ $y;

my $z = '10 little endians';
say 'Equal numeric-ishally' if $x ~~ $z;

my $needle = qr/needle/;

say 'Pattern match' if 'needle' ~~ $needle;

say 'Grep through array' if @haystack ~~ $needle;

say 'Grep through hash keys' if %hayhash ~~ $needle;

say 'Grep through array' if $needle ~~ @haystack;

say 'Array elements exist as hash keys'
    if %hayhash    ~~ @haystack;

say 'Smart match elements' if @straw ~~ @haystack;

say 'Grep through hash keys' if $needle ~~ %hayhash;

say 'Array elements exist as hash keys'
    if @haystack  ~~ %hayhash;

say 'Hash keys identical' if %hayhash ~~ %haymap;
```

Smart match works even if one operand is a *reference* to the given data type:

```
say 'Hash keys identical' if %hayhash ~~ \%hayhash;
```

It's difficult to recommend the use of smart match except in the simplest circumstances, but it can be useful when you have a literal string or number to match against a variable, as in the case of smart match.

# CHAPTER 7

# Objects

When you design a program, you have to approach it from many levels. At the bottom, you have specific details about the problem you're solving. At the top levels, you have to organize the code so it makes sense. Our only hope to manage this complexity is to exploit abstraction (treating similar things similarly) and encapsulation (grouping related details together).

Functions alone are insufficient for large problems. Several techniques group functions into units of related behaviors. One popular technique is *object orientation* (OO), or *object oriented programming* (OOP), where programs work with *objects*–discrete, unique entities with their own identities.

## Moose

Perl's default object system is but minimal but flexible. Its syntax is a little clunky, and it exposes *how* an object system works. You can build great things on top of it, but you or someone else will have to build a lot of code to get what some other languages provide for free.

*Moose* is a complete object system for Perl. It's a complete distribution available from the CPAN–not a part of the core language, but worth installing and using regardless. Moose offers both a simpler way to use an object system as well as advanced features of languages such as Smalltalk and Common Lisp.

Moose objects work with plain vanilla Perl. Within your programs, you can mix and match objects written with Perl's default object system and Moose. Of course, you have to write a lot more code to get what Moose provides for you.

> **Moose Documentation**
>
> See `Moose::Manual` on the CPAN for comprehensive Moose documentation.

## Classes

A Moose object is a concrete instance of a *class*, which is a template describing data and behavior specific to the object. A class generally belongs to a package (Packages, pp. 80), which provides its name:

```
package Cat
{
    use Moose;
}
```

This Cat class *appears* to do nothing, but that's all Moose needs to make a class. Create objects (or *instances*) of the Cat class with the syntax:

```
my $brad = Cat->new;
my $jack = Cat->new;
```

Just as an arrow dereferences a reference, this arrow calls a method on Cat.

## Methods

A *method* is a function associated with a class. A function may belong to a namespace; you've seen that. Similarly, a method belongs to a class.

When you call a method, you do so with an *invocant*. When you call new() on Cat, the name of the class, Cat, is new()'s invocant. Think of this as sending a message to a class: "do whatever new() does." In this case, sending the new message–calling the new() method–returns a new object of the Cat class.

When you call a method on an object, that object is the invocant:

```
my $choco = Cat->new;
$choco->sleep_on_keyboard;
```

A method's first argument is its invocant ($self, by convention). Suppose a Cat can meow():

```
package Cat
{
    use Moose;

    sub meow
    {
```

```
        my $self = shift;
        say 'Meow!';
    }
}
```

Now any `Cat` instance can wake you up in the morning because it hasn't eaten yet:

```
# the cat always meows three times at 6 am
my $fuzzy_alarm = Cat->new;
$fuzzy_alarm->meow for 1 .. 3;
```

Every object can have its own distinct data. (More on this briefly.) Methods which read or write the data of their invocants are *instance methods*; they depend on the presence of an appropriate invocant to work correctly. Methods (such as `meow()`) which do not access instance data are *class methods*. You may invoke class methods on classes and class and instance methods on instances, but you cannot invoke instance methods on classes.

*Constructors*, which *create* instances, are obviously class methods. Moose provides a default constructor for you, named `new()`. That's why you can create a `Cat` object with the minimal class declaration earlier.

Class methods are effectively namespaced global functions. Without access to instance data, they have few advantages over namespaced functions. Most OO code uses instance methods to read and write instance data.

## Attributes

Every Perl object is unique. Objects can contain private data associated with each unique object–you may hear this data called *attributes*, *instance data*, or *object state*. Define an attribute by declaring it as part of the class:

```
package Cat
{
    use Moose;

    has 'name', is => 'ro', isa => 'Str';
}
```

Moose exports the `has()` function for you to use to declare an attribute. In English, this code reads "Cat objects have a `name` attribute. It's read-only, and is a string." The first argument, `'name'`, is the attribute's name. The `is => 'ro'` pair of arguments declares that this attribute is `read only`, so you cannot modify the

167

attribute's value after you've set it. Finally, the `isa => 'Str'` pair declares that the value of this attribute can only be a `string`.

In this example, Moose creates an *accessor* method named `name()` and allows you to pass a `name` parameter to `Cat`'s constructor:

```
for my $name (qw( Tuxie Petunia Daisy ))
{
    my $cat = Cat->new( name => $name );
    say "Created a cat for ", $cat->name;
}
```

Moose's documentation uses parentheses to separate attribute names and characteristics:
```
        has 'name' => ( is => 'ro', isa => 'Str' );
```
This is equivalent to:

```
  has( 'name', 'is', 'ro', 'isa', 'Str' );
```

Moose's approach works nicely for complex declarations:

```
  has 'name' => (
      is         => 'ro',
      isa        => 'Str',

      # advanced Moose options; perldoc Moose
      init_arg   => undef,
      lazy_build => 1,
  );
```

...while this book prefers a low-punctuation approach for simple declarations. Choose the style which offers you the most clarity.

Moose will complain if you try to set `name` to a value which isn't a string. Attributes do not *need* to have types. In that case, anything goes:

```
  package Cat
  {
      use Moose;
```

```
        has 'name', is => 'ro', isa => 'Str';
        has 'age',  is => 'ro';
}

my $invalid = Cat->new( name => 'bizarre',
                        age  => 'purple' );
```

If you add a type to your attribute declaration, Moose will attempt to validate the values assigned to that attribute. Sometimes this strictness is invaluable.

If you mark an attribute as readable *and* writable (with is => rw), Moose will create a *mutator* method which can change that attribute's value:

```
package Cat
{
    use Moose;

    has 'name', is => 'ro', isa => 'Str';
    has 'age',  is => 'ro', isa => 'Int';
    has 'diet', is => 'rw';
}

my $fat = Cat->new( name => 'Fatty',
                    age  => 8,
                    diet => 'Sea Treats' );

say $fat->name, ' eats ', $fat->diet;

$fat->diet( 'Low Sodium Kitty Lo Mein' );
say $fat->name, ' now eats ', $fat->diet;
```

An ro accessor used as a mutator will throw the exception Cannot assign a value to a read-only accessor at ....

Using ro or rw is a matter of design, convenience, and purity. Moose enforces no particular philosophy here. Some people suggest making all instance data ro such that you must pass instance data into the constructor (Immutability, pp. 192). In the Cat example, age() might still be an accessor, but the constructor could take the *year* of the cat's birth and calculate the age itself based on the current year. This approach consolidates validation code and ensure that all created objects have valid data.

Instance data shows some of the value of object orientation. An object contains related data and can perform behaviors with that data. A class describes that data and those behaviors. You can have multiple independent objects with separate instance data and treat all of those objects the same way; they will behave differently depending on their instance data.

## Encapsulation

Moose allows you to declare *which* attributes class instances possess (a cat has a name) as well as the attributes of those attributes (you cannot change a cat's name; you can only read it). Moose itself decides how to *store* those attributes. You can change that if you like, but allowing Moose to manage your storage encourages *encapsulation*: hiding the internal details of an object from external users of that object.

Consider a change to how Cats manage their ages. Instead of passing a value for an age to the constructor, pass in the year of the cat's birth and calculate the age as needed:

```
package Cat
{
    use Moose;

    has 'name',        is => 'ro', isa => 'Str';
    has 'diet',        is => 'rw';
    has 'birth_year',  is => 'ro', isa => 'Int';

    sub age
    {
        my $self = shift;
        my $year = (localtime)[5] + 1900;

        return $year - $self->birth_year;
    }
}
```

While the syntax for *creating* Cat objects has changed, the syntax for *using* Cat objects has not. Outside of Cat, age() behaves as it always has. *How* it works is a detail hidden inside the Cat class.

---

**Compatibility and APIs**

Retain the old syntax for *creating* Cat objects by customizing the generated Cat constructor to allow passing an age parameter. Calculate birth_year from that. See perldoc Moose::Manual::Attributes.

Calculating ages has another advantage. A *default attribute value* will do the right thing when someone creates a new Cat object without passing a birth year:

```
package Cat
{
    use Moose;

    has 'name', is => 'ro', isa => 'Str';
    has 'diet', is => 'rw', isa => 'Str';

    has 'birth_year',
        is      => 'ro',
        isa     => 'Int',
        default => sub { (localtime)[5] + 1900 };
}
```

The default keyword on an attribute takes a function reference[1] which returns the default value for that attribute when constructing a new object. If the code creating an object passes no constructor value for that attribute, the object gets the default value:

```
my $kitten = Cat->new( name => 'Choco' );
```

... and that kitten will have an age of 0 until next year.

## Polymorphism

Encapsulation is useful, but the real power of object orientation is much broader. A well-designed OO program can manage many types of data. When well-designed

---

[1] You can use a simple value such as a number or string directly, but use a function reference for anything more complex.

classes encapsulate specific details of objects into the appropriate places, something curious happens: the code often becomes *less* specific.

Moving the details of what the program knows about individual Cats (the attributes) and what the program knows that Cats can do (the methods) into the Cat class means that code that deals with Cat instances can happily ignore *how* Cat does what it does.

Consider a function which displays details of an object:

```
sub show_vital_stats
{
    my $object = shift;

    say 'My name is ', $object->name;
    say 'I am ',       $object->age;
    say 'I eat ',      $object->diet;
}
```

It's obvious (in context) that this function works if you pass it a Cat object. It's less obvious that it will do the right thing for *any* object with the appropriate three accessors, no matter *how* that object provides those accessors and no matter *what kind* of object it is: Cat, Caterpillar, or Catbird. show_vital_stats() cares that an invocant is valid only in that it supports three methods, name(), age(), and diet() which take no arguments and each return something which can concatenate in a string context. You may have a hundred different classes in your code, none of which have any obvious relationships, but they will work with this function if they conform to this expected behavior.

This property is called *polymorphism*. It means that you can substitute an object of one class for an object of another class if they provide the same external interface.

### Duck Typing

Some languages and environments require you to declare (or at least imply) a formal relationship between two classes before allowing a program to substitute instances for each other. Perl provides ways to enforce these checks, but it does not require them. Its default ad-hoc system lets you treat any two instances with methods of the same name as equivalent. Some people call this *duck typing*, arguing that any object which can quack() is sufficiently duck-like that you can treat it as a duck.

Consider how you might enumerate a zoo's worth of animals without this polymorphic function. The benefit of genericity should be obvious. As well, any specific details about how to calculate the age of an ocelot or octopus can belong in the relevant class–where it matters most.

Of course, the mere existence of a method called name() or age() does not by itself imply the behavior of that object. A Dog object may have an age() which is an accessor such that you can discover $rodney is 11 but $lucky is 6. A Cheese object may have an age() method that lets you control how long to stow $cheddar to sharpen it. age() may be an accessor in one class but not in another:

```
# how old is the cat?
my $years = $zeppie->age;

# store the cheese in the warehouse for six months
$cheese->age;
```

Sometimes it's useful to know *what* an object does and what that *means*.

# Roles

A *role* is a named collection of behavior and state[2]. While a class organizes behaviors and state into a template for objects, a role organizes a named collection of behaviors and state. You can instantiate a class, but not a role. A role is something a class *does*.

Given an Animal which has an age and a Cheese which can age, one difference may be that Animal does the LivingBeing role, while the Cheese does the Storable role:

```
package LivingBeing
{
    use Moose::Role;

    requires qw( name age diet );
}
```

The requires keyword provided by Moose::Role allows you to list methods that this role needs from its composing classes. In other words, anything which

---

[2]See the P6 design documents on roles at http://feather.perl6.nl/syn/S14.html and research on Smalltalk traits at http://scg.unibe.ch/research/traits for copious details.

does this role must supply the name(), age(), and diet() methods. The Cat class must explicitly mark that it performs the role:

```perl
package Cat
{
    use Moose;

    has 'name', is => 'ro', isa => 'Str';
    has 'diet', is => 'rw', isa => 'Str';

    has 'birth_year',
        is      => 'ro',
        isa     => 'Int',
        default => sub { (localtime)[5] + 1900 };

    with 'LivingBeing';

    sub age { ... }
}
```

The with line causes Moose to *compose* the LivingBeing role into the Cat class. Composition ensures all of the attributes and methods of the role are part of the class. LivingBeing requires any composing class to provide methods named name(), age(), and diet(). Cat satisfies these constraints. If LivingBeing were composed into a class which did not provide those methods, Moose would throw an exception.

> **Order Matters!**
>
> The with keyword used to apply roles to a class must occur *after* attribute declaration so that composition can identify any generated accessor methods.

Now all Cat instances will return a true value when queried if they provide the LivingBeing role. Cheese objects should not:

```perl
say 'Alive!' if $fluffy->DOES('LivingBeing');
say 'Moldy!' if $cheese->DOES('LivingBeing');
```

This design technique separates the *capabilities* of classes and objects from the *implementation* of those classes and objects. The birth year calculation behavior of the Cat class could itself be a role:

```
package CalculateAge::From::BirthYear
{
    use Moose::Role;

    has 'birth_year',
        is      => 'ro',
        isa     => 'Int',
        default => sub { (localtime)[5] + 1900 };

    sub age
    {
        my $self = shift;
        my $year = (localtime)[5] + 1900;

        return $year - $self->birth_year;
    }
}
```

Extracting this role from Cat makes the useful behavior available to other classes. Now Cat can compose both roles:

```
package Cat
{
    use Moose;

    has 'name', is => 'ro', isa => 'Str';
    has 'diet', is => 'rw';

    with 'LivingBeing',
         'CalculateAge::From::BirthYear';
}
```

Notice how the age() method of CalculateAge::From::BirthYear satisfies the requirement of the LivingBeing role. Notice also that any check that Cat performs LivingBeing returns a true value. Extracting age() into a role has only changed the details of *how* Cat calculates an age. It's still a LivingBeing.

175

Cat can choose to implement its own age or get it from somewhere else. All that matters is that it provides an age() which satisfies the LivingBeing constraint.

Remember how polymorphism means that you can treat multiple objects with the same behavior in the same way? An object may implement the same behavior in multiple ways. This is *allomorphism*. Pervasive allomorphism can reduce the size of your classes and increase the code shared between them. It also allows you to name specific and discrete collections of behaviors–very useful for testing for capabilities instead of implementations.

To compare roles to other design techniques such as mixins, multiple inheritance, and monkeypatching, see http://www.modernperlbooks.com/mt/2009/04/the-why-of-perl-roles.html.

### Roles and DOES()

When you compose a role into a class, the class and its instances will return a true value when you call DOES() on them:

```
say 'This Cat is alive!'
    if $kitten->DOES( 'LivingBeing' );
```

# Inheritance

Perl's object system supports *inheritance*, which establishes a parent and child relationship between two classes such that one specializes the other. The child class behaves the same way as its parent–it has the same number and types of attributes and can use the same methods. It may have additional data and behavior, but you may substitute any instance of a child where code expects its parent. In one sense, a subclass provides the role implied by the existence of its parent class.

> **Roles versus Inheritance**
>
> Should you use roles or inheritance? Roles provide composition-time safety, better type checking, better factoring of code, and finer-grained control over names and behaviors, but inheritance is more familiar to experienced developers of other languages. Use inheritance when one class truly *extends* another. Use a role when a class needs additional behavior, and when you can give that behavior a meaningful name.

Consider a LightSource class which provides two public attributes (enabled and candle_power) and two methods (light and extinguish):

```perl
package LightSource
{
    use Moose;

    has 'candle_power', is      => 'ro',
                        isa     => 'Int',
                        default => 1;

    has 'enabled', is      => 'ro',
                   isa     => 'Bool',
                   default => 0,
                   writer  => '_set_enabled';

    sub light
    {
        my $self = shift;
        $self->_set_enabled( 1 );
    }

    sub extinguish
    {
        my $self = shift;
        $self->_set_enabled( 0 );
    }
}
```

(Note that enabled's writer option creates a private accessor usable within the class to set the value.)

### Inheritance and Attributes

A subclass of LightSource could define an industrial-strength super candle which provides a hundred times the amount of light:

```perl
package SuperCandle
{
    use Moose;

    extends 'LightSource';

    has '+candle_power', default => 100;
}
```

177

extends takes a list of class names to use as parents of the current class. If that were the only line in this class, SuperCandle objects would behave in the same ways as LightSource objects. A SuperCandle instance would have both the candle_power and enabled attributes as well as the light() and extinguish() methods.

The + at the start of an attribute name (such as candle_power) indicates that the current class does something special with that attribute. Here the super candle overrides the default value of the light source, so any new SuperCandle created has a light value of 100 regular candles.

When you invoke light() or extinguish() on a SuperCandle object, Perl will look in the SuperCandle class for the method. If there's no method by that name in the child class, Perl will look at each parent in turn, recursively. In this case, those methods are in the LightSource class.

Attribute inheritance works similarly (see perldoc Class::MOP).

## Method Dispatch Order

A method call always involves a *dispatch* strategy. This strategy controls how Perl selects the appropriate method. This may seem obvious, given how simple the Cat class is, but much of the power of OO comes from method dispatch.

*Method dispatch order* (or *method resolution order* or *MRO*) is obvious for single-parent classes. Look in the object's class, then its parent, and so on until you find the method or run out of parents. Classes which inherit from multiple parents (*multiple inheritance*)–Hovercraft extends both Boat and Car–require trickier dispatch. Reasoning about multiple inheritance is complex. Avoid multiple inheritance when possible.

Perl uses a depth-first method resolution strategy. It searches the class of the *first* named parent and all of that parent's parents recursively before searching the classes of the current class's immediate parents. The mro pragma (Pragmas, pp. 200) provides alternate strategies, including the C3 MRO strategy which searches a given class's immediate parents before searching any of their parents.

See perldoc mro for more details.

## Inheritance and Methods

As with attributes, subclasses may override methods. Imagine a light that you cannot extinguish:

```
package Glowstick
{
    use Moose;
```

```
    extends 'LightSource';

    sub extinguish {}
}
```

Calling extinguish() on a glowstick does nothing, even though LightSource's method does something. Method dispatch will find the subclass's method. You may not have meant to do this. When you do, use Moose's override to express your intention clearly.

Within an overridden method, Moose's super() allows you to call the overridden method:

```
package LightSource::Cranky
{
    use Carp 'carp';
    use Moose;

    extends 'LightSource';

    override light => sub
    {
        my $self = shift;

        carp "Can't light a lit light source!"
            if $self->enabled;

        super();
    };

    override extinguish => sub
    {
        my $self = shift;

        carp "Can't extinguish unlit light source!"
            unless $self->enabled;

        super();
    };
}
```

This subclass adds a warning when trying to light or extinguish a light source that already has the current state. The super() function dispatches to the nearest parent's implementation of the current method, per the normal Perl method resolution order. (See perldoc Moose::Manual::MethodModifiers for more dispatch options.)

### Inheritance and isa()

Perl's isa() method returns true if its invocant is or extends a named class. That invocant may be the name of a class or an instance of an object:

```
say 'Looks like a LightSource'
    if $sconce->isa( 'LightSource' );

say 'Hominidae do not glow'
    unless $chimpy->isa( 'LightSource' );
```

# Moose and Perl OO

Moose provides many features beyond Perl's default OO. While you *can* build everything you get with Moose yourself (Blessed References, pp. 182), or cobble it together with a series of CPAN distributions, Moose is worth using. It is a coherent whole, with good documentation. Many important projects use it successfully. Its development community is mature and attentive.

Moose takes care of constructors, destructors, accessors, and encapsulation. You must do the work of declaring what you want, but what you get back is safe and easy to use. Moose objects can extend and work with objects from the vanilla Perl system.

Moose also allows *metaprogramming*–manipulating your objects through Moose itself. If you've ever wondered which methods are available on a class or an object or which attributes an object supports, this information is available:

```
my $metaclass = Monkey::Pants->meta;

say 'Monkey::Pants instances have the attributes:';

say $_->name for $metaclass->get_all_attributes;

say 'Monkey::Pants instances support the methods:';

say $_->fully_qualified_name
    for $metaclass->get_all_methods;
```

You can even see which classes extend a given class:

```
my $metaclass = Monkey->meta;

say 'Monkey is the superclass of:';

say $_ for $metaclass->subclasses;
```

See `perldoc Class::MOP::Class` for more information about metaclass operations and `perldoc Class::MOP` for Moose metaprogramming information.

Moose and its *meta-object protocol* (or MOP) offers the possibility of a better syntax for declaring and working with classes and objects in Perl. This is valid code:

```
use MooseX::Declare;

role LivingBeing { requires qw( name age diet ) }

role CalculateAge::From::BirthYear { has 'birth_year',
        is      => 'ro',
        isa     => 'Int',
        default => sub { (localtime)[5] + 1900 };

    method age
    {
        return (localtime)[5] + 1900
                            - $self->birth_year;
    }
}

class Cat with LivingBeing
        with CalculateAge::From::BirthYear
{
    has 'name', is => 'ro', isa => 'Str';
    has 'diet', is => 'rw';
}
```

The `MooseX::Declare` CPAN distribution uses `Devel::Declare` to add new Moose-specific syntax. The `class`, `role`, and `method` keywords reduce the amount of boilerplate necessary to write good object oriented code in Perl. Note specifically the declarative nature of this example, as well as the lack of my `$self = shift;` in `age()`.

If you're using a Perl of 5.14 or newer, `Devel::Declare` is less useful; Perl itself supports a pluggable keyword system. In that case, a syntax-warping module such as `MooseX::Method::Signatures` or `Moops` may be more to your taste.

While Moose is not a part of the Perl core, its popularity ensures that it's available on many OS distributions. Perl distributions such as Strawberry Perl and ActivePerl also include it. Even though Moose is a CPAN module and not a core library, its cleanliness and simplicity make it essential to modern Perl programming.

---

**The Svelte *Alces***

Moose isn't a small library, but it's powerful. The most popular alternative is `Moo`, a slimmer library that's almost completely compatible with Moose. Moo lacks some of the metaprogramming facilities of Moose, but most code doesn't need them. You can easily start a project with Moo and switch to Moose trivially if and when you need the additional power.

---

# Blessed References

Perl's core object system is deliberately minimal. It has only three rules:

- A class is a package.

- A method is a function.

- A (blessed) reference is an object.

You can build anything else out of those three rules. This minimalism can be impractical for larger projects–in particular, the possibilities for greater abstraction through metaprogramming (Code Generation, pp. 234) are awkward and limited. Moose (Moose, pp. 165) is a better choice for modern programs larger than a couple of hundred lines, although lots of legacy code still uses Perl's default OO.

You've seen the first two rules already. The `bless` builtin associates the name of a class with a reference. That reference is now a valid invocant, and Perl will perform method dispatch on it, using the associated class.

A constructor is a method which creates and blesses a reference. By convention, constructors have the name new(), but this is not a requirement. Constructors are also almost always *class methods*.

bless takes two operands, a reference and a class name, and evaluates to the reference. The reference may be any valid reference, empty or not. The class does not have to exist yet. You may even use bless outside of a constructor or a class[3]. A constructor can be as simple as:

```
sub new
{
    my $class = shift;
    bless {}, $class;
}
```

By design, this constructor receives the class name as the method's invocant. You may also hard-code the name of a class, at the expense of flexibility. A parametric constructor allows reuse through inheritance, delegation, or exporting.

The type of reference used is relevant only to how the object stores its own *instance data*. It has no other effect on the resulting object. Hash references are most common, but you can bless any type of reference:

```
my $array_obj  = bless [],           $class;
my $scalar_obj = bless \$scalar,     $class;
my $func_obj   = bless \&some_func,  $class;
```

Moose classes define object attributes declaratively, but Perl's default OO is lax. A class representing basketball players which stores jersey number and position might use a constructor like:

```
package Player
{
    sub new
    {
        my ($class, %attrs) = @_;
        bless \%attrs, $class;
    }
}
```

---

[3]...but you're violating encapsulation to expose the details of object construction outside of a constructor.

... and create players with:

```
my $joel   = Player->new( number => 10,
                          position => 'center' );

my $damian = Player->new( number   => 0,
                          position => 'guard' );
```

The class's methods can access object attributes as hash elements directly:

```
sub format
{
    my $self = shift;
    return '#'       . $self->{number}
         . ' plays ' . $self->{position};
}
```

... but so can any other code, so any change to the object's internal representation may break other code. Accessor methods are safer:

```
sub number   { return shift->{number}   }
sub position { return shift->{position} }
```

... and now you're starting to write yourself what Moose gives you for free. Better yet, Moose encourages people to use accessors instead of direct access by hiding the accessor generation code. Goodbye, temptation.

## Method Lookup and Inheritance

Given a blessed reference, a method call of the form:

```
my $number = $joel->number;
```

... looks up the name of the class associated with the blessed reference $joel–in this case, Player. Next, Perl looks for a function[4] named number() in Player. If no such function exists and if Player extends a parent class, Perl looks in the parent class (and so on and so on) until it finds a number(). If Perl finds number(), it calls that method with $joel as an invocant.

---

[4] Remember that Perl makes no distinction between functions in a namespace and methods.

> ### Keeping Namespaces Clean
>
> The namespace::autoclean CPAN module can help avoid unintentional collisions between imported functions and methods.

Moose provides extends to track inheritance relationships, but Perl uses a package global variable named @ISA. The method dispatcher looks in each class's @ISA to find the names of its parent classes. If InjuredPlayer extends Player, you might write:

```
package InjuredPlayer
{
    @InjuredPlayer::ISA = 'Player';
}
```

The parent pragma (Pragmas, pp. 200) is cleaner[5]:

```
package InjuredPlayer
{
    use parent 'Player';
}
```

Moose has its own metamodel which stores extended inheritance information. This allows Moose to provide additional metaprogramming opportunities.

You may inherit from multiple parent classes:

```
package InjuredPlayer;
{
    use parent qw( Player Hospital::Patient );
}
```

...though the caveats about multiple inheritance and method dispatch complexity apply. Consider instead roles (Roles, pp. 173) or Moose method modifiers.

---

[5]Older code may use the base pragma, but parent superseded base in Perl 5.10.

185

## AUTOLOAD

If there is no applicable method in the invocant's class or any of its superclasses, Perl will next look for an AUTOLOAD() function (AUTOLOAD, pp. 138) in every class according to the selected method resolution order. Perl will invoke any AUTOLOAD() it finds to provide or decline the desired method.

AUTOLOAD() makes multiple inheritance much more difficult to understand.

## Method Overriding and SUPER

As with Moose, you may override methods in basic Perl OO. Unlike Moose, Perl provides no mechanism for indicating your *intent* to override a parent's method. Worse yet, any function you predeclare, declare, or import into the child class may override a method in the parent class by having the same name. Even if you forget to use the override system of Moose, at least it exists. Basic Perl OO offers no such protection.

To override a method in a child class, declare a method with the same name as the method in the parent. Within an overridden method, call the parent method with the SUPER:: dispatch hint:

```
sub overridden
{
    my $self = shift;
    warn 'Called overridden() in child!';
    return $self->SUPER::overridden( @_ );
}
```

The SUPER:: prefix to the method name tells the method dispatcher to dispatch to an overridden method of the appropriate name. You can provide your own arguments to the overridden method, but most code reuses @_. Be careful to shift off the invocant if you do.

---

**The Brokenness of SUPER::**

SUPER:: has a confusing misfeature: it dispatches to the parent of the package into which the overridden method was *compiled*. If you've imported this method from another package, Perl will happily dispatch to the *wrong* parent. The desire for backwards compatibility has kept this misfeature in place. The SUPER module from the CPAN offers a workaround. Moose's super() does not suffer the same problem.

---

## Strategies for Coping with Blessed References

Blessed references may seem minimal and tricky and confusing. They are. Moose is much easier to use, so use it whenever possible. If you do find yourself maintaining code which uses blessed references, or if you can't convince your team to use Moose in full yet, you can work around some of the problems of blessed references with discipline.

- Do not mix functions and methods in the same class.

- Use a single *.pm* file for each class, unless the class is a small, self-contained helper used from a single place.

- Follow standards of vanilla Perl OO, such as naming constructors `new()` and using `$self` as the invocant name in your documentation.

- Use accessor methods pervasively, even within methods in your class. A module such as `Class::Accessor` helps to avoid repetitive boilerplate.

- Avoid `AUTOLOAD()` where possible. If you *must* use it, use function forward declarations (Declaring Functions, pp. 105) to avoid ambiguity.

- Expect that someone, somewhere will eventually need to subclass (or delegate to or reimplement the interface of) your classes. Make it easier for them by not assuming details of the internals of your code, by using the two-argument form of `bless`, and by breaking your classes into the smallest responsible units of code.

- Use helper modules such as `Role::Tiny` to allow better use and reuse.

# Reflection

*Reflection* (or *introspection*) is the process of asking a program about itself as it runs. By treating code as data you can manage code in the same way that you manage data. This is a principle behind code generation (Code Generation, pp. 234).

Moose's `Class::MOP` (Class::MOP, pp. 239) simplifies many reflection tasks for object systems. If you use Moose, its metaprogramming system will help you. If not, several other Perl idioms help you inspect and manipulate running programs.

## Checking that a Module Has Loaded

If you know the name of a module, you can check that Perl believes it has loaded that module by looking in the %INC hash. When Perl loads code with use or require, it stores an entry in %INC where the key is the file path of the module to load and the value is the full path on disk to that module. In other words, loading Modern::Perl effectively does:

```
$INC{'Modern/Perl.pm'} =
    '.../lib/site_perl/5.12.1/Modern/Perl.pm';
```

The details of the path will vary depending on your installation. To test that Perl has successfully loaded a module, convert the name of the module into the canonical file form and test for that key's existence within %INC:

```
sub module_loaded
{
    (my $modname = shift) =~ s!::!/!g;
    return exists $INC{ $modname . '.pm' };
}
```

As with @INC, any code anywhere may manipulate %INC. Some modules (such as Test::MockObject or Test::MockModule) manipulate %INC for good reasons. Depending on your paranoia level, you may check the path and the expected contents of the package yourself.

The Class::Load CPAN module's is_class_loaded() function does all of this for you without making you manipulate %INC.

## Checking that a Package Exists

To check that a package exists somewhere in your program—if some code somewhere has executed a package directive with a given name—check that the package inherits from UNIVERSAL. Anything which extends UNIVERSAL must somehow provide the can() method. If no such package exists, Perl will throw an exception about an invalid invocant, so wrap this call in an eval block:

```
say "$pkg exists" if eval { $pkg->can( 'can' ) };
```

An alternate approach is to grovel through Perl's symbol tables. You're on your own here.

## Checking that a Class Exists

Because Perl makes no strong distinction between packages and classes, the best you can do without Moose is to check that a package of the expected class name exists. You *can* check that the package can() provide new(), but there is no guarantee that any new() found is either a method or a constructor.

## Checking a Module Version Number

Modules do not have to provide version numbers, but every package inherits the VERSION() method from the universal parent class UNIVERSAL (The UNIVERSAL Package, pp. 230):

```
my $version = $module->VERSION;
```

VERSION() returns the given module's version number, if defined. Otherwise it returns undef. If the module does not exist, the method will likewise return undef.

## Checking that a Function Exists

To check whether a function exists in a package, call can() as a class method on the package name:

```
say "$func() exists" if $pkg->can( $func );
```

Perl will throw an exception unless $pkg is a valid invocant; wrap the method call in an eval block if you have any doubts about its validity. Beware that a function implemented in terms of AUTOLOAD() (AUTOLOAD, pp. 138) may report the wrong answer if the function's package has not predeclared the function or overridden can() correctly. This is a bug in the other package.

Use this technique to determine if a module's import() has imported a function into the current namespace:

```
say "$func() imported!" if __PACKAGE__->can( $func );
```

As with checking for the existence of a package, you *can* root around in symbol tables yourself, if you have the patience for it.

## Checking that a Method Exists

There is no foolproof way for reflection to distinguish between a function or a method.

## Rooting Around in Symbol Tables

A *symbol table* is a special type of hash where the keys are the names of package global symbols and the values are typeglobs. A *typeglob* is an internal data structure which can contain any or all of a scalar, an array, a hash, a filehandle, and a function.

Access a symbol table as a hash by appending double-colons to the name of the package. For example, the symbol table for the MonkeyGrinder package is available as %MonkeyGrinder::.

You *can* test the existence of specific symbol names within a symbol table with the exists operator (or manipulate the symbol table to *add* or *remove* symbols, if you like). Yet be aware that certain changes to the Perl core have modified the details of what typeglobs store and when and why.

See the "Symbol Tables" section in perldoc perlmod for more details, then prefer the other techniques in this section for reflection. If you really must manipulate symbol tables and typeglobs, consider using the Package::Stash CPAN module instead.

# Advanced OO Perl

Creating and using objects in Perl with Moose (Moose, pp. 165) is easy. *Designing* good programs is not. You must balance between designing too little and too much. Only practical experience can help you understand the most important design techniques, but several principles can guide you.

## Favor Composition Over Inheritance

Novice OO designs often overuse inheritance to reuse code and to exploit polymorphism. The result is a deep class hierarchy with responsibilities scattered in the wrong places. Maintaining this code is difficult–who knows where to add or edit behavior? What happens when code in one place conflicts with code declared elsewhere?

Inheritance is only one of many tools for OO programmers. It's not always the right tool; it's often the wrong tool. A Car may extend Vehicle::Wheeled (an *is-a relationship*), but Car may better *contain* several Wheel objects as instance attributes (a *has-a relationship*).

Decomposing complex classes into smaller, focused entities (whether classes or roles) improves encapsulation and reduces the possibility that any one class or role does too much. Smaller, simpler, and better encapsulated entities are easier to understand, test, and maintain.

## Single Responsibility Principle

When you design your object system, consider the responsibilities of each entity. For example, an `Employee` object may represent specific information about a person's name, contact information, and other personal data, while a `Job` object may represent business responsibilities. Separating these entities in terms of their responsibilities allows the `Employee` class to consider only the problem of managing information specific to who the person is and the `Job` class to represent what the person does. (Two `Employees` may have a `Job`-sharing arrangement, for example, or one `Employee` may have the CFO and the COO `Jobs`.)

When each class has a single responsibility, you improve the encapsulation of class-specific data and behaviors and reduce coupling between classes.

## Don't Repeat Yourself

Complexity and duplication complicate development and maintenance. The *DRY* principle (Don't Repeat Yourself) is a reminder to seek out and to eliminate duplication within the system. Duplication exists in data as well as in code. Instead of repeating configuration information, user data, and other artifacts within your system, create a single, canonical representation of that information from which you can generate the other artifacts.

This principle helps to reduce the possibility that important parts of your system will get unsynchronized. It also helps you to find the optimal representation of the system and its data.

## Liskov Substitution Principle

The Liskov substitution principle suggests that you should be able to substitute a specialization of a class or a role for the original without violating the API of the original. In other words, an object should be as or more general with regard to what it expects and at least as specific about what it produces as the object it replaces.

Imagine two classes, `Dessert` and its child class `PecanPie`. If the classes follow the Liskov substitution principle, you can replace every use of `Dessert` objects with `PecanPie` objects in the test suite, and everything should pass[6].

---

[6]See Reg Braithwaite's "IS-STRICTLY-EQUIVALENT-TO-A" for more details, http://weblog. raganwald.com/2008/04/is-strictly-equivalent-to.html.

## Subtypes and Coercions

Moose allows you to declare and use types and extend them through subtypes to form ever more specialized descriptions of what your data represents and how it behaves. These type annotations help verify that the data on which you want to work in specific functions or methods is appropriate and even to specify mechanisms by which to coerce data of one type to data of another type.

For example, you may wish to allow people to provide dates to a `Ledger` entry as strings while representing them as `DateTime` instances internally. You can do this by creating a Date type and adding a coercion from string types. See `Moose::Util::TypeConstraints` and `MooseX::Types` for more information.

## Immutability

OO novices often treat objects as if they were bundles of records which use methods to get and set internal values. This simple technique leads to the unfortunate temptation to spread the object's responsibilities throughout the entire system.

With a well-designed object, you tell it *what to do*, not *how to do it*. As a rule of thumb, if you find yourself accessing object instance data (even through accessor methods) outside of the object itself, you may have too much access to an object's internals.

You can prevent this inappropriate access by making your objects immutable. Provide the necessary data to their constructors, then disallow any modifications of this information from outside the class. Expose no methods to mutate instance data. Once you've constructed such an object, you know it's always in a valid state. You can never modify its data to put it in an invalid state.

This takes tremendous discipline, but the resulting systems are robust, testable, and maintainable. Some designs go as far as to prohibit the modification of instance data *within* the class itself, though this is much more difficult to achieve.

# CHAPTER 8

# Style and Efficacy

Quality matters. Programs have bugs. Programs need maintenance and expansion. Programs have multiple programmers.

To program well, we must find the balance between getting the job done now and making our lives easier in the future. We must balance time, resources, and quality. The craft of programming demands that we do that to the best of our ability.

To write Perl well, we must understand the language. We must also cultivate a sense of good taste for the language and the design of programs. The only way to do so is to practice maintaining code and reading and writing great code. This path has no shortcuts, but it does have guideposts.

## Writing Maintainable Perl

*Maintainability* is the nebulous measurement of how easy it is to understand and modify a program. Write some code. Come back to it in six months. How long does it take you to fix a bug or add a feature? That's maintainability.

Maintainability doesn't measure whether you have to look up the syntax for a builtin or a library function. It doesn't measure how someone who has never programmed before will or won't read your code. It's more interesting to ask whether a competent programmer who understands the problem you're trying to solve will find it easy or difficult to modify the program. What problems get in the way of fixing a bug or adding an enhancement correctly?

To write maintainable software, you need experience solving real problems, an understanding of the idioms and techniques and style of your programming language, and good taste. You can develop all of these by concentrating on a few principles:

- *Remove duplication.* Bugs lurk in sections of repeated and similar code when you fix a bug in one piece of code, did you fix it in others? When you update one section, did you update the others?Well-designed systems have little duplication. They use functions, modules, objects, and roles to extract duplicate code into distinct components which accurately model the domain of the problem. The best designs allow you to add features by *removing* code.

- *Name entities well.* Your code tells a story. Every name you choose for a variable, function, module, and class allows you to clarify or obfuscate your intent. Choose your names carefully. If you're having trouble choosing good names, you may need to rethink your design or study your problem in more detail.

- *Avoid unnecessary cleverness.* Concise code is good, when it reveals the intention of the code. Clever code hides your intent behind flashy tricks. Perl allows you to write the right code at the right time. Choose the most obvious solution when possible. Experience and good taste will guide you.Some problems require clever solutions. When this happens, encapsulate this code behind a simple interface and document your cleverness.

- *Embrace simplicity.* If everything else is equal, a simpler program is easier to maintain than its more complex workalike. Simplicity means knowing what's most important and doing just that.Sometimes you need powerful, robust code. Sometimes you need a one-liner. Simplicity means knowing the difference and building only what you need. This is no excuse to avoid error checking or modularity or validation or security. Simple code can use advanced features. Simple code can use CPAN modules, and many of them. Simple code may require work to understand. Yet simple code solves problems effectively, without *unnecessary* work.

# Writing Idiomatic Perl

Perl borrows liberally from other languages. Perl lets you write the code you want to write. C programmers often write C-style Perl, just as Java programmers write Java-style Perl. Effective Perl programmers write Perlish Perl, embracing the language's idioms.

- *Understand community wisdom.* Perl programmers often debate techniques and idioms fiercely. Perl programmers also often share their work, and not just on the CPAN. Pay attention, and gain enlightenment on the tradeoffs between various ideals and styles.CPAN developers, Perl Mongers, and mailing list participants have hard-won experience solving problems in myriad ways. Talk to them. Read their code. Ask questions. Learn from them and let them learn from you.

- *Follow community norms.* Perl is a community of toolsmiths. We solve broad problems, including static code analysis (`Perl::Critic`), reformatting (`Perl::Tidy`), and private distribution systems (`CPAN::Mini`, `Carton`, `Pinto`). Take advantage of the CPAN infrastructure; follow the CPAN model of writing, documenting, packaging, testing, and distributing your code.

- *Read code.* Join a mailing list such as Perl Beginners (http://learn.perl.org/faq/beginners.html), browse PerlMonks (http://perlmonks.org/), and otherwise immerse yourself in the community[1]. Read code and try to answer questions–even if you never post them, this is a great opportunity to learn.

# Writing Effective Perl

Writing maintainable code means designing maintainable code. Good design comes from good habits:

- *Write testable code.* Writing an effective test suite exercises the same design skills as writing effective code. Code is code. Good tests also give you the confidence to modify a program while keeping it running correctly.

- *Modularize.* Enforce encapsulation and abstraction boundaries. Find the right interfaces between components. Name things well and put them where they belong. Modularity forces you to think about patterns and abstractions in your code to understand how everything fits together. Find the pieces that don't fit well. Improve them until they do.

- *Follow sensible coding standards.* Effective guidelines discuss error handling, security, encapsulation, API design, project layout, and other facets of maintainable code. Excellent guidelines help developers communicate with each other with code. Your job is to solve problems with code. Let your code speak clearly.

- *Exploit the CPAN.* Perl programmers solve problems. Then we share those solutions. The CPAN is a force multiplier; search it first for a solution or partial solution to your problem. Invest time in research to find full or partial solutions you can reuse. It will pay off.If you find a bug, report it. Patch it, if possible. Fix a typo. Ask for a feature. Say "Thank you!" We are better together than we are separately. We are powerful and effective when we reuse code.

---

[1] See http://www.perl.org/community.html.

When you're ready–when you create something new or fix something old in a reusable way–share your code. Join us. We solve problems.

# Exceptions

Good programmers anticipate the unexpected. Files that should exist won't. A huge disk that will never fill up will. The always-up network goes down. The unbreakable database breaks. Exceptions happen. Robust software must handle them. If you can recover, great! If you can't, log the relevant information and retry.

Perl handles exceptional conditions through *exceptions*: a dynamically-scoped control flow mechanism designed to raise and handle errors.

## Throwing Exceptions

Suppose you want to write a log file. If you can't open the file, something has gone wrong. Use die to throw an exception[2]:

```
sub open_log_file
{
    my $name = shift;
    open my $fh, '>>', $name
        or die "Can't open logging file '$name': $!";
    return $fh;
}
```

die() sets the global variable $@ to its operand and immediately exits the current function *without returning anything*. This thrown exception will continue up the call stack (Controlled Execution, pp. 252) until something catches it. If nothing catches the exception, the program will exit with an error.

Exception handling uses the same dynamic scope (Dynamic Scope, pp. 122) as local symbols.

## Catching Exceptions

Sometimes allowing an exception to end the program is useful. A program run as a timed process might throw an exception when the error logs have filled, causing an SMS to go out to administrators. Yet not all exceptions should be fatal. Your

---

[2]...or let autodie (The autodie Pragma, pp. 278) add it for you, in this case.

program might need to recover from some exceptions. Other exceptions might only give you a chance to save your user's work and exit cleanly.

Use the block form of the `eval` operator to catch an exception:

```
# log file may not open
my $fh = eval { open_log_file( 'monkeytown.log' ) };
```

If the file open succeeds, `$fh` will contain the filehandle. If it fails, `$fh` will remain undefined, and program flow will continue.

The block argument to `eval` introduces a new scope, both lexical and dynamic. If `open_log_file()` called other functions and something eventually threw an exception, this `eval` could catch it.

An exception handler is a blunt tool. It will catch all exceptions thrown in its dynamic scope. To check which exception you've caught (or if you've caught an exception at all), check the value of $@. Be sure to `localize` $@ before you attempt to catch an exception, as $@ is a global variable:

```
local $@;

# log file may not open
my $fh = eval { open_log_file( 'monkeytown.log' ) };

# caught exception
if (my $exception = $@) { ... }
```

Copy $@ to a lexical variable immediately to avoid the possibility of subsequent code clobbering the global variable $@. You never know what else has used an `eval` block elsewhere and reset $@.

$@ usually contains a string describing the exception. Inspect its contents to see whether you can handle the exception:

```
if (my $exception = $@)
{
    die $exception
        unless $exception =~ /^Can't open logging/;
    $fh = log_to_syslog();
}
```

Rethrow an exception by calling `die()` again. Pass the existing exception or a new one as necessary.

Applying regular expressions to string exceptions can be fragile, because error messages may change over time. This includes the core exceptions that Perl itself throws. Instead of throwing an exception as a string, you may use a reference–even a blessed reference–with `die`. This allows you to provide much more information in your exception: line numbers, files, and other debugging information. Retrieving information from a data structure is much easier than parsing data out of a string. Catch these exceptions as you would any other exception.

The CPAN distribution `Exception::Class` makes creating and using exception objects easy:

```
package Zoo::Exceptions
{
    use Exception::Class
        'Zoo::AnimalEscaped',
        'Zoo::HandlerEscaped';
}

sub cage_open
{
    my $self = shift;
    Zoo::AnimalEscaped->throw
        unless $self->contains_animal;
    ...
}

sub breakroom_open
{
    my $self = shift;
    Zoo::HandlerEscaped->throw
        unless $self->contains_handler;
    ...
}
```

## Exception Caveats

Though throwing exceptions is relatively simple, catching them is less so. Using `$@` correctly requires you to navigate several subtle risks:

- Unlocalized uses further down the dynamic scope may modify `$@`

- `$@` may contain an object which returns a false value in boolean context

- A signal handler (especially the DIE signal handler) may change $@

- The destruction of an object during scope exit may call `eval` and change $@

Perl 5.14 fixed some of these issues. They occur rarely, but they're often difficult to diagnose and to fix. The `Try::Tiny` CPAN distribution improves the safety of exception handling *and* the syntax[3].

`Try::Tiny` is easy to use:

```
use Try::Tiny;

my $fh = try   { open_log_file( 'monkeytown.log' ) }
         catch { log_exception( $_ ) };
```

`try` replaces `eval`. The optional `catch` block executes only when `try` catches an exception. `catch` receives the caught exception as the topic variable `$_`.

## Built-in Exceptions

Perl itself throws several exceptional conditions. `perldoc perldiag` lists several "trappable fatal errors". Some are syntax errors that Perl produces during failed compilations, but you can catch the others during runtime. The most interesting are:

- Using a disallowed key in a locked hash (Locking Hashes, pp. 77)

- Blessing a non-reference (Blessed References, pp. 182)

- Calling a method on an invalid invocant (Moose, pp. 165)

- Failing to find a method of the given name on the invocant

- Using a tainted value in an unsafe fashion (Taint, pp. 243)

- Modifying a read-only value

- Performing an invalid operation on a reference (References, pp. 83)

Of course you can also catch exceptions produced by `autodie` (The autodie Pragma, pp. 278) and any lexical warnings promoted to exceptions (Registering Your Own Warnings, pp. 213).

---

[3]`Try::Tiny` inspired improvements to Perl 5.14's exception handling.

# Pragmas

Most Perl modules which provide new functions or define classes (Moose, pp. 165). Others, such as `strict` or `warnings`, influence the behavior of the language itself. This second class of module is a *pragma*. By convention, pragmas have lower-case names to differentiate them from other modules.

## Pragmas and Scope

Pragmas work by exporting specific behavior or information into the lexical scopes of their callers. You've seen how declaring a lexical variable makes a symbol name available within a scope. Using a pragma makes its behavior effective within a scope as well:

```
{
    # $lexical not visible; strict not in effect
    {
        use strict;
        my $lexical = 'available here';
        # $lexical is visible; strict is in effect
    }
    # $lexical again invisible; strict not in effect
}
```

Just as lexical declarations affect inner scopes, pragmas maintain their effects within inner scopes:

```
# file scope
use strict;

{
    # inner scope, but strict still in effect
    my $inner = 'another lexical';
}
```

## Using Pragmas

use a pragma as you would any other module. Pragmas take arguments, such as a minimum version number to use or a list of arguments to change the pragma's behavior:

```
# require variable declarations, prohibit barewords
use strict qw( subs vars );
```

```
# rely on the semantics of the 2012 book
use Modern::Perl '2012';
```

Sometimes you need to *disable* all or part of those effects within a further nested lexical scope. The no builtin performs an unimport (Importing, pp. 111), which undoes the effects of a well-behaved pragma. For example, to disable the protection of strict when you need to do something symbolic:

```
use Modern::Perl; # or use strict;

{
    no strict 'refs';
    # manipulate the symbol table here
}
```

## Useful Pragmas

Perl includes several useful core pragmas.

- the strict pragma enables compiler checking of symbolic references, bareword use, and variable declaration.

- the warnings pragma enables optional warnings for deprecated, unintended, and awkward behaviors.

- the utf8 pragma tells the parser to use the UTF-8 encoding to understand the source code of the current file.

- the autodie pragma enables automatic error checking of system calls and builtins.

- the constant pragma allows you to create compile-time constant values (though see the CPAN's Const::Fast for an alternative).

- the vars pragma allows you to declare package global variables, such as $VERSION or @ISA (Blessed References, pp. 182).

- the feature pragma allows you to enable and disable newer features of Perl individually. Where use 5.14; enables all of the Perl 5.14 features and the strict pragma, use feature ':5.14'; does the same. This pragma is more useful to *disable* individual features in a lexical scope.

- the less pragma demonstrates how to write a pragma.

As you might suspect from `less`, you can write your own lexical pragmas in pure Perl. `perldoc perlpragma` explains how to do so, while the explanation of `$^H` in `perldoc perlvar` explains how the feature works.

The CPAN has begun to gather non-core pragmas:

- `autovivification` disables autovivification (Autovivification, pp. 94)

- `indirect` prevents the use of indirect invocation (Indirect Objects, pp. 262)

- `autobox` enables object-like behavior for Perl's core types (scalars, references, arrays, and hashes).

- `perl5i` combines and enables many experimental language extensions into a coherent whole.

These tools are not widely used yet, but they have their champions. `autovivification` and `indirect` can help you write more correct code. `autobox` and `perl5i` are experiments with what Perl might one day become; they're worth playing with in small projects.

# CHAPTER 9

# Managing Real Programs

A book can teach you to write small programs to solve example problems. You can learn a lot of syntax that way.

To write real programs to solve real problems, you must learn to *manage* code written in your language. How do you organize code? How do you know that it works? How can you make it robust in the face of errors? What makes code concise, clear, and maintainable? Modern Perl helps you answer all of those questions.

## Testing

You've already tested your code, if you've ever run it, noticed something wasn't working quite right, made a change, and then ran it again. *Testing* is the process of verifying that your software behaves as intended. Effective testing automates that process. Rather than relying on humans to perform repeated manual checks perfectly, let the computer do it.

Perl provides great tools to help you write the right tests.

### Test::More

Perl testing begins with the core module `Test::More` and its `ok()` function. `ok()` takes two parameters, a boolean value and a string which describes the test's purpose:

```
ok(   1, 'the number one should be true'       );
ok(   0, '... and zero should not'             );
ok(  '', 'the empty string should be false'    );
ok( '!', '... and a non-empty string should not' );

done_testing();
```

Any condition you can test in your program can eventually become a binary value. Every test *assertion* is a simple question with a yes or no answer: does this code behave as I intended? A complex program may have thousands of individual conditions. That's fine. You can test every one of those conditions, if you're willing to put in the work. Isolating specific behaviors into individual assertions helps you debug errors of coding and errors of understanding, especially as you modify the code in the future.

The function `done_testing()` tells `Test::More` that the program has executed all of the assertions you expected to run. If the program encountered a runtime exception or otherwise exited unexpectedly before the call to `done_testing()`, the test framework will notify you that something went wrong. Without a mechanism like `done_testing()`, how would you *know*? Admittedly this example code is too simple to fail, but code that's too simple to fail fails far more often than you want.

---

`Test::More` allows an optional *test plan* to count the number of individual assertions you plan to run:

```
use Test::More tests => 4;

ok(    1, 'the number one should be true'            );
ok(    0, '... and zero should not'                  );
ok(   '', 'the empty string should be false'         );
ok(  '!', '... and a non-empty string should not' );
```

The `tests` argument to `Test::More` sets the test plan for the program. This is a safety net. If fewer than four tests ran, something went wrong. If more than four tests ran, something went wrong. `done_testing()` is easier, but sometimes an exact count can be useful.

---

## Running Tests

This example test file is a complete Perl program which produces the output:

```
ok 1 - the number one should be true
not ok 2 - ... and zero should not
#    Failed test '... and zero should not'
#    at truth_values.t line 4.
not ok 3 - the empty string should be false
#    Failed test 'the empty string should be false'
#    at truth_values.t line 5.
```

```
ok 4 - ... and a non-empty string should not
1..4
# Looks like you failed 2 tests of 4.
```

This output uses a test output format called *TAP*, the *Test Anything Protocol* (http://testanything.org/). Failed TAP tests produce diagnostic messages as a debugging aid.

This output of this small example is easy to understand, but it can get complicated quickly. In most cases, you want to know either that everything passed or the specifics of any failures. The core module TAP::Harness interprets TAP. Its related program prove runs tests and displays only the most pertinent information:

```
$ prove truth_values.t
truth_values.t .. 1/?
#   Failed test '... and zero should not'
#   at truth_values.t line 4.

#   Failed test 'the empty string should be false'
#   at truth_values.t line 5.
# Looks like you failed 2 tests of 4.
truth_values.t .. Dubious, test returned 2
    (wstat 512, 0x200)
Failed 2/4 subtests

Test Summary Report
-------------------
truth_values.t (Wstat: 512 Tests: 4 Failed: 2)
  Failed tests:  2-3
```

That's a lot of output to display what is already obvious: the second and third tests fail because zero and the empty string evaluate to false. Fortunately, it's easy to fix those failing tests with boolean coercion (Boolean Coercion, pp. 78):

```
ok(   ! 0, '... and zero should not'            );
ok(   ! '', 'the empty string should be false' );
```

With those two changes, prove now displays:

```
$ prove truth_values.t
truth_values.t .. ok
All tests successful.
```

See `perldoc prove` for other test options, such as running tests in parallel (`-j`), automatically adding *lib/* to Perl's include path (`-l`), recursively running all test files found under *t/* (`-r t`), and running slow tests first (`--state=slow,save`). The bash shell alias `proveall` may prove useful:

```
alias proveall='prove -j9 --state=slow,save -lr t'
```

## Better Comparisons

Even though the heart of all automated testing is the boolean condition "is this true or false?", reducing everything to that boolean condition is tedious and the diagnostics could be better. `Test::More` provides several other convenient assertion functions.

The `is()` function compares two values using Perl's `eq` operator. If the values are equal, the test passes:

```
is(          4, 2 + 2, 'addition should work' );
is( 'pancake',    100, 'pancakes are numeric' );
```

As you might expect, the first test passes and the second fails with a diagnostic message:

```
t/is_tests.t .. 1/2
#   Failed test 'pancakes are numeric'
#   at t/is_tests.t line 8.
#          got: 'pancake'
#     expected: '100'
# Looks like you failed 1 test of 2.
```

Where `ok()` only provides the line number of the failing test, `is()` displays the expected and received values.

`is()` applies implicit scalar context to its values (Prototypes, pp. 265). This means, for example, that you can check the number of elements in an array without explicitly evaluating the array in scalar context[1]:

```
my @cousins = qw( Rick Kristen Alex
                  Kaycee Eric Corey );
is @cousins, 6, 'I should have only six cousins';
```

---

[1] ...and you can omit the parenthesis.

... though some people prefer to write `scalar @cousins` for the sake of clarity.

`Test::More`'s corresponding `isnt()` function compares two values using the `ne` operator, and passes if they are not equal. It also provides scalar context to its operands.

Both `is()` and `isnt()` apply *string comparisons* with the `eq` and `ne` operators. This almost always does the right thing, but for complex values such as objects with overloading (Overloading, pp. 240) or dual vars (Dualvars, pp. 80), use the `cmp_ok()` function which requires you to provide a specific comparison operator:

```
cmp_ok( 100, $cur_balance, '<=',
        'I should have at least $100' );

cmp_ok( $monkey, $ape, '==',
        'Simian numifications should agree' );
```

Classes and objects provide their own interesting ways to interact with tests. Test that a class or object extends another class (Inheritance, pp. 176) with `isa_ok()`:

```
my $chimpzilla = RobotMonkey->new;
isa_ok( $chimpzilla, 'Robot' );
isa_ok( $chimpzilla, 'Monkey' );
```

`isa_ok()` provides its own diagnostic message on failure.

`can_ok()` verifies that a class or object can perform the requested method (or methods):

```
can_ok( $chimpzilla, 'eat_banana' );
can_ok( $chimpzilla, 'transform', 'destroy_tokyo' );
```

The `is_deeply()` function compares two references to ensure that their contents are equal:

```
use Clone;

my $numbers   = [ 4, 8, 15, 16, 23, 42 ];
my $clonenums = Clone::clone( $numbers );

is_deeply( $numbers, $clonenums,
     'clone() should produce identical items' );
```

If the comparison fails, Test::More will do its best to provide a reasonable diagnostic indicating the position of the first inequality between the structures. See the CPAN modules Test::Differences and Test::Deep for more configurable tests.

Test::More has several more test functions, but these are the most useful.

## Organizing Tests

CPAN distributions should include a *t/* directory containing one or more test files named with the *.t* suffix. When you build a distribution with Module::Build or ExtUtils::MakeMaker, the testing step runs all of the *t/\*.t* files, summarizes their output, and succeeds or fails on the results of the test suite as a whole. There are no concrete guidelines on how to manage the contents of individual *.t* files, though two strategies are popular:

- Each *.t* file should correspond to a *.pm* file

- Each *.t* file should correspond to a feature

A hybrid approach is the most flexible; one test can verify that all of your modules compile, while other tests demonstrate that each module behaves as intended. As your project grows, the second approach is easier to manage. Keep your test files small and focused and they'll be easier to maintain.

Separate test files can also speed up development. If you're adding the ability to breathe fire to your RobotMonkey, you may want only to run the *t/breathe_fire.t* test file. When you have the feature working to your satisfaction, run the entire test suite to verify that local changes have no unintended global effects.

## Other Testing Modules

Test::More relies on a testing backend known as Test::Builder. The latter module manages the test plan and coordinates the test output into TAP. This design allows multiple test modules to share the same Test::Builder backend. Consequently, the CPAN has hundreds of test modules available–and they can all work together in the same program.

- Test::Fatal helps test that your code throws (and does not throw) exceptions appropriately. You may also encounter Test::Exception.

- Test::MockObject and Test::MockModule allow you to test difficult interfaces by *mocking* (emulating but producing different results).

- `Test::WWW::Mechanize` helps test web applications, while `Plack::Test`, `Plack::Test::Agent`, and the subclass `Test::WWW::Mechanize::PSGI` can do so without using an external live web server.

- `Test::Database` provides functions to test the use and abuse of databases. `DBICx::TestDatabase` helps test schemas built with `DBIx::Class`.

- `Test::Class` offers an alternate mechanism for organizing test suites. It allows you to create classes in which specific methods group tests. You can inherit from test classes just as your code classes inherit from each other. This is an excellent way to reduce duplication in test suites. See Curtis Poe's excellent `Test::Class` series[2]. The newer `Test::Routine` distribution offers similar possibilities through the use of Moose (Moose, pp. 165).

- `Test::Differences` tests strings and data structures for equality and displays any differences in its diagnostics. `Test::LongString` adds similar assertions.

- `Test::Deep` tests the equivalence of nested data structures (Nested Data Structures, pp. 92).

- `Devel::Cover` analyzes the execution of your test suite to report on the amount of your code your tests actually exercises. In general, the more coverage the better–though 100% coverage is not always possible, 95% is far better than 80%.

- `Test::Most` gathers several useful test modules into one parent module. It saves time and effort.

See the Perl QA project (http://qa.perl.org/) for more information about testing in Perl.

# Handling Warnings

While there's more than one way to write a working Perl program, some of those ways can be confusing, unclear, and even incorrect. Perl's optional warnings system can help you avoid these situations.

---

[2]http://www.modernperlbooks.com/mt/2009/03/organizing-test-suites-with-testclass.html

## Producing Warnings

Use the `warn` builtin to emit a warning:

```
warn 'Something went wrong!';
```

`warn` prints a list of values to the STDERR filehandle (Input and Output, pp. 213). Perl will append the filename and line number of the `warn` call unless the last element of the list ends in a newline.

The core `Carp` module extends Perl's warning mechanisms. Its `carp()` function reports a warning from the perspective of the calling code. Given a function like:

```
use Carp 'carp';

sub only_two_arguments
{
    my ($lop, $rop) = @_;
    carp( 'Too many arguments provided' ) if @_ > 2;
    ...
}
```

...the arity (Arity, pp. 100) warning will include the filename and line number of the *calling* code, not `only_two_arguments()`. Carp's `cluck()` is similar, but it produces a backtrace of *all* function calls up to the current function.

Carp's verbose mode adds backtraces to all warnings produced by `carp()` and `croak()` (Reporting Errors, pp. 112) throughout the entire program:

```
$ perl -MCarp=verbose my_prog.pl
```

Use `Carp` when writing modules (Modules, pp. 223) instead of `warn` or `die`.

## Enabling and Disabling Warnings

Sometimes older code uses the `-w` command-line argument. `-w` enables warnings throughout the program, even in external modules written and maintained by other people. It's all or nothing—though it can help you if you have the time and energy to eliminate warnings and potential warnings throughout the entire codebase.

The modern approach is to use the `warnings` pragma[3]. This enables warnings in *lexical* scopes. If you've used `warnings` in a scope, you're indicating that the code should not normally produce warnings.

---

[3] ...or an equivalent such as use `Modern::Perl;`.

> **Global Warnings Flags**
>
> The -W flag enables warnings throughout the program unilaterally, regardless of any use of `warnings`. The -X flag *disables* warnings throughout the program unilaterally. Neither is common.

All of -w, -W, and -X affect the value of the global variable $^W. Code written before the `warnings` pragma[4] may `localize` $^W to suppress certain warnings within a given scope.

## Disabling Warning Categories

To disable selective warnings within a scope, use `no warnings;` with an argument list. Omitting the argument list disables all warnings within that scope.

`perldoc perllexwarn` lists all of the warnings categories your version of Perl understands. Most of them represent truly interesting conditions, but some may be actively unhelpful in your specific circumstances. For example, the `recursion` warning will occur if Perl detects that a function has called itself more than a hundred times. If you are confident in your ability to write recursion-ending conditions, you may disable this warning within the scope of the recursion (though tail calls may be better; Tail Calls, pp. 117).

If you're generating code (Code Generation, pp. 234) or locally redefining symbols, you may wish to disable the `redefine` warnings.

Some experienced Perl hackers disable the `uninitialized` value warnings in string-processing code which concatenates values from many sources. If you're careful about initializing your variables, you may never need to disable this warning, but sometimes the warning gets in the way of writing concise code in your local style.

## Making Warnings Fatal

If your project considers warnings as onerous as errors, you can make them fatal. To promote *all* warnings into exceptions within a lexical scope:

```
use warnings FATAL => 'all';
```

---

[1]Perl 5.6.0, spring 2000, so you know it's old.

You may also make specific categories of warnings fatal, such as the use of deprecated constructs:

```
use warnings FATAL => 'deprecated';
```

With proper discipline, this can produce very robust code–but be cautious. Many warnings come from runtime conditions. If your test suite fails to identify all of the warnings you might encounter, your program may exit from uncaught runtime exceptions. Keep in mind that newer versions of Perl may add new warnings and that custom warnings will also be fatal (Registering Your Own Warnings, pp. 213). If you enable fatal warnings, do so only in code that you control and never in library code you expect other people to use.

## Catching Warnings

If you're willing to work for it, you can catch warnings as you would exceptions. The %SIG variable[5] contains handlers for out-of-band signals raised by Perl or your operating system. Assign a function reference to $SIG{__WARN__} to catch a warning:

```
{
    my $warning;
    local $SIG{__WARN__} = sub { $warning .= shift };

    # do something risky
    ...

    say "Caught warning:\n$warning" if $warning;
}
```

Within the warning handler, the first argument is the warning's message. Admittedly, this technique is less useful than disabling warnings lexically–but it can come to good use in test modules such as Test::Warnings from the CPAN, where the actual text of the warning is important.

Beware that %SIG is global. localize it in the smallest possible scope, but understand that it's still a global variable.

---

[5]See perldoc perlvar.

## Registering Your Own Warnings

The `warnings::register` pragma allows you to create your own warnings so that users of your code can enable and disable them in lexical scopes. From a module, use the `warnings::register` pragma:

```
package Scary::Monkey;

use warnings::register;
```

This will create a new warnings category named after the package `Scary::Monkey`. Enable these warnings with `use warnings 'Scary::Monkey'` and disable them with `no warnings 'Scary::Monkey'`.

Use `warnings::enabled()` to test if the caller's lexical scope has enabled a warning category. Use `warnings::warnif()` to produce a warning only if warnings are in effect. For example, to produce a warning in the `deprecated` category:

```
package Scary::Monkey;

use warnings::register;

sub import
{
    warnings::warnif( 'deprecated',
        'empty imports from ' . __PACKAGE__ .
        ' are now deprecated' )
    unless @_;
}
```

See `perldoc perllexwarn` for more details.

# Files

Most programs must interact with the real world somehow, mostly by reading, writing, and otherwise manipulating files. Perl's origin as a tool for system administrators has produced a language well suited for text processing.

## Input and Output

A *filehandle* represents the current state of one specific channel of input or output. Every Perl program has three standard filehandles available, STDIN (the input to the program), STDOUT (the output from the program), and STDERR (the error output

213

from the program). By default, everything you print or say goes to STDOUT, while errors and warnings goes to STDERR. This separation of output allows you to redirect useful output and errors to two different places–an output file and error logs, for example.

Use the open builtin to get a filehandle. To open a file for reading:

```
open my $fh, '<', 'filename'
    or die "Cannot read '$filename': $!\n";
```

The first operand is a lexical which will contain the resulting filehandle. The second operand is the *file mode*, which determines the type of the filehandle operation (reading, writing, or appending, for example). The final operand is the name of the file. If the open fails, the die clause will throw an exception, with the reason for failure in the $! magic variable.

You may open files for writing, appending, reading and writing, and more. Some of the most important file modes are:

| Symbols | Explanation |
| --- | --- |
| < | Open for reading |
| > | Open for writing, clobbering existing contents if the file exists and creating a new file otherwise. |
| >> | Open for writing, appending to any existing contents and creating a new file otherwise. |
| +< | Open for both reading and writing. |
| -\| | Open a pipe to an external process for reading. |
| \|- | Open a pipe to an external process for writing. |

Table 9.1: File Modes

You can even create filehandles which read from or write to plain Perl scalars, using any existing file mode:

```
open my $read_fh,  '<', \$fake_input;
open my $write_fh, '>', \$captured_output;

do_something_awesome( $read_fh, $write_fh );
```

perldoc perlopentut explains in detail more exotic uses of open, including its ability to launch and control other processes, as well as the use of sysopen for finer-grained control over input and output. `perldoc perlfaq5` includes working code for many common IO tasks.

---

**Remember autodie?**

Assume all of the examples in this section have use `autodie`; enabled, and so can safely elide error handling. If you choose not to use `autodie`, remember to check the return values of all system calls to handle errors appropriately.

---

## Unicode, IO Layers, and File Modes

In addition to the file mode, you may add an *IO encoding layer* which allows Perl to encode to or decode from a Unicode encoding. For example, if you know you're going to read a file written in the UTF-8 encoding:

```
open my $in_fh,  '>:encoding(UTF-8)', $infile;
```

... or to write to a file using the UTF-8 encoding:

```
open my $out_fh, '<:encoding(UTF-8)', $outfile;
```

### Two-argument open

Older code often uses the two-argument form of open(), which jams the file mode with the name of the file to open:

```
open my $fh, "> $some_file"
    or die "Cannot write to '$some_file': $!\n";
```

Perl must extract the file mode from the filename. That's a risk; anytime Perl has to guess at what you mean, it may guess incorrectly. Worse, if $some_file came from untrusted user input, you have a potential security problem, as any unexpected characters could change how your program behaves.

The three-argument open() is a safer replacement for this code.

215

> ### The Many Names of DATA
>
> The special package global DATA filehandle represents the current file. When Perl finishes compiling the file, it leaves DATA open and pointing to the end of the compilation unit *if* the file has a __DATA__ or __END__ section. Any text which occurs after that token is available for reading from DATA. The entire file is available if you use seek to rewind the filehandle. This is useful for short, self-contained programs. See perldoc perldata for more details.

## Reading from Files

Given a filehandle opened for input, read from it with the readline builtin, also written as <>. A common idiom reads a line at a time in a while() loop:

```
open my $fh, '<', 'some_file';

while (<$fh>)
{
    chomp;
    say "Read a line '$_'";
}
```

In scalar context, readline reads a single line of the file and returns it, or undef< if it's reached the end of file (eof()). Each iteration in this example returns the next line or undef. This while idiom explicitly checks the definedness of the variable used for iteration, such that only the end of file condition ends the loop. In other words, this is shorthand for:

```
open my $fh, '<', 'some_file';

while (defined($_ = <$fh>))
{
    chomp;
    say "Read a line '$_'";
    last if eof $fh;
}
```

> **Why use while and not for?**
>
> for imposes list context on its operand. In the case of readline, Perl will read the *entire* file before processing *any* of it. while performs iteration and reads a line at a time. When memory use is a concern, use while.

Every line read from readline includes the character or characters which mark the end of a line. In most cases, this is a platform-specific sequence consisting of a newline (\n), a carriage return (\r), or a combination of the two (\r\n). Use chomp to remove it.

The cleanest way to read a file line-by-line in Perl is:

```
open my $fh, '<', $filename;

while (my $line = <$fh>)
{
    chomp $line;
    . . .
}
```

Perl accesses files in text mode by default. If you're reading *binary* data, such as a media file or a compressed file–use binmode before performing any IO. This will force Perl to treat the file data as pure data, without modifying it in any way[6]. While Unix-like platforms may not always *need* binmode, portable programs play it safe (Unicode and Strings, pp. 30).

### Writing to Files

Given a filehandle open for output, print or say to it:

```
open my $out_fh, '>', 'output_file.txt';

print $out_fh "Here's a line of text\n";
say   $out_fh "... and here's another";
```

Note the lack of comma between the filehandle and the subsequent operand.

---

[6]Modifications include translating \n into the platform-specific newline sequence.

> ### Filehandle Disambiguation
>
> Damian Conway's *Perl Best Practices* recommends enclosing the filehandle in curly braces as a habit. This is necessary to disambiguate parsing of a filehandle contained in an aggregate variable, and it won't hurt anything in the simpler cases.

Both `print` and `say` take a list of operands. Perl uses the magic global `$,` as the separator between list values. Perl also uses any value of `$\` as the final argument to `print` or `say`. Thus these two lines of code produce the same result:

```
my @princes = qw( Corwin Eric Random ... );

print @princes;
print join( $,, @princes ) . $\;
```

### Closing Files

When you've finished working with a file, `close` its filehandle explicitly or allow it to go out of scope. Perl will close it for you. The benefit of calling `close` explicitly is that you can check for–and recover from–specific errors, such as running out of space on a storage device or a broken network connection.

As usual, `autodie` handles these checks for you:

```
use autodie qw( open close );

open my $fh, '>', $file;

...

close $fh;
```

### Special File Handling Variables

For every line read, Perl increments the value of the variable `$.`, which serves as a line counter.

`readline` uses the current contents of `$/` as the line-ending sequence. The value of this variable defaults to the most appropriate line-ending character sequence for text files on your current platform. The word *line* is a misnomer, however. You can set $/ to contain any sequence of characters[7] This is useful for highly-structured data in which you want to read a *record* at a time.

Given a file with records separated by two blank lines, set $/ to \n\n to read a record at a time. chomp on a record read from the file will remove the double-newline sequence.

Perl *buffers* its output by default, performing IO only when the amount of pending output exceeds a threshold. This allows Perl to batch up expensive IO operations instead of always writing very small amounts of data. Yet sometimes you want to send data as soon as you have it without waiting for that buffering–especially if you're writing a command-line filter connected to other programs or a line-oriented network service.

The $| variable controls buffering on the currently active output filehandle. When set to a non-zero value, Perl will flush the output after each write to the filehandle. When set to a zero value, Perl will use its default buffering strategy.

> **Automatic Flushing**
>
> Files default to a fully-buffered strategy. STDOUT when connected to an active terminal–but *not* another program–uses a line-buffered strategy, where Perl will flush STDOUT every time it encounters a newline in the output.

Instead of cluttering your code with a global variable, use the autoflush() method on a lexical filehandle:

```
open my $fh, '>', 'pecan.log';
$fh->autoflush( 1 );
```

. . .

As of Perl 5.14, you can use any method provided by IO::File on a filehandle. You do not need to load IO::File explicitly. In Perl 5.12, you must load IO::File yourself.

IO::File's input_line_number() and input_record_separator() methods do the job of $. and $/ on individual filehandles. See the documentation for IO::File, IO::Handle, and IO::Seekable.

---

[7]...but, sadly, not a regular expression. Maybe by 5.22.

## Directories and Paths

Working with directories is similar to working with files, except that you cannot *write* to directories[8]. Open a directory handle with the `opendir` builtin:

```
opendir my $dirh, '/home/monkeytamer/tasks/';
```

The `readdir` builtin reads from a directory. As with `readline`, you may iterate over the contents of directories one at a time or you may assign them to an array in one swoop:

```
# iteration
while (my $file = readdir $dirh)
{
    ...
}

# flatten into a list, assign to array
my @files = readdir $otherdirh;
```

Perl 5.12 added a feature where `readdir` in a `while` sets `$_`:

```
use 5.012;

opendir my $dirh, 'tasks/circus/';

while (readdir $dirh)
{
    next if /^\./;
    say "Found a task $_!";
}
```

The curious regular expression in this example skips so-called *hidden files* on Unix and Unix-like systems, where a leading dot prevents them from appearing in directory listings by default. It also skips the two special files . and .., which represent the current directory and the parent directory respectively.

The names returned from `readdir` are *relative* to the directory itself. In other words, if the *tasks/* directory contains three files named *eat*, *drink*, and *be_monkey*,

---

[8]Instead, you save and move and rename and remove files.

`readdir` will return `eat`, `drink`, and `be_monkey` and *not tasks/eat, tasks/drink,* and *task/be_monkey.* In contrast, an *absolute* path is a path fully qualified to its filesystem.

Close a directory handle by letting it go out of scope or with the `closedir` builtin.

## Manipulating Paths

Perl offers a Unixy view of your filesystem and will interpret Unix-style paths appropriately for your operating system and filesystem. If you're using Microsoft Windows, you can use the path *C:/My Documents/Robots/Bender/* just as easily as you can use the path *C:\My Documents\Robots\Caprica Six\.*

Even though Perl uses Unix file semantics consistently, cross-platform file manipulation is much easier with a module. The core `File::Spec` module family lets you manipulate file paths safely and portably. It's a little clunky, but it's well documented.

The `Path::Class` distribution on the CPAN has a nicer interface. Use the `dir()` function to create an object representing a directory and the `file()` function to create an object representing a file:

```
use Path::Class;

my $meals = dir( 'tasks', 'cooking' );
my $file  = file( 'tasks', 'health', 'robots.txt' );
```

You can get File objects from directories and vice versa:

```
my $lunch      = $meals->file( 'veggie_calzone' );
my $robots_dir = $robot_list->dir;
```

You can even open filehandles to directories and files:

```
my $dir_fh    = $dir->open;
my $robots_fh = $robot_list->open( 'r' )
                  or die "Open failed: $!";
```

Both `Path::Class::Dir` and `Path::Class::File` offer further useful behaviors—though beware that if you use a `Path::Class` object of some kind with an operator or function which expects a string containing a file path, you need to stringify the object yourself. This is a persistent but minor annoyance. (If you find it burdensome, try `Path::Tiny` as an alternative.)

```
my $contents = read_from_filename( "$lunch" );
```

## File Manipulation

Besides reading and writing files, you can also manipulate them as you would directly from a command line or a file manager. The file test operators, collectively called the -X operators, examine file and directory attributes. To test that a file exists:

```
say 'Present!' if -e $filename;
```

The -e operator has a single operand, the name of a file or a file or directory handle. If the file exists, the expression will evaluate to a true value. perldoc -f -X lists all other file tests; the most popular are:

-f

, which returns a true value if its operand is a plain file

-d

, which returns a true value if its operand is a directory

-r

, which returns a true value if the file permissions of its operand permit reading by the current user

-s

, which returns a true value if its operand is a non-empty file

Look up the documentation for any of these operators with perldoc -f -r, for example.

The rename builtin can rename a file or move it between directories. It takes two operands, the old path of the file and the new path:

```
rename 'death_star.txt', 'carbon_sink.txt';

# or if you're stylish:
rename 'death_star.txt' => 'carbon_sink.txt';
```

There's no core builtin to copy a file, but the core File::Copy module provides both copy() and move() functions. Use the unlink builtin to remove one or more files. (The delete builtin deletes an element from a hash, not a file from the filesystem.) These functions and builtins all return true values on success and set $! on error.

---

**Better than `File::Spec`**

`Path::Class` provides convenience methods to check certain file attributes as well as to remove files completely and portably.

---

Perl tracks its current working directory. By default, this is the active directory from where you launched the program. The core `Cwd` module's `cwd()` function returns the name of the current working directory. The builtin `chdir` attempts to change the current working directory. Working from the correct directory is essential to working with files with relative paths.

---

**Switching Directories**

If you love the command-line tools `pushd` and `popd`, try `File::pushd`.

---

# Modules

Many people consider the CPAN (The CPAN, pp. 15) to be Perl's best advantage. The CPAN is a system for finding and installing modules. A *module* is a package contained in its own file and loadable with `use` or `require`. A module must be valid Perl code. It must end with an expression which evaluates to a true value so that the Perl parser knows it has loaded and compiled the module successfully. There are no other requirements, only strong conventions.

When you load a module, Perl splits the package name on double-colons (`::`) and turns the components of the package name into a file path. This means that `use StrangeMonkey;` causes Perl to search for a file named *StrangeMonkey.pm* in every directory in `@INC`, in order, until it finds one or exhausts the list.

Similarly, `use StrangeMonkey::Persistence;` causes Perl to search for a file named `Persistence.pm` in every directory named *StrangeMonkey/* present in every directory in `@INC`, and so on. `use StrangeMonkey::UI::Mobile;` causes Perl to search for a relative file path of *StrangeMonkey/UI/Mobile.pm* in every directory in `@INC`.

The resulting file may or may not contain a package declaration matching its filename–there is no such technical *requirement*–but it's easier to understand that way.

> ### perldoc Tricks
>
> `perldoc -l Module::Name` will print the full path to the relevant *.pm* file, if that file contains *documentation* in POD form. `perldoc -lm Module::Name` will print the full path to the *.pm* file. `perldoc -m Module::Name` will display the contents of the *.pm* file.

## Using and Importing

When you load a module with `use`, Perl loads it from disk, then calls its `import()` method, passing any arguments you provided. By convention, a module's `import()` method takes a list of names and exports functions and other symbols into the calling namespace. This is merely convention; a module may decline to provide an `import()`, or its `import()` may perform other behaviors. Pragmas (Pragmas, pp. 200) such as `strict` use arguments to change the behavior of the calling lexical scope instead of exporting symbols:

```
use strict;
# ... calls strict->import()

use CGI ':standard';
# ... calls CGI->import( ':standard' )

use feature qw( say switch );
# ... calls feature->import( qw( say switch ) )
```

The `no` builtin calls a module's `unimport()` method, if it exists, passing any arguments. This is most common with pragmas which introduce or modify behavior through `import()`:

```
use strict;
# no symbolic references or barewords
# variable declaration required

{
    no strict 'refs';
    # symbolic references allowed
    # strict 'subs' and 'vars' still in effect
}
```

Both use and no take effect during compilation, such that:

```
use Module::Name qw( list of arguments );
```

...is the same as:

```
BEGIN
{
    require 'Module/Name.pm';
    Module::Name->import( qw( list of arguments ) );
}
```

Similarly:

```
no Module::Name qw( list of arguments );
```

...is the same as:

```
BEGIN
{
    require 'Module/Name.pm';
    Module::Name->unimport(qw( list of arguments ));
}
```

...including the require of the module.

> **Missing Methods Never Missed**
>
> If import() or unimport() does not exist in the module, Perl will not give an error message. They are truly optional.

You *may* call import() and unimport() directly, though outside of a BEGIN block it makes little sense to do so; after compilation has completed, the effects of import() or unimport() may have little effect.

Both use and require are case-sensitive. While Perl knows the difference between strict and Strict, your combination of operating system and file system may not. If you were to write use Strict;, Perl would not find *strict.pm* on a case-sensitive filesystem. With a case-insensitive filesystem, Perl would happily load *Strict.pm*, but nothing would happen when it tried to call Strict->import(). (*strict.pm* declares a package named strict.)

Portable programs are careful about case even if they don't have to be.

## Exporting

A module can make package global symbols available to other packages through a process known as *exporting*–often by calling import() implicitly or directly.

The core module Exporter is the standard way to export symbols from a module. Exporter relies on the presence of package global variables–@EXPORT_OK and @EXPORT in particular–which contain a list of symbols to export when requested.

Consider a StrangeMonkey::Utilities module which provides several standalone functions usable throughout the system:

```
package StrangeMonkey::Utilities;

use Exporter 'import';

our @EXPORT_OK = qw( round translate screech );

...
```

Any other code now can use this module and, optionally, import any or all of the three exported functions. You may also export variables:

```
push @EXPORT_OK, qw( $spider $saki $squirrel );
```

Export symbols by default by listing them in @EXPORT instead of @EXPORT_OK:

```
our @EXPORT = qw( monkey_dance monkey_sleep );
```

...so that any use StrangeMonkey::Utilities; will import both functions. Be aware that specifying symbols to import will *not* import default symbols; you only get what you request. To load a module without importing any symbols, use an explicit empty list:

```
# make the module available, but import() nothing
use StrangeMonkey::Utilities ();
```

Regardless of any import lists, you can always call functions in another package with their fully-qualified names:

```
StrangeMonkey::Utilities::screech();
```

226

---

**Simplified Exporting**

The CPAN module `Sub::Exporter` provides a nicer interface to export functions without using package globals. It also offers more powerful options. However, `Exporter` can export variables, while `Sub::Exporter` only exports functions.

## Organizing Code with Modules

Perl does not require you to use modules, packages, or namespaces. You may put all of your code in a single *.pl* file, or in multiple *.pl* files you `require` as necessary. You have the flexibility to manage your code in the most appropriate way, given your development style, the formality and risk and reward of the project, your experience, and your comfort with deploying code.

Even so, a project with more than a couple of hundred lines of code benefits from module organization:

- Modules help to enforce a logical separation between distinct entities in the system.

- Modules provide an API boundary, whether procedural or OO.

- Modules suggest a natural organization of source code.

- The Perl ecosystem has many tools devoted to creating, maintaining, organizing, and deploying modules and distributions.

- Modules provide a mechanism of code reuse.

Even if you do not use an object-oriented approach, modeling every distinct entity or responsibility in your system with its own module keeps related code together and separate code separate.

# Distributions

A *distribution* is a collection of metadata and modules (Modules, pp. 223) which forms a single redistributable, testable, and installable unit. The easiest way to configure, build, package, test, and install Perl code is to follow the CPAN's conventions. These conventions govern how to package a distribution, how to resolve its dependencies, where to install software, how to verify that it works, how to display documentation, and how to manage a repository. All of these guidelines have arisen from the rough consensus of thousands of contributors working on tens of thousands of projects. A distribution built to CPAN standards can be tested on several versions of Perl on several different hardware platforms within a few hours of its uploading, with errors reported automatically to authors–all without human intervention.

You may choose never to release any of your code as public CPAN distributions, but you *can* use CPAN tools and conventions to manage even private code. The Perl community has built amazing infrastructure; why not take advantage of it?

## Attributes of a Distribution

Besides one or more modules, a distribution includes several other files and directories:

- *Build.PL* or *Makefile.PL*, a driver program used to configure, build, test, bundle, and install the distribution.

- *MANIFEST*, a list of all files contained in the distribution. This helps tools verify that a bundle is complete.

- *META.yml* and/or *META.json*, a file containing metadata about the distribution and its dependencies.

- *README*, a description of the distribution, its intent, and its copyright and licensing information.

- *lib/*, the directory containing Perl modules.

- *t/*, a directory containing test files.

- *Changes*, a human-readable log of every significant change to the distribution.

A well-formed distribution must contain a unique name and single version number (often taken from its primary module). Any distribution you download from the public CPAN should conform to these standards. The public CPANTS service (http://cpants.perl.org/) evaluates each uploaded distribution against packaging guidelines and conventions and recommends improvements. Following the CPANTS guidelines doesn't mean the code works, but it does mean that the CPAN packaging tools should understand the distribution.

# CPAN Tools for Managing Distributions

The Perl core includes several tools to manage distributions:

- CPAN.pm is the official CPAN client. While by default this client installs distributions from the public CPAN, you can also use your ownpoint them to your own repository instead of or in addition to the public repository.

- Module::Build is a pure-Perl tool suite for configuring, building, installing, and testing distributions. It works with *Build.PL* files.

- ExtUtils::MakeMaker is a legacy tool which Module::Build intends to replace. It is still in wide use, though it is in maintenance mode and receives only critical bug fixes. It works with *Makefile.PL* files.

- Test::More (Testing, pp. 203) is the basic and most widely used testing module used to write automated tests for Perl software.

- TAP::Harness and prove (Running Tests, pp. 204) run tests and interpret and report their results.

In addition, several non-core CPAN modules make your life easier as a developer:

- App::cpanminus is a configuration-free CPAN client. It handles the most common cases, uses little memory, and works quickly.

- App::perlbrew helps you to manage multiple installations of Perl. Install new versions of Perl for testing or production, or to isolate applications and their dependencies.

- CPAN::Mini and the cpanmini command allow you to create your own (private) mirror of the public CPAN. You can inject your own distributions into this repository and manage which versions of the public modules are available in your organization.

- Dist::Zilla automates away common distribution tasks. While it uses either Module::Build or ExtUtils::MakeMaker, it can replace *your* use of them directly. See http://dzil.org/ for an interactive tutorial.

- Test::Reporter allows you to report the results of running the automated test suites of distributions you install, giving their authors more data on any failures.

- Carton and Pinto are two newer projects which help manage and install code's dependencies. Neither is in widespread use yet, but they're both under active development.

## Designing Distributions

The process of designing a distribution could fill a book (see Sam Tregar's *Writing Perl Modules for CPAN*), but a few design principles will help you. Start with a utility such as `Module::Starter` or `Dist::Zilla`. The initial cost of learning the configuration and rules may seem like a steep investment, but the benefit of having everything set up the right way (and in the case of `Dist::Zilla`, *never going out of date*) relieves you of tedious busywork.

A distribution should follow several non-code guidelines:

- *Each distribution performs a single, well-defined purpose.* That purpose may even include gathering several related distributions into a single installable bundle. Decompose your software into individual distributions to manage their dependencies appropriately and to respect their encapsulation.

- *Each distribution contains a single version number.* Version numbers must always increase. The semantic version policy (http://semver.org/) is sane and compatible with Perl's approach.

- *Each distribution provides a well-defined API.* A comprehensive automated test suite can verify that you maintain this API across versions. If you use a local CPAN mirror to install your own distributions, you can re-use the CPAN infrastructure for testing distributions and their dependencies. You get easy access to integration testing across reusable components.

- *Distribution tests are useful and repeatable.* The CPAN infrastructure supports automated test reporting. Use it!

- *Interfaces are simple and effective.* Avoid the use of global symbols and default exports; allow people to use only what they need. Do not pollute their namespaces.

# The UNIVERSAL Package

Perl's builtin `UNIVERSAL` package is the ancestor of all other packages–in the object-oriented sense (Moose, pp. 165). `UNIVERSAL` provides a few methods for its children to use, inherit, or override.

## The VERSION() Method

The `VERSION()` method returns the value of the `$VERSION` variable of the invoking package or class. If you provide a version number as an optional parameter, the method will throw an exception if the queried `$VERSION` is not equal to or greater than the parameter.

Given a `HowlerMonkey` module of version 1.23:

```
my $hm = HowlerMonkey->new;

say HowlerMonkey->VERSION;       # prints 1.23
say $hm->VERSION;                # prints 1.23
say $hm->VERSION( 0.0  );        # prints 1.23
say $hm->VERSION( 1.23 );        # prints 1.23
say $hm->VERSION( 2.0  );        # exception!
```

There's little reason to override `VERSION()`.

## The DOES() Method

The `DOES()` method supports the use of roles (Roles, pp. 173) in programs. Pass it an invocant and the name of a role, and the method will return true if the appropriate class somehow does that role—whether through inheritance, delegation, composition, role application, or any other mechanism.

The default implementation of `DOES()` falls back to `isa()`, because inheritance is one mechanism by which a class may do a role. Given a `Cappuchin`:

```
say Cappuchin->DOES( 'Monkey'       );  # prints 1
say $cappy->DOES(     'Monkey'      );  # prints 1
say Cappuchin->DOES( 'Invertebrate' );  # prints 0
```

Override `DOES()` if you manually consume a role or otherwise somehow provide allomorphic equivalence.

## The can() Method

The `can()` method takes a string containing the name of a method. It returns a reference to the function which implements that method, if it exists. Otherwise, it returns a false value. You may call this on a class, an object, or the name of a package. In the latter case, it returns a reference to a function, not a method[9].

Given a class named `SpiderMonkey` with a method named `screech`, get a reference to the method with:

```
if (my $meth = SpiderMonkey->can( 'screech' )) {...}
```

---

[9] ...not that you can tell the difference, given only a reference.

This technique leads to the pattern of checking for a method's existence before dispatching to it:

```
if (my $meth = $sm->can( 'screech' )
{
    # method; not a function
    $sm->$meth();
}
```

Use can() to test if a package implements a specific function or method:

```
use Class::Load;

die "Couldn't load $module!"
    unless load_class( $module );

if (my $register = $module->can( 'register' ))
{
    # function; not a method
    $register->();
}
```

> **Module::Pluggable**
>
> The CPAN module Class::Load simplifies the work of loading classes by name. Similarly, Module::Pluggable takes most of the work out of building and managing plugin systems. Get to know both distributions.

## The isa() Method

The isa() method takes a string containing the name of a class or the name of a core type (SCALAR, ARRAY, HASH, Regexp, IO, and CODE). Call it as a class method or an instance method on an object. isa() returns a true value if its invocant is or derives from the named class, or if the invocant is a blessed reference to the given type.

Given an object $pepper (a hash reference blessed into the Monkey class, which inherits from the Mammal class):

```
say $pepper->isa( 'Monkey' );   # prints 1
say $pepper->isa( 'Mammal' );   # prints 1
```

```
say $pepper->isa( 'HASH'    );   # prints 1
say Monkey->isa( 'Mammal'   );   # prints 1

say $pepper->isa( 'Dolphin' );   # prints 0
say $pepper->isa( 'ARRAY'   );   # prints 0
say Monkey->isa( 'HASH'     );   # prints 0
```

Any class may override isa(). This can be useful when working with mock objects (see Test::MockObject and Test::MockModule on the CPAN) or with code that does not use roles (Roles, pp. 173). Be aware that any class which *does* override isa() generally has a good reason for doing so.

---

**Does a Class Exist?**

While both UNIVERSAL::isa() and UNIVERSAL::can() are methods (Method-Function Equivalence, pp. 270), you may *safely* use the latter as a function solely to determine whether a class exists in Perl. If UNIVERSAL::can( $classname, 'can' ) returns a true value, someone somewhere has defined a class of the name $classname. That class may not be usable, but it does exist.

---

# Extending UNIVERSAL

It's tempting to store other methods in UNIVERSAL to make it available to all other classes and objects in Perl. Avoid this temptation; this global behavior can have subtle side effects, especially in code you didn't write and don't maintain, because it is unconstrained.

With that said, occasional abuse of UNIVERSAL for *debugging* purposes and to fix improper default behavior may be excusable. For example, Joshua ben Jore's UNIVERSAL::ref distribution makes the nearly-useless ref() operator usable. The UNIVERSAL::can and UNIVERSAL::isa distributions can help you debug anti-polymorphism bugs (Method-Function Equivalence, pp. 270). Perl::Critic can detect those and other problems.

Outside of very carefully controlled code and very specific, very pragmatic situations, there's no reason to put code in UNIVERSAL directly. There are almost always much better design alternatives.

# Code Generation

Novice programmers write more code than they need to write, partly from unfamiliarity with languages, libraries, and idioms, but also due to inexperience. They start by writing long lists of procedural code, then discover functions, then parameters, then objects, and–perhaps–higher-order functions and closures.

As you become a better programmer, you'll write less code to solve the same problems. You'll use better abstractions. You'll write more general code. You can reuse code–and when you can add features by deleting code, you'll achieve something great.

Writing programs to write programs for you–*metaprogramming* or *code generation*–allows you to build reusable abstractions. While you can make a huge mess, you can also build amazing things. For example, metaprogramming techniques make Moose possible (Moose, pp. 165).

The AUTOLOAD technique (AUTOLOAD, pp. 138) for missing functions and methods demonstrates this technique in a specific form: Perl's function and method dispatch system allows you to control what happens when normal lookup fails.

## eval

The simplest code generation technique is to build a string containing a snippet of valid Perl and compile it with the string `eval` operator. Unlike the exception-catching block `eval` operator, string `eval` compiles the contents of the string within the current scope, including the current package and lexical bindings.

A common use for this technique is providing a fallback if you can't (or don't want to) load an optional dependency:

```
eval { require Monkey::Tracer }
    or eval 'sub Monkey::Tracer::log {}';
```

If Monkey::Tracer is not available, this code defines a log() function which will do nothing. This simple example is deceptive, because getting eval right takes some work. You must handle quoting issues to include variables within your evald code. Add more complexity to interpolate some variables but not others:

```
sub generate_accessors
{
    my ($methname, $attrname) = @_;

    eval <<"END_ACCESSOR";
sub get_$methname
```

234

```
    {
        my \$self = shift;
        return \$self->{$attrname};
    }

    sub set_$methname
    {
        my (\$self, \$value) = \@_;
        \$self->{$attrname}  = \$value;
    }
END_ACCESSOR
}
```

Woe to those who forget a backslash! Good luck convincing your syntax highlighter what's happening! Worse yet, each invocation of string `eval` builds a new data structure representing the entire code. Compiling code isn't free, either. Yet even with its limitations, this technique is simple and useful.

## Parametric Closures

While building accessors and mutators with `eval` is straightforward, closures (Closures, pp. 130) allow you to add parameters to generated code at compilation time *without* requiring additional evaluation:

```
sub generate_accessors
{
    my $attrname = shift;

    my $getter = sub
    {
        my $self = shift;
        return $self->{$attrname};
    };

    my $setter = sub
    {
        my ($self, $value) = @_;
        $self->{$attrname} = $value;
    };

    return $getter, $setter;
}
```

This code avoids unpleasant quoting issues and compiles each closure only once. It even uses less memory by sharing the compiled code between all closure instances. All that differs is the binding to the $attrname lexical. In a long-running process or a class with a lot of accessors, this technique can be very useful.

Installing into symbol tables is reasonably easy, if ugly:

```
my ($get, $set) = generate_accessors( 'pie' );

no strict 'refs';
*{ 'get_pie' } = $get;
*{ 'set_pie' } = $set;
```

The odd syntax of an asterisk[10] dereferencing a hash refers to a symbol in the current *symbol table*, which is the section of the current namespace which contains globally-accessible symbols such as package globals, functions, and methods. Assigning a reference to a symbol table entry installs or replaces that entry. To promote an anonymous function to a method, store that function's reference in the symbol table.

Assigning to a symbol table symbol with a string, not a literal variable name, is a symbolic reference. You must disable strict reference checking for the operation. Many programs have a subtle bug in similar code, as they assign and generate in a single line:

```
no strict 'refs';

*{ $methname } = sub {
    # subtle bug: strict refs disabled here too
};
```

This example disables strictures for the outer block *as well as the body of the function itself.* Only the assignment violates strict reference checking, so disable strictures for that operation alone:

```
{
    my $sub = sub { ... };

    no strict 'refs';
```

---

[10]Think of it as a *typeglob sigil*, where a *typeglob* is Perl jargon for "symbol table".

```
    *{ $methname } = $sub;
}
```

If the name of the method is a string literal in your source code, rather than the
contents of a variable, you can assign to the relevant symbol directly:

```
{
    no warnings 'once';
    (*get_pie, *set_pie) =
        generate_accessors( 'pie' );
}
```

Assigning directly to the glob does not violate strictures, but mentioning each
glob only once *does* produce a "used only once" warning you can disable with the
warnings pragma.

> **Symbol Tables Simplified**
>
> Use the CPAN module Package::Stash instead of manipulating symbol
> tables yourself.

## Compile-time Manipulation

Unlike code written explicitly as code, code generated through string eval gets
compiled at runtime. Where you might expect a normal function to be available
throughout the lifetime of your program, a generated function might not be available when you expect it.

Force Perl to run code–to generate other code–during compilation by wrapping
it in a BEGIN block. When the Perl parser encounters a block labeled BEGIN, it
parses and compiles the entire block, then runs it (unless it has syntax errors).
When it finishes, parsing will continue as if there had been no interruption.

The difference between writing:

```
sub get_age    { ... }
sub set_age    { ... }

sub get_name   { ... }
sub set_name   { ... }
```

```
sub get_weight { ... }
sub set_weight { ... }
```

...and:

```
sub make_accessors { ... }

BEGIN
{
    for my $accessor (qw( age name weight ))
    {
        my ($get, $set) =
            make_accessors( $accessor );

        no strict 'refs';
        *{ 'get_' . $accessor } = $get;
        *{ 'set_' . $accessor } = $set;
    }
}
```

...is primarily one of maintainability.

Within a module, any code outside of functions executes when you use it, because of the implicit BEGIN Perl adds around the `require` and `import` (Importing, pp. 111). Any code outside of a function but inside the module will execute *before* the `import()` call occurs. If you `require` the module, there is no implicit BEGIN block. After parsing finishes, Perl will run code outside of the functions.

Beware of the interaction between lexical *declaration* (the association of a name with a scope) and lexical *assignment*. The former happens during compilation, while the latter occurs at the point of execution. This code has a subtle bug:

```
use UNIVERSAL::require;

# buggy; do not use
my $wanted_package = 'Monkey::Jetpack';

BEGIN
{
    $wanted_package->require;
    $wanted_package->import;
}
```

... because the BEGIN block will execute *before* the assignment of the string value to $wanted_package occurs. The result will be an exception from attempting to invoke the require() method[11] on an undefined value.

## Class::MOP

Unlike installing function references to populate namespaces and to create methods, there's no simple way to create classes at runtime in Perl. Moose comes to the rescue, with its bundled Class::MOP library. It provides a *meta object protocol*—a mechanism for creating and manipulating an object system by manipulating objects.

Rather than writing your own fragile string eval code or trying to poke into symbol tables manually, you can manipulate the entities and abstractions of your program with objects and methods.

To create a class:

```
use Class::MOP;

my $class = Class::MOP::Class->create(
            'Monkey::Wrench'
        );
```

Add attributes and methods to this class when you create it:

```
my $class = Class::MOP::Class->create(
    'Monkey::Wrench' =>
    (
        attributes =>
        [
            Class::MOP::Attribute->new('$material'),
            Class::MOP::Attribute->new('$color'),
        ]
        methods =>
        {
            tighten => sub { ... },
            loosen  => sub { ... },
        }
    ),
);
```

---

[11]UNIVERSAL::require adds a require() method to UNIVERSAL.

... or to the metaclass (the object which represents that class) once created:

```
$class->add_attribute(
    experience => Class::MOP::Attribute->new('$xp')
);

$class->add_method( bash_zombie => sub { ... } );
```

You can inspect the metaclass:

```
my @attrs = $class->get_all_attributes;
my @meths = $class->get_all_methods;
```

Similarly `Class::MOP::Attribute` and `Class::MOP::Method` allow you to create and manipulate and introspect attributes and methods.

# Overloading

Perl is not a pervasively object oriented language. Its core data types (scalars, arrays, and hashes) are not objects with methods, but you *can* control the behavior of your own classes and objects, especially when they undergo coercion or contextual evaluation. This is *overloading*.

Overloading is subtle but powerful. An interesting example is overloading how an object behaves in boolean context. In boolean context, an object will evaluate to a true value, unless you overload boolification.

---
**Overloading Boolean Context**

Why overload boolean context? Suppose you're using the Null Object pattern (http://www.c2.com/cgi/wiki?NullObject) to make your own objects appear false in boolean context.

---

You can overload what the object does for almost every operation or coercion: stringification, numification, boolification, iteration, invocation, array access, hash access, arithmetic operations, comparison operations, smart match, bitwise operations, and even assignment. Stringification, numification, and boolification are the most important and most common.

## Overloading Common Operations

The overload pragma associates functions with overloadable operations. Passing argument pairs, where the key is the name of a type of overload and the value is a function reference. A Null class which overloads boolean evaluation so that it always evaluates to a false value might resemble:

```
package Null
{
    use overload 'bool' => sub { 0 };

    ...

}
```

It's easy to add a stringification:

```
package Null
{
    use overload
        'bool' => sub { 0 },
        '""'   => sub { '(null)' };
}
```

Overriding numification is more complex, because arithmetic operators tend to be binary ops (Arity, pp. 100). Given two operands both with overloaded methods for addition, which overloading should take precedence? The answer needs to be consistent, easy to explain, and understandable by people who haven't read the source code of the implementation.

perldoc overload attempts to explain this in the sections labeled *Calling Conventions for Binary Operations* and *MAGIC AUTOGENERATION*, but the easiest solution is to overload numification (keyed by '0+') and tell overload to use the provided overloads as fallbacks where possible:

```
package Null
{
    use overload
        'bool'   => sub { 0 },
        '""'     => sub { '(null)' },
        '0+'     => sub { 0 },
        fallback => 1;
}
```

Setting `fallback` to a true value lets Perl use any other defined overloads to compose the requested operation when possible. If that's not possible, Perl will act as if there were no overloads in effect. This is often what you want.

Without `fallback`, Perl will only use the specific overloadings you have provided. If someone tries to perform an operation you have not overloaded, Perl will throw an exception.

## Overload and Inheritance

Subclasses inherit overloadings from their ancestors. They may override this behavior in one of two ways. If the parent class uses overloading as shown, with function references provided directly, a child class *must* override the parent's overloaded behavior by using `overload` directly.

If you're writing a parent class, use the *name* of a method rather than a function reference. That'll allow child classes to prove their own overloadings by overriding the named methods:

```
package Null
{
    use overload
        'bool'   => 'get_bool',
        '""'     => 'get_string',
        '0+'     => 'get_num',
        fallback => 1;
}
```

Any child class can do something different for boolification by overriding `get_-bool()`, for example.

## Uses of Overloading

Overloading may seem like a tempting tool to use to produce symbolic shortcuts for new operations, but it's rare for a good reason. The `IO::All` CPAN distribution pushes this idea to its limit. In return, you get a simple and elegant API. Yet for every brilliant API refined through the appropriate use of overloading, a dozen more messes congeal. Sometimes the best code eschews cleverness in favor of simplicity.

Overriding addition, multiplication, and even concatenation on a `Matrix` class makes sense, only because the existing notation for those operations is pervasive. A new problem domain without that established notation is a poor candidate for overloading, as is a problem domain where you have to squint to make Perl's existing operators match a different notation.

Damian Conway's *Perl Best Practices* suggests one other use for overloading: to prevent the accidental abuse of objects. For example, overloading numification to croak() for objects which have no reasonable single numeric representation can help you find and fix real bugs.

# Taint

Some Perl features can help you write secure programs. These tools are no substitute for careful thought and planning, but they *reward* caution and understanding and can help you avoid subtle mistakes.

## Using Taint Mode

*Taint mode* (or *taint*) is a sticky piece of metadata attached to all data which comes from outside of your program. Any data derived from tainted data is also tainted. You may use tainted data within your program, but if you use it to affect the outside world–if you use it insecurely–Perl will throw a fatal exception.

perldoc perlsec explains taint mode in copious detail.

Launch your program with the -T command-line argument to enable taint mode. If you use this argument on the #! line of a program, you must run the program directly. If you run it as perl mytaintedappl.pl and neglect the -T flag, Perl will exit with an exception–by the time Perl encounters the flag on the #! line, it's missed its opportunity to taint the environment data which makes up %ENV, for example.

## Sources of Taint

Taint can come from two places: file input and the program's operating environment. The former is anything you read from a file or collect from users in the case of web or network programming. The latter includes any command-line arguments, environment variables, and data from system calls. Even operations such as reading from a directory handle produce tainted data.

The tainted() function from the core module Scalar::Util returns true if its argument is tainted:

```
die 'Oh no! Tainted data!'
    if Scalar::Util::tainted( $suspicious_value );
```

## Removing Taint from Data

To remove taint, you must extract known-good portions of the data with a regular expression capture. That captured data will be untainted.

For example, if your user input consists of a US telephone number, you can untaint it with:

```
die 'Number still tainted!'
    unless $number =~ /(\(/d{3}\) \d{3}-\d{4})/;

my $safe_number = $1;
```

The more specific your pattern is about what you allow, the more secure your program can be. The opposite approach of *denying* specific items or forms runs the risk of overlooking something harmful. Far better to disallow something that's safe but unexpected than that to allow something harmful which appears safe. Even so, nothing prevents you from writing a capture for the entire contents of a variable—but in that case, why use taint?

## Removing Taint from the Environment

The superglobal %ENV represents environment variables for the system. This data is tainted because forces outside of the program's control can manipulate values there. Any environment variable which modifies how Perl or the shell finds files and directories is an attack vector. A taint-sensitive program should delete several keys from %ENV and set $ENV{PATH} to a specific and well-secured path:

```
delete @ENV{ qw( IFS CDPATH ENV BASH_ENV ) };
$ENV{PATH} = '/path/to/app/binaries/';
```

If you do not set $ENV{PATH} appropriately, you will receive messages about its insecurity. If this environment variable contained the current working directory, or if it contained relative directories, or if the directories specified had world-writable permissions, a clever attacker could hijack system calls to perpetrate mischief.

For similar reasons, @INC does not contain the current working directory under taint mode. Perl will also ignore the PERL5LIB and PERLLIB environment variables. Use the lib pragma or the -I flag to perl to add library directories to the program.

## Taint Gotchas

Taint mode is all or nothing. It's either on or off. This sometimes leads people to use permissive patterns to untaint data, and gives the illusion of security. In that case, taint is busywork which provides no real security. Review your untainting rules carefully.

Unfortunately, not all modules handle tainted data appropriately. This is a bug which CPAN authors should take seriously. If you have to make legacy code taint-safe, consider the use of the -t flag, which enables taint mode but reduces taint violations from exceptions to warnings. This is not a substitute for full taint mode, but it allows you to secure existing programs without the all or nothing approach of -T.

# CHAPTER 10

# Perl Beyond Syntax

Baby Perl can solve a lot of your problems, but it will only take you so far. Effective programmers understand how Perl's features interact and combine. This fluent Perl takes advantage of the language's natural patterns and idioms. The result of Perlish thinking is concise, powerful, and useful code.

## Idioms

Every language has common patterns of expression, or *idioms*. The earth revolves, but we speak of the sun rising or setting. We brag about clever hacks and cringe at nasty hacks as we sling code.

Perl idioms are language features or design techniques. They're mannerisms and mechanisms that give your code a Perlish accent. You don't have to use them, but they play to Perl's strengths.

### The Object as `$self`

Perl's object system (Moose, pp. 165) treats the invocant of a method as a mundane parameter. Regardless of whether you invoke a class or an instance method, the first element of @_ is always the invocant. By convention, most Perl code uses `$class` as the name of the class method invocant and `$self` for the name of the object invocant. This convention is strong enough that useful extensions such as `MooseX::Method::Signatures` assume you will use `$self` as the name of object invocants.

### Named Parameters

Perl loves lists. Lists are a fundamental element of Perl. List flattening and binding lets you chain together multiple expressions to manipulate data in many ways to produce the results you want.

While Perl's argument passing simplicity (everything flattens into @_) is occasionally too simple, assigning from @_ in list context allows you to unpack named parameters as pairs. The fat comma (Declaring Hashes, pp. 68) operator turns an ordinary list into an obvious list of pairs of arguments:

```
make_ice_cream_sundae(
    whipped_cream => 1,
    sprinkles     => 1,
    banana        => 0,
    ice_cream     => 'mint chocolate chip',
);
```

Within the function, code unpacks these parameters into a hash and treats that hash as if it were a single argument:

```
sub make_ice_cream_sundae
{
    my %args    = @_;
    my $dessert = get_ice_cream( $args{ice_cream} );

    . . .
}
```

---
**Hash or Hash Ref?**

*Perl Best Practices* suggests passing hash references instead. This allows Perl to perform caller-side validation of the hash reference. In other words, if you pass the wrong number of arguments, you'll get an error where you *call* the function.

---

This technique works well with `import()` (Importing, pp. 111) or other methods; process as many parameters as you like before slurping the remainder into a hash:

```
sub import
{
    my ($class, %args)  = @_;
    my $calling_package = caller();

    . . .
}
```

# The Schwartzian Transform

The *Schwartzian transform* is an elegant demonstration of Perl's pervasive list handling as an idiom borrowed from Lisp. Suppose you have a Perl hash which associates the names of your co-workers with their phone extensions:

```perl
my %extensions =
(
    '000' => 'Damian',
    '002' => 'Wesley',
    '012' => 'LaMarcus',
    '042' => 'Robin',
    '088' => 'Nic',
);
```

> **Hash Key Quoting Rules**
>
> Fat comma hash key quoting only works on things that look like barewords. With the leading zero, these keys look like octal numbers. Almost everyone makes this mistake.

To sort this list by name alphabetically, you must sort the hash by its values, not its keys. Getting the values sorted correctly is easy:

```perl
my @sorted_names = sort values %extensions;
```

... but you need an extra step to preserve the association of names and extensions, hence the Schwartzian transform. First, convert the hash into a list of data structures which is easy to sort–in this case, two-element anonymous arrays:

```perl
my @pairs = map  { [ $_, $extensions{$_} ] }
            keys %extensions;
```

`sort` takes the list of anonymous arrays and compares their second elements (the names) as strings:

```perl
my @sorted_pairs = sort { $a->[1] cmp $b->[1] }
                   @pairs;
```

249

The block provided to sort takes its arguments in two package-scoped (Scope, pp. 119) variables: $a and $b[1]. The sort block takes its arguments two at a time. The first becomes the contents of $a and the second the contents of $b. If $a should come before $b in the results, the block must return -1. If both values sort to the same position, the block must return 0. Finally, if $a should come after $b in the results, the block should return 1. Any other return values are errors.

---

**Know Your Data**

Reversing the hash *in place* would work if no one had the same name. This particular data set presents no such problem, but code defensively.

---

The cmp operator performs string comparisons and the <=> performs numeric comparisons. Given @sorted_pairs, a second map operation converts the data structure to a more usable form:

```
my @formatted_exts = map { "$_->[1], ext. $_->[0]" }
                          @sorted_pairs;
```

...and now you can print the whole thing:

```
say for @formatted_exts;
```

The Schwartzian transformation uses Perl's pervasive list processing to get rid of the temporary variables:

```
say for
    map  { " $_->[1], ext. $_->[0] "            }
    sort {    $a->[1] cmp    $b->[1]            }
    map  { [ $_      =>      $extensions{$_} ]  }
         keys %extensions;
```

Read the expression from right to left, in the order of evaluation. For each key in the extensions hash, make a two-item anonymous array containing the key and the value from the hash. Sort that list of anonymous arrays by their second elements, the values from the hash. Format a string of output from those sorted arrays.

---

[1] See perldoc -f sort for an extensive discussion of the implications of this scoping.

The Schwartzian transform pipeline of `map-sort-map` transforms a data structure into another form easier for sorting and then transforms it back into another form.

While this sorting example is simple, consider the case of calculating a cryptographic hash for a large file. The Schwartzian transform is especially useful because it effectively caches any expensive calculations by performing them once in the rightmost `map`.

## Easy File Slurping

`local` is essential to managing Perl's magic global variables. You must understand scope (Scope, pp. 119) to use `local` effectively–but if you do, you can use tight and lightweight scopes in interesting ways. For example, to slurp files into a scalar in a single expression:

```
my $file = do { local $/; <$fh> };

# or
my $file; { local $/; $file = <$fh> };
```

`$/` is the input record separator. `localizing` it sets its value to `undef`, pending assignment. As the value of the separator is undefined, Perl happily reads the entire contents of the filehandle in one swoop. Because a do block evaluates to the value of the last expression evaluated within the block, this evaluates to the data read from the filehandle: the contents of the file. At the end of the expression, `$/` has reverted to its previous state and `$file` contains the contents of the file.

The second example avoids a second copy of the string containing the file's contents; it's not as pretty, but it uses the least amount of memory.

---

**File::Slurp**

This useful example is admittedly maddening for people who don't understand both `local` and scoping. The `File::Slurp` module from the CPAN is a worthy (and often faster) alternative.

---

## Handling Main

Perl requires no special syntax for creating closures (Closures, pp. 130). You can close over a lexical variable inadvertently. Many programs commonly set up several file-scoped lexical variables before handing off processing to other functions.

It's tempting to use these variables directly, rather than passing values to and returning values from functions, especially as programs grow. Unfortunately, these programs may come to rely on subtleties of what happens when during Perl's compilation process–a variable you *thought* would be initialized to a specific value may not get initialized until much later.

To avoid this, wrap the main code of your program in a single function, `main()`. Encapsulate your variables to their proper scopes. Then add a single line to the beginning of your program, after you've used all of the modules and pragmas you need:

```
#!/usr/bin/perl

use Modern::Perl;

...

exit main( @ARGV );

sub main {
    ...

    # successful exit
    return 0;
}
```

Calling `main()` *before* anything else in the program forces you to be explicit about initialization and order of compilation. Calling `exit` with `main()`'s return value prevents any other bare code from running.

## Controlled Execution

The effective difference between a program and a module is in its intended use. Users invoke programs directly, while programs load modules after execution has already begun. Yet a module and a program are both Perl code. Making a module executable is easy. So is making a program behave as a module (useful for testing parts of an existing program without formally making a module). All you need to do is to discover *how* Perl began to execute a piece of code.

`caller`'s single optional argument is the number of call frames (Recursion, pp. 115) which to report. `caller(0)` reports information about the current call frame. To allow a module to run correctly as a program *or* a module, put all executable code in functions, add a `main()` function, and write a single line at the start of the module:

```
main() unless caller(0);
```

If there's *no* caller for the module, someone invoked it directly as a program (with `perl path/to/Module.pm` instead of `use Module;`).

---

**Improved Caller Inspection**

The eighth element of the list returned from `caller` in list context is a true value if the call frame represents `use` or `require` and `undef` otherwise. While that's more accurate, few people use it.

---

## Postfix Parameter Validation

The CPAN has several modules which help verify the parameters of your functions; `Params::Validate` and `MooseX::Params::Validate` are two good options. Simple validation is easy even without those modules.

Suppose your function takes exactly two arguments. You *could* write:

```
use Carp 'croak';

sub groom_monkeys
{
    if (@_ != 2)
    {
        croak 'Can only groom two monkeys!';
    }
    ...
}
```

... but from a linguistic perspective, the consequences are more important than the check and deserve to be at the *start* of the expression:

```
croak 'Can only groom two monkeys!' unless @_ == 2;
```

This early return technique–especially with postfix conditionals–can simplify the rest of the code. Each such assertion is effectively a single row in a truth table.

253

## Regex En Passant

Many Perl idioms rely on the fact that expressions evaluate to values:

```
say my $ext_num = my $extension = 42;
```

While that code is obviously clunky, it demonstrates how to use the value of one expression in another expression. This isn't a new idea; you've likely used the return value of a function in a list or as an argument to another function before. You may not have realized its implications.

Suppose you want to extract a first name from a first name plus surname combination with a precompiled regular expression in $first_name_rx:

```
my ($first_name) = $name =~ /($first_name_rx)/;
```

In list context, a successful regex match returns a list of all captures (Capturing, pp. 153, and Perl assigns the first one to $first_name.

To remove all non-word characters to create a useful user name for a system account, you could write:

```
(my $normalized_name = $name) =~ tr/A-Za-z//dc;
```

> **/r in Perl 5.14**
>
> Perl 5.14 added the non-destructive substitution modifier /r, so that you can write my $normalized_name = $name =~ tr/A-Za-z//dcr;.

First, assign the value of $name to $normalized_name. The parentheses affect the precedence so that assignment happens first. The assignment expression evaluates to the *variable* $normalized_name. That variable becomes the first operand to the transliteration operator.

This technique works on other in-place modification operators:

```
my $age = 14;
(my $next_age = $age)++;

say "I am $age, but next year I will be $next_age";
```

## Unary Coercions

Perl's type system almost always does the right thing when you choose the correct operators. Use the string concatenation operator and Perl will treat both operands as strings. Use the addition operator and Perl will treat both operands as numeric.

Occasionally you have to give Perl a hint about what you mean with a *unary coercion* to force the evaluation of a value a specific way.

To ensure that Perl treats a value as numeric, add zero:

```
my $numeric_value = 0 + $value;
```

To ensure that Perl treats a value as a boolean, double negate it:

```
my $boolean_value = !! $value;
```

To ensure that Perl treats a value as a string, concatenate it with the empty string:

```
my $string_value = '' . $value;
```

Though the need for these coercions is vanishingly rare, you should understand these idioms if you encounter them. While it may look like it would be safe to remove a "useless" + 0 from an expression, doing so may well break the code.

# Global Variables

Perl provides several *super global variables* that are truly global, not scoped to a package or file. Unfortunately, their global availability means that any direct or indirect modifications may have effects on other parts of the program–and they're terse. Experienced Perl hackers have memorized some of them. Few people have memorized all of them. Only a handful are ever useful. `perldoc perlvar` contains the exhaustive list of these variables.

## Managing Super Globals

As Perl evolves, it moves more global behavior into lexical behavior, so that you can avoid many of these globals. When you can't avoid them, use `local` in the smallest possible scope to constrain any modifications. You are still susceptible to any changes code you *call* makes to those globals, but you reduce the likelihood of surprising code *outside* of your scope. As the easy file slurping idiom (Easy File Slurping, pp. 251) demonstrates, `local` is often the right approach:

```
my $file; { local $/; $file = <$fh> };
```

The effect of localizing $/ lasts only through the end of the block. There is a low chance that any Perl code will run as a result of reading lines from the filehandle[2] and change the value of $/ within the do block.

Not all cases of using super globals are this easy to guard, but this often works.

Other times you need to *read* the value of a super global and hope that no other code has modified it. Catching exceptions with an eval block is susceptible at least one race condition where DESTROY() methods invoked on lexicals that have gone out of scope may reset $@:

```
local $@;

eval { ... };

if (my $exception = $@) { ... }
```

Copy $@ *immediately* after catching an exception to preserve its contents. See also Try::Tiny instead (Exception Caveats, pp. 198).

## English Names

The core English module provides verbose names for punctuation-heavy super globals. Import them into a namespace with:

```
use English '-no_match_vars';
```

This allows you to use the verbose names documented in perldoc perlvar within the scope of this pragma.

Three regex-related super globals ($&, $`, and $') impose a global performance penalty for *all* regular expressions within a program. If you forget the -no_-match_vars import, your program will suffer the penalty even if you don't explicitly read from those variables. Modern Perl programs can use the @- variable instead of them.

## Useful Super Globals

Most modern Perl programs can get by with using only a couple of the super globals. You're most likely to encounter only a few of these variables in real programs.

---

[2]A tied filehandle (Tie, pp. 273) is one of the few possibilities.

- $/ (or $INPUT_RECORD_SEPARATOR from the English pragma) is a string of zero or more characters which denotes the end of a record when reading input a line at a time. By default, this is your platform-specific newline character sequence. If you undefine this value, Perl will attempt to read the entire file into memory. If you set this value to a *reference* to an integer, Perl will try to read that many *bytes* per record (so beware of Unicode concerns). If you set this value to an empty string (' '), Perl will read in a paragraph at a time, where a paragraph is a chunk of text followed by an arbitrary number of newlines.

- $. ($INPUT_LINE_NUMBER) contains the number of records read from the most recently-accessed filehandle. You can read from this variable, but writing to it has no effect. Localizing this variable will localize the filehandle to which it refers.

- $| ($OUTPUT_AUTOFLUSH) governs whether Perl will flush everything written to the currently selected filehandle immediately or only when Perl's buffer is full. Unbuffered output is useful when writing to a pipe or socket or terminal which should not block waiting for input. This variable will coerce any values assigned to it to boolean values.

- @ARGV contains the command-line arguments passed to the program.

- $! ($ERRNO) is a dualvar (Dualvars, pp. 80) which contains the result of the *most recent* system call. In numeric context, this corresponds to C's errno value, where anything other than zero indicates an error. In string context, this evaluates to the appropriate system error string. Localize this variable before making a system call (implicitly or explicitly) to avoid overwriting the appropriate value for other code elsewhere. Perl's internals make system calls sometimes, so the value of this variable can change out from under you. Copy it *immediately* after causing a system call to get accurate results.

- $" ($LIST_SEPARATOR) is a string used to separate array and list elements interpolated into a string.

- %+ contains named captures from successful regular expression matches (Named Captures, pp. 153).

- $@ ($EVAL_ERROR) contains the value thrown from the most recent exception (Catching Exceptions, pp. 196).

- $0 ($PROGRAM_NAME) contains the name of the program currently executing. You may modify this value on some Unix-like platforms to change the

name of the program as it appears to other programs on the system, such as
ps or top.

- $$ ($PID) contains the process id of the currently running instance of the
  program, as the operating system understands it. This will vary between
  fork()ed programs and *may* vary between threads in the same program.

- @INC holds a list of filesystem paths in which Perl will look for files to load
  with use or require. See perldoc -f require for other items this array
  can contain.

- %SIG maps OS and low-level Perl signals to function references used to
  handle those signals. Trap the standard Ctrl-C interrupt by catching the INT
  signal, for example. See perldoc perlipc for more information about
  signals and signal handling.

## Alternatives to Super Globals

IO and exceptions are the worst perpetrators of action at a distance. Use Try::Tiny
(Exception Caveats, pp. 198) to insulate you from the tricky semantics of proper
exception handling. localize and copy the value of $! to avoid strange behaviors
when Perl makes implicit system calls. Use IO::File and its methods on lexical
filehandles (Special File Handling Variables, pp. 218) to limit unwanted global
changes to IO behavior.

# CHAPTER 11

# What to Avoid

Perl isn't perfect. Some features are difficult to use correctly and others seemed great but don't work all that well. A few features combine with others in strange ways with weird edge cases. Knowing Perl's rough edges will help you avoid them, when possible, and avoid rough edges when you must use them.

## Barewords

Perl is a malleable language. You can write programs in whichever creative, maintainable, obfuscated, or bizarre fashion you prefer. Good programmers write code that they want to maintain, but Perl won't decide for you what *you* consider maintainable.

Perl's parser understands Perl's builtins and operators. It uses sigils to identify variables and other punctuation to recognize function and method calls. Yet sometimes the parser has to guess what you mean, especially when you use a *bareword*–an identifier without a sigil or other syntactically significant punctuation.

### Good Uses of Barewords

Though the `strict` pragma (Pragmas, pp. 200) rightly forbids ambiguous barewords, some barewords are acceptable.

#### Bareword hash keys

Hash keys in Perl are usually *not* ambiguous because the parser can identify them as string keys; `pinball` in `$games{pinball}` is obviously a string.

Occasionally this interpretation is not what you want, especially when you intend to *evaluate* a builtin or a function to produce the hash key. To make these cases clear, pass arguments to the function or use parentheses, or prepend a unary plus to force the evaluation of the builtin:

```
# the literal 'shift' is the key
my $value = $items{shift};
```

```
# the value produced by shift is the key
my $value = $items{shift @_}

# the function returns the key
my $value = $items{myshift( @_ )}

# unary plus uses the builtin shift
my $value = $items{+shift};
```

## Bareword package names

Package names are also barewords. If your naming conventions rule that package names have initial capitals and functions do not, you'll rarely encounter naming collisions. Even still, Perl must determine how to parse Package->method. Does it mean "call a function named Package() and call method() on its return value?" or "Call a method named method() in the Package namespace?" The answer depends on the code you've already compiled.

Force the parser to treat Package as a package name by appending the package separator (::)[1] or make it a literal string:

```
# probably a class method
Package->method;

# definitely a class method
Package::->method;

# a slightly less ugly class method
'Package'->method;
```

## Bareword named code blocks

The special named code blocks AUTOLOAD, BEGIN, CHECK, DESTROY, END, INIT, and UNITCHECK are barewords which *declare* functions without the sub builtin. You've seen this before (Code Generation, pp. 234):

```
package Monkey::Butler;

BEGIN { initialize_simians( __PACKAGE__ ) }
```

---

[1]Even among people who understand why this works, very few people do it.

```
sub AUTOLOAD { ... }
```

While you *can* declare AUTOLOAD() without using sub, few people do.

### Bareword constants

Constants declared with the constant pragma are usable as barewords:

```
# don't use this for real authentication
use constant NAME     => 'Bucky';
use constant PASSWORD => '|38fish!head74|';

return unless $name eq NAME && $pass eq PASSWORD;
```

These constants do *not* interpolate in double-quoted strings.

Constants are a special case of prototyped functions (Prototypes, pp. 265). When you predeclare a function with a prototype, the parser will treat all subsequent uses of that bareword specially–and will warn about ambiguous parsing errors. All other drawbacks of prototypes still apply.

## Ill-Advised Uses of Barewords

No matter how cautiously you code, barewords still produce ambiguous code. You can avoid the worst abuses, but you will encounter several types of barewords in legacy code.

### Bareword hash values

Some old code may not take pains to quote the *values* of hash pairs:

```
# poor style; do not use
my %parents =
(
    mother => Annette,
    father => Floyd,
);
```

When neither the Floyd() nor Annette() functions exist, Perl will interpret these barewords as strings. strict 'subs' will produce an error in this situation.

### Bareword function calls

Code written without strict 'subs' may use bareword function names. Adding parentheses will make the code pass strictures. Use perl -MO=Deparse,-p (see perldoc B::Deparse) to discover how Perl parses them, then parenthesize accordingly.

### Bareword filehandles

Prior to lexical filehandles (Filehandle References, pp. 90), all file and directory handles used barewords. You can almost always safely rewrite this code to use lexical filehandles. Perl's parser recognizes the special exceptions of STDIN, STDOUT, and STDERR.

### Bareword sort functions

Finally, the second operand of the sort builtin can be the *name* of a function to use for sorting. While this is rarely ambiguous to the parser, it can confuse *human* readers. The alternative of providing a function reference in a scalar is little better:

```
# bareword style
my @sorted = sort compare_lengths @unsorted;

# function reference in scalar
my $comparison = \&compare_lengths;
my @sorted     = sort $comparison @unsorted;
```

The second option avoids the use of a bareword, but the result is longer. Unfortunately, Perl's parser *does not* understand the single-line version due to the special parsing of sort; you cannot use an arbitrary expression (such as taking a reference to a named function) where a block or a scalar might otherwise go.

```
# does not work
my @sorted = sort \&compare_lengths @unsorted;
```

In both cases, the way sort invokes the function and provides arguments can be confusing (see perldoc -f sort for the details). Where possible, consider using the block form of sort instead. If you must use either function form, add a comment about what you're doing and why.

# Indirect Objects

Perl has no operator new. A constructor is anything which returns an object. By convention, constructors are class methods named new(), but you can name these methods (or even use *functions*). Several old Perl OO tutorials promote the use of C++ and Java-style constructor calls:

```
my $q = new CGI;  # DO NOT USE
```

... instead of the obvious method call:

```
my $q = CGI->new;
```

These syntaxes produce equivalent behavior, except when they don't.

## Bareword Indirect Invocations

In the indirect object form (more precisely, the *dative* case) of the first example, the verb (the method) precedes the noun to which it refers (the object). This is fine in spoken languages, but it introduces parsing ambiguities in Perl.

Because the method's name is a bareword (Barewords, pp. 259), the parser uses several heuristics to figure out the proper interpretation of this code. While these heuristics are well-tested and *almost* always correct, their failure modes are confusing. Things get worse when you pass arguments to a constructor:

```
# DO NOT USE
my $obj = new Class( arg => $value );
```

In this example, the *name* of the class looks like a function call. Perl *can* disambiguate many of these cases, but its heuristics depend on which package names the parser has seen, which barewords it has already resolved (and how it resolved them), and the *names* of functions already declared in the current package. For an exhaustive list of these conditions, you have to read the source code of Perl's parser–not something the average Perl programmer wants to do.

Imagine running afoul of a prototyped function (Prototypes, pp. 265) with a name which just happens to conflict somehow with the name of a class or a method called indirectly. This is rare[2], but so unpleasant to debug that it's worth avoiding indirect invocations.

---

[2]It's happened to your author when using the JSON module.

## Indirect Notation Scalar Limitations

Another danger of the indirect syntax is that the parser expects a single scalar expression as the object. Printing to a filehandle stored in an aggregate variable *seems* obvious, but it is not:

```
# DOES NOT WORK AS WRITTEN
say $config->{output} 'Fun diagnostic message!';
```

Perl will attempt to call `say` on the `$config` object.

`print`, `close`, and `say`–all builtins which operate on filehandles–operate in an indirect fashion. This was fine when filehandles were package globals, but lexical filehandles (Filehandle References, pp. 90) make the indirect object syntax problems obvious. To solve this, disambiguate the subexpression which produces the intended invocant:

```
say {$config->{output}} 'Fun diagnostic message!';
```

## Alternatives to Indirect Notation

Direct invocation notation does not suffer this ambiguity problem. To construct an object, call the constructor method on the class name directly:

```
my $q   = Plack::Request->new;
my $obj = Class->new( arg => $value );
```

This syntax *still* has a bareword problem in that if you have a function named `Request` in the `Plack` namespace, Perl will interpret the bareword class name as a call to the function, as:

```
sub Plack::Request;

# you wrote Plack::Reuqest->new, but Perl saw
my $q = Plack::Request()->new;
```

While this happens rarely, you can disambiguate classnames by appending the package separator ( :: ) or by explicitly marking class names as string literals:

```
# package separator
my $q = Plack::Request::->new;

# unambiguously a string literal
my $q = 'Plack::Request'->new;
```

Almost no one ever does this.

For the limited case of filehandle operations, the dative use is so prevalent that you can use the indirect invocation approach if you surround your intended invocant with curly brackets. If you're using Perl 5.14 or newer (or if you load IO::File or IO::Handle), you can use methods on lexical filehandles[3].

The CPAN module Perl::Critic::Policy::Dynamic::NoIndirect (a plugin for Perl::Critic) can analyze your code to find indirect invocations. The CPAN module indirect can identify and prohibit their use in running programs:

```
# warn on indirect use
no indirect;

# throw exceptions on their use
no indirect ':fatal';
```

# Prototypes

A *prototype* is a piece of metadata attached to a function or variable. A function prototype changes how Perl's parser understands it.

Prototypes allow users to define their own functions which behave like builtins. Consider the builtin push, which takes an array and a list. While Perl would normally flatten the array and list into a single list passed to push, the parser knows to treat the array as a *container*, not to flatten its values. In effect, this is like passing a reference to an array and a list of values to push. The parser's behavior allows push to modify the values of the container.

Function prototypes attach to function declarations:

```
sub foo       (&@);
sub bar       ($$) { ... }
my  $baz = sub (&&) { ... };
```

Any prototype attached to a forward declaration must match the prototype attached to the function declaration. Perl will give a warning if this is not true. Strangely you may omit the prototype from a forward declaration and include it for the full declaration–but there's no reason to do so.

The builtin prototype takes the name of a function and returns a string representing its prototype.

---

[3]Almost no one does this for print and say.

To see the prototype of a builtin, use the CORE:: form of the builtin's name as the operand to prototype:

```
$ perl -E "say prototype 'CORE::push';"
\@@
$ perl -E "say prototype 'CORE::keys';"
\%
$ perl -E "say prototype 'CORE::open';"
*;$@
```

prototype will return undef for those builtins whose functions you cannot emulate:

```
say prototype 'CORE::system' // 'undef'
# undef; cannot emulate builtin system

say prototype 'CORE::prototype' // 'undef'
# undef; builtin prototype has no prototype
```

Remember push?

```
$ perl -E "say prototype 'CORE::push';"
\@@
```

The @ character represents a list. The backslash forces the use of a *reference* to the corresponding argument. This prototype means that push takes a reference to an array and a list of values. You might write mypush as:

```
sub mypush (\@@)
{
    my ($array, @rest) = @_;
    push @$array, @rest;
}
```

Other prototype characters include $ to force a scalar argument, % to mark a hash (most often used as a reference), and & to identify a code block. See perldoc perlsub for more information.

## The Problem with Prototypes

Prototypes change how Perl parses your code and how Perl coerces arguments to your functions. While these prototypes may superficially resemble function signatures in other languages, they are very different. They do not document the number or types of arguments functions expect, nor do they map arguments to named parameters.

Prototype coercions work in subtle ways, such as enforcing scalar context on incoming arguments:

```
sub numeric_equality($$)
{
    my ($left, $right) = @_;
    return $left == $right;
}

my @nums = 1 .. 10;

say 'They're equal, whatever that means!'
    if numeric_equality @nums, 10;
```

... but only work on simple expressions:

```
sub mypush(\@@);

# compilation error: prototype mismatch
# (expects array, gets scalar assignment)
mypush( my $elems = [], 1 .. 20 );
```

To debug this, users of mypush must know both that a prototype exists, and the limitations of the array prototype.

> **Debugging Prototype Errors**
>
> If you think this error message is inscrutable, wait until you see the *complicated* prototype errors.

## Good Uses of Prototypes

Prototypes *do* have a few good uses that outweigh their problems. For example, you can use a prototyped function to override one of Perl's builtins. First check that you *can* override the builtin by examining its prototype in a small test program. Then use the subs pragma to tell Perl that you plan to override a builtin, and finally declare your override with the correct prototype:

```
use subs 'push';

sub push (\@@) { ... }
```

Beware that the subs pragma is in effect for the remainder of the *file*, regardless of any lexical scoping.

The second reason to use prototypes is to define compile-time constants. When Perl encounters a function declared with an empty prototype (as opposed to *no* prototype) *and* this function evaluates to a single constant expression, the optimizer will turn all calls to that function into constants instead of function calls:

```
sub PI () { 4 * atan2(1, 1) }
```

All subsequent code will use the calculated value of pi in place of the bareword PI or a call to PI(), with respect to scoping and visibility.

The core pragma `constant` handles these details for you. The `Const::Fast` module from the CPAN creates constant scalars which you can interpolate into strings.

A reasonable use of prototypes is to extend Perl's syntax to operate on anonymous functions as blocks. The CPAN module `Test::Exception` uses this to good effect to provide a nice API with delayed computation[4]. Its `throws_ok()` function takes three arguments: a block of code to run, a regular expression to match against the string of the exception, and an optional description of the test:

```
use Test::More;
use Test::Exception;

throws_ok
    { my $unobject; $unobject->yoink }
    qr/Can't call method "yoink" on an undefined/,
```

---

[4]See also `Test::Fatal`

```
    'Method on undefined invocant should fail';

done_testing();
```

The exported throws_ok() function has a prototype of &$;$. Its first argument is
a block, which becomes an anonymous function. The second argument is a scalar.
The third argument is optional.

Careful readers may have spotted the absence of a comma after the block. This is
a quirk of Perl's parser, which expects whitespace after a prototyped block, not the
comma operator. This is a drawback of the prototype syntax. If that bothers you,
use throws_ok() without taking advantage of the prototype:

```
use Test::More;
use Test::Exception;

throws_ok(
    sub { my $unobject; $unobject->yoink() },
    qr/Can't call method "yoink" on an undefined/,
    'Method on undefined invocant should fail' );

done_testing();
```

A final good use of prototypes is when defining a custom named function to use
with sort[5]:

```
sub length_sort ($$)
{
    my ($left, $right) = @_;
    return length($left) <=> length($right);
}

my @sorted = sort length_sort @unsorted;
```

The prototype of $$ forces Perl to pass the sort pairs in @_. sort's documentation
suggests that this is slightly slower than using the package globals $a and $b, but
using lexical variables often makes up for any speed penalty.

---

[5]Ben Tilly suggested this example.

269

# Method-Function Equivalence

Perl's object system is deliberately minimal (Blessed References, pp. 182). Because a class is a package, Perl does not distinguish between a function and a method stored in a package. The same builtin, sub, declares both. Perl will happily dispatch to a function called as a method. Likewise, you can invoke a method as if it were a function–fully-qualified, exported, or as a reference–if you pass in your own invocant manually.

Invoking the wrong thing in the wrong way causes problems.

## Caller-side

Consider a class with several methods:

```
package Order;

use List::Util 'sum';

...

sub calculate_price
{
    my $self = shift;
    return sum( 0, $self->get_items );
}
```

Given an Order object $o, the following invocations of this method *may* seem equivalent:

```
my $price = $o->calculate_price;

# broken; do not use
my $price = Order::calculate_price( $o );
```

Though in this simple case, they produce the same output, the latter violates object encapsulation by avoiding method lookup.

If $o were instead a subclass or allomorph (Roles, pp. 173) of Order which overrode calculate_price(), bypassing method dispatch would call the wrong method. Any change to the implementation of calculate_price(), such as a modification of inheritance or delegation through AUTOLOAD()–might break calling code.

270

Perl has one circumstance where this behavior may seem necessary. If you force method resolution without dispatch, how do you invoke the resulting method reference?

```
my $meth_ref = $o->can( 'apply_discount' );
```

There are two possibilities. The first is to discard the return value of the `can()` method:

```
$o->apply_discount if $o->can( 'apply_discount' );
```

The second is to use the reference itself with method invocation syntax:

```
if (my $meth_ref = $o->can( 'apply_discount' ))
{
    $o->$meth_ref();
}
```

When `$meth_ref` contains a function reference, Perl will invoke that reference with `$o` as the invocant. This works even under strictures, as it does when invoking a method with a scalar containing its name:

```
my $name = 'apply_discount';
$o->$name();
```

There is one small drawback in invoking a method by reference; if the structure of the program changes between storing the reference and invoking the reference, the reference may no longer refer to the most appropriate method. If the `Order` class has changed such that `Order::apply_discount` is no longer the right method to call, the reference in `$meth_ref` will not have updated.

When you use this invocation form, limit the scope of the references.

## Callee-side

Because Perl makes no distinction between functions and methods at the point of declaration and because it's *possible* (however inadvisable) to invoke a given function as a function or a method, it's possible to write a function callable as either.

The CGI module has these two-faced functions. Every one of them must apply several heuristics to determine whether the first argument is an invocant. This causes problems. It's difficult to predict exactly which invocants are potentially valid for a given method, especially when you may have to deal with subclasses. Creating an API that users cannot easily misuse is more difficult too, as is your documentation burden. What happens when one part of the project uses the procedural interface and another uses the object interface?

If you *must* provide a separate procedural and OO interface to a library, create two separate APIs.

# Automatic Dereferencing

Perl can automatically dereference certain references on your behalf. Given an array reference in `$arrayref`, you can write:

```
push $arrayref, qw( list of values );
```

Given an expression which returns an array reference, you can do the same:

```
push $houses{$location}[$closets], \@new_shoes;
```

The same goes for the array operators pop, shift, unshift, splice, keys, values, and each and the hash operators keys, values, and each. If the reference provided is not of the proper type–if it does not dereference properly–Perl will throw an exception. While this may seem more dangerous than explicitly dereferencing references directly, it is in fact the same behavior:

```
my $ref = sub { ... };

# will throw an exception
push  $ref, qw( list of values );

# will also throw an exception
push @$ref, qw( list of values );
```

Unfortunately, this automatic dereferencing has two problems. First, it only works on plain variables. If you have a blessed array or hash, a tied hash, or an object with array or hash overloading, Perl will throw a runtime exception instead of dereferencing the reference.

Second, remember that each, keys, and values can operate on both arrays and hashes. You can't look at:

```
my @items = each $ref;
```

... and tell whether @items contains a list of key/value pairs or index/value pairs, because you don't know whether you should expect $ref to refer to a hash or an array. Yes, choosing good variable names will help, but this code is intrinsically confusing.

Neither of these drawbacks make this syntax *unusable* in general, but its rough edges and potential for confusing readers make it less useful than it could be.

# Tie

Where overloading (Overloading, pp. 240) allows you to customize the behavior of classes and objects for specific types of coercion, a mechanism called *tying* allows you to customize the behavior of primitive variables (scalars, arrays, hashes, and filehandles). Any operation you might perform on a tied variable translates to a specific method call on an object.

The tie builtin originally allowed you to use disk space instead of RAM for hashes and arrays, so that Perl could use data larger than available memory. The core module Tie::File allows you to do this, in effect treating files as if they were arrays.

The class to which you tie a variable must conform to a defined interface for a specific data type. Read perldoc perltie for an overview, then see the core modules Tie::StdScalar, Tie::StdArray, and Tie::StdHash for specific details. Start by inheriting from one of those classes, then override any specific methods you need to modify.

---

**When Class and Package Names Collide**

If tie weren't confusing enough, Tie::Scalar, Tie::Array, and Tie::Hash define the necessary interfaces to tie scalars, arrays, and hashes, but Tie::StdScalar, Tie::StdArray, and Tie::StdHash provide the default implementations.

---

## Tying Variables

To tie a variable:

```
use Tie::File;
tie my @file, 'Tie::File', @args;
```

The first argument is the variable to tie. The second is the name of the class into which to tie it. @args is an optional list of arguments required for the tying function. In the case of Tie::File, @args should contain a valid filename.

Tying functions resemble constructors: TIESCALAR, TIEARRAY(), TIEHASH(), or TIEHANDLE() for scalars, arrays, hashes, and filehandles respectively. Each function returns a new object which represents the tied variable. Both tie and tied return this object, though most people use tied in a boolean context.

## Implementing Tied Variables

To implement the class of a tied variable, inherit from a core module such as Tie::StdScalar[6], then override the specific methods for the operations you want to change. In the case of a tied scalar, these are likely FETCH and STORE, possibly TIESCALAR(), and probably not DESTROY().

Here's a class which logs all reads from and writes to a scalar:

```perl
package Tie::Scalar::Logged
{
    use Modern::Perl;

    use Tie::Scalar;
    use parent -norequire => 'Tie::StdScalar';

    sub STORE
    {
        my ($self, $value) = @_;
        Logger->log("Storing <$value> (was [$$self])",
        $$self = $value;
    }

    sub FETCH
    {
        my $self = shift;
        Logger->log("Retrieving <$$self>", 1);
        return $$self;
    }
}
```

---

[6]Tie::StdScalar lacks its own *.pm* file, so write use Tie::Scalar;.

Assume that the Logger class method log() takes a string and the number of frames up the call stack of which to report the location.

Within the STORE() and FETCH() methods, $self works as a blessed scalar. Assigning to that scalar reference changes the value of the scalar and reading from it returns its value.

Similarly, the methods of Tie::StdArray and Tie::StdHash act on blessed array and hash references, respectively. Again, perldoc perltie explains the methods tied variables support, such as reading or writing multiple values at once.

---

**Isn't tie Fun?**

The -norequire option prevents the parent pragma from attempting to load a file for Tie::StdScalar, as that module is part of the file *Tie/Scalar.pm*. This is messy but necessary.

---

## When to use Tied Variables

Tied variables seem like fun opportunities for cleverness, but they can produce confusing interfaces. Unless you have a very good reason for making objects behave as if they were builtin data types, avoid creating your own ties. tied variables are often much slower than builtin data types.

With that said, tied variables can help you debug tricky code (use the logged scalar to help you understand *where* a value changes) or to make certain impossible things possible (access large files without running out of memory). Tied variables are less useful as the primary interfaces to objects; it's often too difficult and constraining to try to fit your whole interface to that supported by tie().

A final word of warning is a sad indictment of lazy programming: a lot of code goes out of its way to *prevent* use of tied variables, often by accident. This is unfortunate, but library code is sometimes fast and lazy with what it expects, and you can't always fix it.

# CHAPTER 12

# What's Missing

Perl isn't perfect, but it is malleable–in part because no single configuration is ideal for every programmer and every purpose. Some useful behaviors are available as core libraries. More are available from the CPAN. Effective Perl programmers take full advantage of the options available to them.

## Missing Defaults

Perl's language design process has always tried to combine practicality with expandability, but it was as impossible to predict the future in 1994 as it is in 2014. Perl 5 expanded the language and made the CPAN possible, but it also retained backwards compatibility with most Perl 1 code written as far back as 1987.

The best Perl code of 2014 is very different from the best Perl code of 1994 or the best Perl code of 1987.

Although Perl includes an extensive core library, it's not comprehensive. Many of the best modules are available outside of the core, from the CPAN (The CPAN, pp. 15). The `Task::Kensho` meta-distribution includes several other distributions which represent the best the CPAN has to offer. When you need to solve a problem, look there first.

There are still plenty of gems in the core, however.

### The strict Pragma

The `strict` pragma (Pragmas, pp. 200) allows you to forbid (or re-enable) various powerful language constructs which offer potential for accidental abuse.

`strict` forbids symbolic references, requires variable declarations (Lexical Scope, pp. 119), and prohibits the use of undeclared barewords (Barewords, pp. 259). While symbolic references are occasionally necessary (Using and Importing, pp. 224), the use of a variable as a variable name offers the possibility of subtle errors of action at a distance–or, worse, the possibility of poorly-validated user input manipulating private data for malicious purposes.

Requiring variable declarations helps to detect typos in variable names and encourages proper scoping of lexical variables. It's easier to see the intended scope of a lexical variable if all variables have my or our declarations in the appropriate scope.

strict takes effect in lexical scopes. See perldoc strict for more details.

## The warnings Pragma

The warnings pragma (Handling Warnings, pp. 209) controls the reporting of various warning classes, such as attempting to stringify the undef value or using the wrong type of operator on values. It also warns about the use of deprecated features.

The most useful warnings explain that Perl had trouble understanding what you meant and had to guess at the proper interpretation. Even though Perl often guesses correctly, disambiguation on your part will ensure that your programs run correctly.

The warnings pragma takes effect in lexical scopes. See perldoc perllexwarn and perldoc warnings for more details.

> **Asking for More Help**
>
> If you use both warnings with diagnostics, you'll get expanded diagnostic messages for each warning present in your programs, straight out of perldoc perldiag. It's a great help when learning Perl, but be sure to disable diagnostics before deploying your program, lest you fill up your logs or expose debugging information to users.

### IO::File **and** IO::Handle

Before Perl 5.14, lexical filehandles were objects of the IO::Handle class, but you had to load IO::Handle explicitly before you could call methods on them. As of Perl 5.14, lexical filehandles are instances of IO::File and Perl loads it for you.

Add use IO::Handle; to code running on Perl 5.12 or earlier if you call methods on lexical filehandles.

## The autodie Pragma

Perl leaves error handling (or error ignoring) up to you. If you forget to check the return value of every open() call, for example, you could try to read from a closed filehandle–or worse, lose data as you try to write to one. The `autodie` pragma changes this for you. If you write:

```
use autodie;

open my $fh, '>', $file;
```

... an unsuccessful `open()` call will throw an exception. Given that the most appropriate approach to a failed system call is throwing an exception, this pragma can remove a lot of boilerplate code and allow you the peace of mind of knowing that you haven't forgotten to check a return value. See `perldoc autodie` for more information.

## Perl Version Numbers

If you encounter a piece of Perl code without knowing when it was written or who wrote it, can you tell which version of Perl it requires? If you have a lot of experience with Perl both before and after the release of Perl 5.10, you might remember which version added `say` and when `autodie` entered the core. Otherwise, you might have to guess, trawl through `perldelta` files, or use `CPAN::MinimumVersion` from the CPAN.

There's no requirement for you to add the minimum required Perl version number to all new code you write, but it *can* clarify your intentions. For example, if you've tested your code with Perl 5.12 and use only features present in Perl 5.12, write:

```
use 5.012;
```

... and you'll document your intent. You'll also make it easier for tools to identify the particular features of Perl you may or may not use in this code. If someone comes along later and proves that the code works just fine on Perl 5.10, you can change the version number–and you'll do so based on practical evidence.

# Index

285

289